DISCARD UNIV

W9-BDA-838

Date Due

HARVARD POLITICAL STUDIES

EQUALITY IN POLITICAL PHILOSOPHY

PUBLISHED UNDER THE DIRECTION OF THE
DEPARTMENT OF GOVERNMENT IN
HARVARD UNIVERSITY

EQUALITY

IN

POLITICAL PHILOSOPHY

SANFORD A. LAKOFF

HARVARD UNIVERSITY PRESS
CAMBRIDGE, MASSACHUSETTS
1964

Distributed in Great Britain by Oxford University Press, London

Publication of this book has been aided
by a grant from the Ford Foundation

Library of Congress Catalog Card Number: 64-13425
Printed in the United States of America

For Margaret D. Clark

Preface

A WORK OF this scope, tracking a grand but elusive theme over many centuries, would quickly become unmanageable if it were not somehow circumscribed. The reader deserves to be forewarned of at least some of the limitations he will encounter. As the title indicates, this is a study of the discussion of equality in political philosophy. It does not examine in any but a cursory way the appearance of egalitarian ideas and sentiments at the less rarefied levels of political controversy. It does not deal with egalitarian movements or with the application of egalitarian ideas in various societies. Important as these matters are to a full understanding of egalitarianism as a phenomenon of history, they remain outside the bounds of this study.

Nor will an effort be made in these pages to expound a new philosophy of equality; our purpose is only to examine those already offered. We shall follow chronological order, but not primarily to trace the filiation of ideas from one philosopher to another or to examine the relationship between ideas and environment. Our purpose is to demonstrate, with the help of textual explication most of all, the recurrence of several patterns of egalitarian thought throughout modern history. The chapters and the book as a whole have been designed with these patterns in mind. The reader should therefore not expect a compendium of egalitarian thought or comprehensive accounts of the work of the philosophers studied. Rousseau, for example, is represented here only by his second *Discourse*, although a full account of Rousseau's position would have to reconcile that early work with his later *Social Contract* and constitutional projects. The interpretation of Hegel would also be very different if later works were included in our treatment. The reader's indulgence for these and other limitations is entreated. An exposition that would transcend them must await an even more ambitious effort than this.

During the years in which this study has come to fruition, first as a doctoral dissertation and now as a book, I have incurred many debts in connection with it. Some of these are to the personnel of various institutions. For fellowship assistance I am grateful to the Committee on Scholarships and the Sheldon Fund at Harvard, which awarded me a Sinclair Kennedy Travelling Fellowship, and to the Committee on Legal and Political Philosophy of the Social Science Research Council. A grant from the Rockefeller Foundation to the Department of Government at Harvard helped defray the costs of typing the manuscript. Although I have used libraries elsewhere, my principal debt is to Widener Library.

I am indebted to the following publishers for permission to quote copyright material: Fortress Press, for quotations from Luther's *Three Treatises* (Philadelphia, 1943); James Clarke & Co. Ltd., for quotations from Calvin's *Institutes of the Christian Religion*, translated by H. Beveridge (London, 1953); J. M. Dent & Sons, Ltd. and E. P. Dutton & Co. Inc., for quotations from Rousseau's *The Social Contract and the Discourses*, translated by G. D. H. Cole (Everyman's Library, New York, 1950); Liveright Publishing Corp. and The Hogarth Press, Ltd., for quotations from Freud's *Group Psychology and the Analysis of the Ego*, translated by J. Strachey (New York, 1949); The University of Chicago Press, for quotations from Hegel's *Early Theological Writings*, translated by T. M. Knox and R. Kroner (Chicago, 1951).

I have also been exceedingly fortunate in my teachers, particularly those who have contributed to my training in the study of social thought. I acknowledge them with the keenest appreciation: David S. Berkowitz, Lewis Coser, Carl J. Friedrich, Louis Hartz, Max Lerner, Frank E. Manuel, Philip Rieff, and Jacob Taubes. George H. Williams guided my study of Thomas Müntzer in his seminar on Church History at the Harvard Divinity School. James Luther Adams, also of the Divinity School, called my attention to a number of obscure but valuable sources. William Y.

Elliott kindly encouraged me to draw out the implications of the study in presentations to his seminar on modern political thought. An earlier draft received valuable criticism from Robert G. Mc-Closkey and Stephen R. Graubard, as well as from others already mentioned. Hubert Forbes and Robert H. Binstock helped with various chores to enable me to meet a thesis submission date, and Leon Jacobson's assiduous labors assisted greatly in the preparation of the manuscript for publication. Elma S. Leavis, who typed the manuscript, patiently maintained her customary sharp watch for my inaccuracies. Those errors and doubtful judgments that remain are of course solely my responsibility.

Finally, I have the pleasure of dedicating this book to Margaret D. Clark, who guided the first steps of my thought and who for many years has devoted the singular gifts of her mind and spirit to the education of the people of my native city, Bayonne, New Jersey. Her active participation in the affairs of government, her equally intense pursuit of the arduous joys of creativity and contemplation, and her warm compassion for all humanity's ills remain an inspiration to me, as to all her students.

SANFORD A. LAKOFF

Cambridge, Mass.
December, 1963

Contents

EQUALITY IN POLITICAL PHILOSOPHY

CHAPTER ONE

Three Concepts of Equality

EW TERMS of political discourse have had as long a life and as important a role in the making of modern history as the idea of equality. From the earliest outcropping of social controversy to the clash of ideologies in our own day it has continued to arouse great expectations and grave apprehensions. It would be too much to expect that an idea carrying such passionate appeal and such symbolic force should be easy to define to everyone's satisfaction. Nevertheless, a number of worthy efforts have been made to pierce the veil of ambiguity surrounding the term, and it may be well to begin this inquiry by considering some that have been made before.

When the French revolutionaries made "Liberty, Equality, Fraternity" the slogan of their cause, they did not take the trouble to provide an elaborate exegesis. The Declaration of the Rights of Man and of the Citizen offered concrete illustrations of what the slogan was intended to convey, but many of the parties to the Revolution looked upon the Declaration as a statement of minimal objectives, and, in any case, the demands put forward did not explain the premises from which they were derived. The American founding fathers had been only a little more explicit. When they wrote in the Declaration of Independence the words "all men are created equal," they were careful to add immediately afterward that "they are endowed by their Creator with

certain unalienable Rights," among them "Life, Liberty and the
pursuit of Happiness." But even this qualification did not prevent
later generations of Americans from developing conflicting interpretations when the issue of equality became the subject of
profound moral and political disagreement, notably in the conflict
over slavery. Stephen A. Douglas charged Abraham Lincoln in
their celebrated debates with misreading the intent of the framers.
The pronouncement on equality in the Declaration of Independence, Douglas asserted, had been meant to apply only to
white Europeans and not to Negroes, Indians, or immigrants from
Asia. Lincoln answered, with an admirable display of clear thinking and spare eloquence:

I think the authors of that notable instrument intended to include *all*
men, but they did not intend to declare all men equal *in all respects*.
They did not mean to say all were equal in color, size, intellect, moral
developments, or social capacity. They defined with tolerable distinctness in what respects they did consider all men created equal—equal
with 'certain inalienable rights, among which are life, liberty, and the
pursuit of happiness.' This they said, and this they meant. They did
not mean to assert the obvious untruth that all were then actually
enjoying that equality, nor yet that they were about to confer it
immediately upon them. In fact, they had no power to confer such a
boon. They meant simply to declare the right, so that enforcement of
it might follow as fast as circumstances should permit.[1]

When he was pressed by Douglas to say whether the Negro was
actually created equal to the white man, Lincoln repeated what
he had said before and added:

Certainly the negro is not our equal in color—perhaps not in many
other respects; still, in the right to put into his mouth the bread that his
own hands have earned, he is the equal of every other man, white or
black. In pointing out that more has been given you, you can not be
justified in taking away the little which has been given him. All I
ask for the negro is that if you do not like him, let him alone. If God
gave him but little, that little let him enjoy.[2]

It took a civil war and a number of constitutional amendments
to secure the political acceptance, at least in principle, of Lincoln's
interpretation. But the emancipation of the Negro did not put an
end to the controversy over equality in the nineteenth century.
Especially in England and the United States, equality was the
subject of lively controversy among men of letters and students of

political economy. In 1870, when Sir Erskine May published his *History of Democracy* blaming the troubles of France on the agitation for social equality, Matthew Arnold was moved to counterattack. The trouble with the English, he said, was that they subscribed to the "religion of inequality." Gladstone, he noted, had spoken the truth in observing that "there is no broad political idea which has entered less into the formation of the political system of this country than equality." If anything, the English had a "love of inequality," evident in their admiration for courtly show and in the envy of the rich.[3] This love of inequality fostered a universal preoccupation with objects and attainments unworthy of civilized man and degraded a large segment of the population to a level at which far too few were able to fulfill their potentialities as human beings. Inequality, said Arnold, "materializes our upper class, vulgarises our middle class, brutalises our lower."[4]

A few years later, in 1873, Sir James Fitzjames Stephen, who had been in India when conflict over radical ideals broke out in the English press, set down his social philosophy in *Liberty, Equality, Fraternity*.[5] In these largely critical reflections, aimed to rebut the new "Religion of Humanity," Stephen rejected the utilitarian view that equality was one of the principal criteria of social justice and the basis for universal suffrage ("one man one vote"). He insisted that equality was only rightly understood as the common opportunity to achieve unequal status and reward.

In 1890 Leslie Stephen set out to clarify the subject of "social equality" in the hope of laying the tired controversy to rest.[6] All dogmatic assertions of equality, whether in nature or society, were to be rejected. Properly speaking, the term was to be understood to mean, as John Stuart Mill had already established, that the good of society lay in making it possible for the greatest number of individuals to develop their capacities to the fullest without regard to the circumstances of their birth or social origin. Valuable as was this effort at clarification, especially in comparison to the thickly rhetorical arguments made before, it was plainly inadequate. In the same period, for example, American readers were learning from William Graham Sumner that equality meant one thing, and from Edward Bellamy that it meant something else again. Sumner, expounding the views of the Spencerian Liberals, put the issue boldly: "The State gives equal rights and equal chances just because it does not mean to give anything else. It sets each man on his feet, and gives him leave to run . . ."[7] Bellamy, in his *Equality* (1897), written as a sequel to the vision of the future offered in his more popular utopian novel, *Looking Backward* (1887), put his understanding of equality in terms closer to the view of a Marxian Socialist. To realize the ideal of the Declaration of Independence, Bellamy declared, it would be necessary for the government to control the economic system, to use "the collective social machinery for the indefinite promotion of the welfare of the people at large."[8] In France, meanwhile, the sociologist Celestin Bouglé wrote a book with a promising title, *Les idées égalitaires*, in which, however, he put together all ideas of equality, modern and classical, in order to see what it was in social conditions that produced egalitarianism, and ignored philosophic distinctions.[9]

By the turn of the century this succession of efforts intended to clarify the issue had only succeeded in promoting the doubtful but widely held conviction that there was a serious conflict between liberty and equality. A book[10] with this conflict for its theme appeared in America in 1925, and it may safely be said to have echoed conventional opinion. In 1931, however, R. H. Tawney expressed the views of a rapidly growing segment of educated opinion when he denied that equality and liberty were necessarily incompatible and proposed a number of specific social reforms in the course of a book entitled *Equality*.[11] Equality, Tawney held, was no danger to liberty so long as it stood for the effort to remove the barriers imposed by social organization on the benign expression of individual differences.

Tawney's work was more an exhortation to the British Labour Party to lead the way toward the expansion of opportunity and social welfare programs than it was an academic effort to resolve diverging interpretations of equality. The war against fascism indirectly stimulated two works more analytical in nature. One was a booklet by the English historian David Thomson, who followed Tawney in emphasizing the interdependence of liberty and equality and also made the worthwhile suggestion that in the course of history equality seemed to have been extended gradually from the sphere of ethics to that of law, then to religious belief, politics, and society, and finally, in the twentieth century, to economics.[12] The other study was made by Henry Alonzo Myers, a student of literature and philosophy, whose book was addressed to the American controversy over equality. Perhaps the most valuable contribution of Myers' study is his insight into the reflection of egalitarian doctrines in early American literature. Hawthorne, Myers points out, had a conception of equality in keeping with Puritan pessimism ("we are sinners all alike"), while Melville believed that God balanced the lot of every man ("thou just Spirit of Equality, which hast spread one royal mantle of humanity over all my kind!"), and Whitman put forth a buoyantly optimistic and humane egalitarianism.[13]

Finally, and most important to the thesis of the present study, is the recent inquiry into the philosophic meaning of equality conducted by two distinguished British students of the history of social thought, Sir Isaiah Berlin and Richard Wollheim, in a brief but stimulating discussion published in 1956. In hope of clearing up the confusion surrounding the term, Berlin called upon historians of ideas to "isolate the pure ore of egalitarianism proper from those alloys which the admixture of other attitudes and ideals has at various times generated."[14] In other words, what Berlin proposed was that students of the problem concentrate on discovering or formulating a single universally acceptable idea of equality.

With all due respect to Berlin, it must be said that such an enterprise would be doomed to failure. It may be that a single idea of equality could be designed to suit the purposes of ethics or theology, but for politics a single, all-embracing idea of equality would dispel no confusion at all. The difficulty is that "to isolate the pure ore of egalitarianism proper" would be to arrive at a purely formal statement to the effect that all men are or ought to be equal in some respects. As Lincoln recognized, to say no more than that men are "equal" is to suggest that they are identical without specifying how or why. Conceivably the statement might be intended to mean that men are identical in any and all respects; but this is by no means a necessary inference. If one were to assemble a compendium of egalitarian thought, it would soon be apparent that there is a need to distinguish between the common formal understanding of equality and the different substantive ones—between the statement "all men are equal" and the specification of the respects (perhaps quite limited in number) in which they are to be considered equals. One proponent may assert that by equality he merely means to suggest identity in legal or political rights. Another may say that equality requires the possession of property in common. Still another may say that he intends the term to denote a physical or natural identity which does not necessarily contain a prescription for political or economic justice. To the historian of ideas, therefore, it is of the utmost importance to distinguish between the formal proposition and the substantive notions of equality which have in the course of time introduced themselves into the wide-open arms of the formal statement.

The philosopher who propounds a particular understanding of equality is free to consider it absolute and universal; but the historian of ideas, faced with conflicting claims, can only consider them all valid in their own terms. *Formally* there is one idea of equality; *substantively* there are many. Berlin may, if he likes, consider a "true egalitarian" someone who insists, as some Bolsheviks are said to have done in the early days of the Russian Revolution, that an orchestra ought not to have a conductor.[15] To the historian of ideas, however, this musically subversive suggestion is one for which the Socialist egalitarianism of Marx cannot be fairly indicted. To make equality a synonym for the absence of all distinctions is not to define any of the real proposals of equality but only to prepare an attack upon absurd caricatures of them all.

The supposition that there must be a "pure" egalitarianism leads Berlin also to suggest that in the case of Liberal egalitarianism, as presumably in other cases, "the criterion of equality has plainly been influenced by *something other* than the mere desire for *equality as such* . . ." For Liberalism such influence derives from "the desire for liberty, or the full development of human resources, or the belief that men desire to be as rich or as powerful or as famous as they can make themselves—beliefs which are not connected with the desire for equality at all." [16] It would be more accurate to say, as Karl Mannheim had already noted in his essay on Conservatism,[17] that without these "extra" desires equality would simply be without meaning for a Liberal. It is only when the term is used with these specifications in mind that it is not an empty formality but a Liberal principle. It is not as though there would be a conflict between equality and the other elements unless equality were modified or compromised to admit them. Wollheim has rightly pointed out that the equality of Liberalism, as an equality of rights, makes an independent notion of freedom superfluous, insofar as freedom refers to the possession of these rights by all.[18] Liberal equality, in other words, is the perfectly happy marriage of a formal statement with a substantive one. What is peculiarly Liberal is the substantive one. Plainly, when a Liberal argues for equality, he means an equality of rights which would not include the right of a majority to trample on the rights of individuals. The Liberal doctrine of equality is simply a specification of many if not all of the values which characterize Liberalism generally.

It follows that it is also impossible to treat equality as though it were a single "unit-idea" in the sense proposed by A. O. Lovejoy.[19] In his rigorous statement of the peculiar province of the history of ideas, a statement which deserves serious attention, Lovejoy proposes a distinction between unit-ideas and the systems of thought in which they are embedded at various times. The test of whether a given idea is a unit-idea is whether it can sustain a detachment from any and all of these systems without losing essential characteristics. By such a test there is no single unit-idea of equality, save for the purely formal statement. Are there perhaps a number of "unit-ideas"—a number of substantive versions of equality which are recurrent and which may be abstracted from different systems and yet retain essential characteristics?

It is the contention of this study that there are indeed three unit-ideas of equality, or, to use a more commonplace description, three concepts of equality—concepts which are present in their essential elements from earliest times but which are only made explicit and propounded in opposition to each other in the course of modern history.

In an important if limited sense, the history of the idea of equality reflects the changing character of Western civilization. If the philosophers of antiquity and the theologians of the Middle Ages held equality to be an intimation of ultimate perfection but not an appropriate standard for existing society, it was because economic, political, and cultural circumstances combined to make inequality seem a synonym for order and natural necessity. Only when the long tradition of hierarchy and privilege began to be challenged successfully in religious and secular affairs, and only when speculation was no longer circumscribed by the assumption of a cosmic hierarchy, did the varieties of modern egalitarian philosophy slowly but dramatically emerge. The record of their subsequent development is in the same important if limited sense the record of the aspirations of the modern Western nations to fashion a new, egalitarian civilization, a "new order of the ages," as the Americans proudly proclaimed.

The philosophers themselves were also, of course, important agents of the aspirations they recorded. As a moral science, political philosophy offered nothing less than a secular alternative to theology. Although the modern discussion of equality appeared first in the theological disputations of the Reformation, it was in the new mode of political philosophy that it received definitive expression. From the start equality was a subject approached from several different points of view. In time these differences crystallized into three distinct traditions. Properly speaking, the designations by which these traditions are known—Liberal, Conservative and Socialist—belong to the nineteenth century. It was only in the aftermath of the democratic revolutions of the late eighteenth century that adherents of all three traditions came into such sharp conflict on such common grounds that they could fairly invite classification. The root concepts, however, extend farther back in time.

In at least one of its essential elements the Liberal concept of equality may be traced to the belief of certain Stoic philosophers in the universality of human reason. The individualism which is apparent in the Liberal advocacy of competitive equality and which accompanies the belief in universal rationality does not arise until much later. Similarly the essential elements of the Conservative concept of equality may be found as early as Plato's *Republic*, where the demand for equality is said to derive from the promptings of envy and appetite in human nature and to call for the levelling of all distinctions in society. The Conservative concept of equality gives rise in the course of history to a variety of responses, but at the base of argument there is always just this identification of equality with depravity in human nature and mass dictatorship in society. A Socialist conception of equality may be said to arise, again in essential elements, in early visions of a Golden Age and in designs for perfect communities, such as that which Plato drew for his guardians, and those which monastic and sectarian groups set as their standard of aspiration. These early examples, however, tend to involve an asceticism and a concern for leisure that are later replaced by an emphasis on material goods and labor.

For a long time these various notions of equality were thought to apply only in an ultimate sense or within strictly limited conditions. It is only with the Protestant Reformation that they begin to take shape as ethical conceptions with immediate bearing upon actual conditions. At first the three concepts of equality appear in religious terms and with relation chiefly to the organization of the church. From these religious grounds they are transferred in seventeenth century thought to a social setting. By the end of the eighteenth century all three concepts have acquired a certain distinctness and rest almost entirely on secular philosophic premises.

In the nineteenth century the existence of the three traditions is made perfectly clear as they are brought into conflict with one another. For the first time it becomes an easy matter to identify and distinguish adherents of each point of view. The Socialist camp included some relatively individualistic egalitarians, but it was mainly composed of those who believed collectivism to be the true expression of equality. As a rule they believed that natural rights egalitarianism was at best only a step in the right direction and at worst a class interest disguised as a universal principle. The Liberals found themselves in the customary middle ground of the meliorist, fending off attacks from both left and right, as they crusaded to extend the principle of equal freedom to more and more areas. While the Socialists denounced them as lackeys of the propertied classes, others opposed to any radical change accused them of opening the way for a thoroughgoing attack upon all distinctions, bound to end in communism and tyranny. The Conservative standard identified a rather more motley assemblage of anxious and angry souls. Their common cause was resistance to all "levelling" and vulgarizing tendencies, their common conviction a belief that the demand for equality was inspired by envy and appetite rather than a sense of justice. Some of those who expounded a Conservative view of equality clung to the wish for a restoration of aristocracy, but others were so impressed by the degeneracy around them that their social vision was entirely defined by melancholy reflections on equality.

By the middle and later decades of the nineteenth century Liberals fell out over the question of whether *laissez faire* served or inhibited "equal freedom," and over the related question of whether popular government promoted or undermined individual autonomy. Those who shared the Conservative view of equality proposed a variety of alternatives to the levelling tendency, ranging from the effort to modify democracy to a flight into romantic individualism. Freud was to provide a synthesis of these tangents of Conservative thought in a prescription harking back to Plato's *Republic*. The solution, as he conceived it, was to appease the demand for equality by promoting a psychological sense of social solidarity while at the same time fostering a new aristocracy of the enlightened which would provide the necessary leadership and maintain order. Among Socialists, Marxian orthodoxy succeeded in fixing a firm philosophic unity even in the midst of continual splintering over policies and personalities. Even so, serious intellectual problems were raised by the Socialist inquiry into the meaning of equality and into the possibility of bringing true communism to fruition. In time such inherent conflicts and doubts came to inhibit the philosophic impulse among adherents of all three schools of thought.

By the end of the century the argument that had blazed with such intensity both among the rival traditions and within each of them came to an almost abrupt end. As political philosophy in general was superseded by the effort to construct empirical social sciences, the philosophic discussion of equality waned to the point of utter disappearance. Philosophic Liberalism became Liberal political economy, the Conservative impulse passed into historical sociology and psychology, and "Scientific Socialism" virtually displaced the more speculative versions. The varieties of egalitarianism, when they appeared at all, would do so thereafter almost exclusively in scientific dress, eventually in all the subdisciplines of the social sciences.

Whether the demise of the philosophic discussion is to be lamented, and what are the implications to be drawn from the tradition of inquiry we are about to trace, are questions that must wait until we have examined in more detail the sequence of development that has only been sketched so far.

Ultimate and Operative: The Classical Dualism

EQUALITY IS a word with both a venerable ancestry and a prodigious burden of inherited meanings. From earliest times it has stood as a component of perhaps the most influential ethical legacy of classical civilization, the striving after justice for all. This ideal, however, was from the first a wholly inadequate instrument for many of the sentiments and schemes put forward in the name of equality. Neither Greek *isonomia* nor Roman *aequitas*, circumscribed as they were by the limitations of legal procedure, could satisfy the demands or contain the longings of those who, even under the protection of the law, felt in some way excluded from what was held to be essential to humanity and civilization. The law might mete out equal justice to all offenders, but the acts it punished were often proscribed only to sanction and protect inequalities of rank and fortune. While the outsiders remained the inarticulate, they could only voice their protests, their hurt, and their resentment through specific appeals for relief and amelioration or in more nearly ultimate, more symbolic, visions of a total renovation of the existing order. Few philosophers spoke for the outcast until the appearance of the Stoic school, and even then the cries of the underprivileged echoed faintly in the councils of the learned.

The Stoic philosophers who in Roman captivity introduced egalitarianism in philosophic terms were, as outsider-intellectuals, well fitted for this historical role. Yet, when their fragmentary work is examined closely, it is by no means clear that Stoic egalitarianism was quite as much in advance of its times as is sometimes imagined. Nor is it fair to the magnificent honesty of the Platonic dialogues or to the grand synthetic achievement of Aristotle to say that before the Stoics equality was always treated in a derogatory way. Egalitarian ideals are of course also expressed in prophetic Judaism and in the ethics of Christianity. In neither of these instances, however, is there an unambiguous and systematic effort to invalidate earthly distinctions except with reference to the ultimate source and destiny of all being, expressed in the belief in the equality of souls before God.

Inadequate definitions of egalitarianism have had the unfortunate effect of greatly oversimplifying the interpretation of its earliest expressions. "There is no change in political theory so startling in its completeness," A. J. Carlyle could write, "as the change from the theory of Aristotle to the later philosophical view represented by Cicero and Seneca. Over against Aristotle's view of the natural inequality of human nature we find set out the theory of the natural equality of human nature."[1] The theory of human nature, however, is only one aspect of political theory in general and of egalitarianism in particular. Aristotle's denial of the humanity of the slave did not prevent him from distinguishing political relations from relations of master and slave and from advocating a form of equality in politics. The Greek Stoics, on the other hand, despite their strongly egalitarian view of human nature and human reason, were for the most part indifferent to politics altogether and therefore, strictly speaking, had no theory of political equality at all. And their Roman successors conceived of the egalitarian state of nature as a condition of the past irrelevant to actual society.[2]

A more comprehensive view of political thought indicates no such startling change in classical history or in the even longer history of both classical and medieval thought. On the contrary there is a remarkable degree of continuity in the discussion of equality throughout these periods. Classical and medieval theorists tend to take a dualistic position with regard to equality which is not at all modified by the contributions of Stoicism and Christianity. In virtually all of the premodern theories, including the Stoic and the Christian, equality and inequality are held together in the same systems of thought. Among the constant motifs of classical and medieval thought are a number of antiegalitarian themes, among them the advocacy of hierarchy on the ground of a gradation in human natures (or by analogy from the superiority of soul to body), and the association of equality with the reign of appetite expressing itself in envy and libertinism. These social and political beliefs are often related to more general systematic assumptions, such as those which assert that the order of the universe is hierarchical or that all creatures and natural phenomena are ranked in orders of perfection, or that, while man is a creature capable of reason and virtue, most men are driven to evil by their passions. In the same systems of thought egalitarian motifs find expression in the persistent myth of the Golden Age; in the Judaeo-Christian belief in a period of original innocence; in the distributive justice of Aristotle; in the communism of Plato's guardians; in Christian indifference to worldly distinctions; and in the communism of monastic orders and certain of the heretical sects.

For the most part, equality and inequality are held together in such a way that they tend to coexist without being subjected to an attempt at integration. The one major attempt at a reconciliation in a form applicable to the whole of existing society was suggested by Plato and developed by Aristotle through the device of proportional equality. By proposing that authority be distributed according to some standard, depending upon the character of the society, Aristotle combined a belief in equality with a belief in the necessity and value of hierarchical organization. Aquinas made a less successful effort at a partial reconciliation in suggesting that slavery be considered merely an "addition" to the natural law.[3] Outside of these attempts, the general tendency of premodern thought is to consider inequality the necessary order of actual society as a whole and equality the ideal order either of a remote and irrevocable past or of those exceptional individuals capable of extraordinary wisdom, asceticism, and virtue.

A comparison of Plato and Aristotle will indicate the difference between the coexistence of equality and inequality and the attempt to integrate them. For Plato, equality in the form of communism has a positive value either as an impractical ideal (the *Laws*) or as a condition of which only the best are capable (*Republic*). The Athenian Stranger, in the *Laws*, prefaces his quite different practical suggestions with this declaration of principle:

The first and highest form of the state and of the government and of the law is that in which there prevails most widely the ancient saying, that "Friends have all things in common." Whether there is anywhere now, or ever will be, this communion of women and children and of property, in which the private and the individual is altogether banished from life, and things which are by nature private, such as eyes and ears and hands, have become common, and in some way see and hear and act in common, and all men express praise and blame and feel joy and sorrow on the same occasions, and whatever laws there are unite the city to the utmost,—whether all this is possible or not, I say that no man, acting upon any other principle, will ever constitute a state which will be truer or more exalted in virtue.[4]

Otherwise, equality carries only the negative attributes of corruption. In the *Republic* Plato's political doctrine is rigorously constructed upon the basis of an organic functional-natural hierarchy. In nature men are not equal: the physician and the carpenter are as differently constituted as male and female; nor are all men born with the same capacity for learning.[5] Order in society is attained by relating each class of people with its appropriate function and in relating the functional classes according to the rank ascribed to each. Order, or temperance, is the "harmony of the weaker and the stronger, and the middle class," in whatever respects weakness and strength may be said to consist,[6] and justice is the recognition of this order in the laws. Democracy errs against nature, and therefore against temperance and justice, in dispensing "a sort of equality to equals and unequals alike," making no distinctions of quality. It does not order but only assimilates the greatest variety of natures and manners, and holds them together in a profane pantheon always in danger of collapsing from its unsound construction. Anyone in search of a constitution to govern a society could go to democracy as "to a bazaar at which they sell them, and pick out the one that suits him," since democracy combines all sorts of elements indiscriminately.[7] The life of democratic man "has neither law nor order, and this distracted existence he terms joy and bliss and freedom. . ."[8]

Democratic equality is thus not a value among other values, but an attack upon all value, all order. Sons become equal to fathers, the metic and the citizen have identical rights, the stranger is equal to the native, and the slave is equal to his purchaser. The master fears and flatters his students, and the students lose respect for their teachers. The young man is as "venerable" as the oldest, and the old adopt the manners of the young. Even the animals mimic the democratic behavior of the people: "the horses and asses have a way of marching along with all the rights and dignities of freemen; and they will run at anybody who comes in their way if he does not leave the road clear for them: and all things are ready to burst with liberty."[9]

Plato's critique of democracy applies also to that stage of the degeneration from perfection which is designated oligarchy. Oligarchy is established when an error in eugenics creates a number of guardians who abandon ascetic communism for the sake of material acquisition and finally succeed in overthrowing the remnant of true guardians. From that moment appetite is in the saddle. Ambition and avarice replace learning, virtue, and simplicity, and wealth becomes the only recognized standard of value. Oligarchy is only the first phase of the domination of appetite. It is succeeded by democracy because the criterion of wealth cannot produce effective leadership and because the *polis* comes to be divided into groups of have's and have not's, sharing the same materialist aspirations. The revolt of the poor and the debtors overthrows the wealthy oligarchs and establishes the second phase of appetite.[10] If oligarchy overthrew every standard but wealth, democracy levels even this last barrier to total anarchy. The final term of the development is the passage from democracy to tyranny, the ultimate stage of degeneration. An "excess of liberty . . . seems to pass into excess of slavery."[11]

Plato's critique of equality, like his affirmation of inequality, is the *locus classicus* for all aristocratic antiegalitarian thought. Gregory Vlastos has suggested that Plato's political doctrines are intimately associated with his cosmology. Plato's views concerning slavery, the state, man, and the world, Vlastos observes, all illustrate a single hierarchic pattern.[12] Informing all of these particular views is the two-world theory. The body is the slave or servant of the soul as the mortal is the servant of the divine and as the mechanical realm is the servant of purpose. In the *Timaeus* Plato sees this analogy symbolized physiologically: the head is shaped like the universe and the neck is an isthmus and boundary separating and relating the head and the body. Cosmic order is maintained because teleology governs mechanical necessity—significantly, Vlastos points out, by "persuasion." Plato's opponents, the Ionian physicists, oppose his cosmological theories and also his political theories. Plato, in fact, "imputes to them not only mechanistic cosmology, but also the contract theory of the state." Just as physical bodies move themselves in a self-regulating system of nature, the Ionians are said to argue, so human laws are not absolute commands but man-made agreements.[13]

This association of Plato's political and cosmological theory bears interesting implications, not only for Plato's critique of the conventionalist theory expounded by Glaucon and Thrasymachus in the *Republic*,[14] but also for the change from classical to modern thinking about equality. It is reasonable to suppose that once the belief in social hierarchy lost the support of cosmology (as it may well have seemed after the Copernican revolution), that belief became more difficult to maintain. The modern social contract theories, like the early conventionalist arguments, present an egalitarian notion of society more compatible with a view of nature as a nonhierarchical interplay of forces.

Perhaps because he accepted neither Plato's cosmology nor his two-world theory, and because he regarded teleology as a potential within nature, Aristotle could reject the belief in natural equality and yet at the same time retain equality as a principle of social organization. Like Plato, Aristotle held that ruling and being ruled is the condition of all natural objects and that among rational creatures rule should be assigned to those superior in reason.[15] Since it is impossible a priori to separate men into ranks until their various potentialities are put in evidence, it is essential that the *polis* be ordered according to the principle of distributive justice. In the absolutely best *polis*, rights and privileges would be available to all but distributed according to individual contributions to the welfare of the community. Thus all would participate in the advantages of the *polis*, but in a measure equal to their individual merit, and authority would be bestowed upon those who demonstrate superiority in reason.[16] The best *practical* state would take into account not only merit but birth and wealth. This *polis*, the "polity," would therefore be a mixed constitution blending democracy and oligarchy under the general scheme of all justice—proportional equality. Arithmetical or numerical equality would be appropriate only if all men were identical in nature and in their contribution to the welfare of the state. Since on neither count will there be identity, the constitution must take the differences into account;[17] at the same time Aristotle recognizes that extreme inequalities in property and power are both dangerous and unjust. It is a "sorry thing" that men should live in penury, and "it is difficult for men who have suffered that fate not to be revolutionaries."[18] Democracy is valuable because the populace in a well-ordered state is more to be relied upon for prudence than a single ruler or even a few rulers, and because, while statecraft is an art, it is one of those arts in which often the consumers are better judges of the product than the maker himself. "The diner—not the cook—will be the best judge of the feast."[19]

Aristotle's attempt to combine elements of hierarchy and social aristocracy with elements of equality presents a major contrast not only with the ideals of Plato's *Republic*, but with most of classical and medieval political theory as well.[20] Plato's theory is most in accord with the dominant trend of thought. The natural order of the universe and therefore of all human institutions is hierarchical: this principle underlies what is by far the major tendency in pre-Reformation political theory in regard to the problem of equality. This natural order is regarded as the divinely prescribed, original, and unchanging constitution of the universe. As Augustine put it, "From heaven to earth, from the visible to the invisible, some things are good, others better than others. In this they are unequal, so that all kinds of things might be."[21] The influential works of the Pseudo-Dionysius, originally reputed to be early patristic but later revealed to be a fifth century forgery, indicate that even after the impact of Christianity had been felt for some time the belief in hierarchical order was by no means diminished. According to Pseudo-Dionysius, the universe is a series of concentric circles in which a hierarchic system mediates between God and man. The rays of the sun reach all men, no matter which circle they inhabit, but the circles are not equidistant from the source of light. Those nearer God are the more perfect; they are therefore given rule over the others.[22] If the superior is deceived, if he is unjust to subordinates, he must still be venerated and assisted as a superior. The slave who hits his master is always wrong, like the child who hits his father.[23] The social relations of inequality are thus regarded as sacred natural relations, even though God's love reaches all men equally.

The persistence of antiegalitarian thought, however, did not rule out the survival of the egalitarian elements in their specifically premodern form. Premodern egalitarian thought may be distinguished from the later varieties by a number of characteristics. Equality is often conceived as the rule for an ideal state located in some distant or mythic past beyond recovery; or else it is held up as a condition to which only the best may aspire. Usually equality of property and equality in social relations are assumed to go together, but the communism envisioned is often ascetic. This asceticism is joined to an exaltation of contemplative leisure and a disdain of labor and other physical forms of activity. Not all of these characteristics are present in each manifestation of premodern egalitarian thought, but, taken together, these are the dominant motifs.

The earliest expression of these premodern egalitarian themes is probably contained in the Greek myth of a Golden Age. The Roman Saturnalia indicates the sense in which this myth came to be understood, as well as the attitude it expressed in celebrating the "brief return" to the Golden Age of Saturn, or Chronos.[24] Pompeius Trogus, in the first century A.D., describes the festival in terms of the Roman version of the Greek myth:

The first inhabitants of Italy were the Aborigines, whose king, Saturn, is said to have been so just that there were no slaves under him nor any private property, but all things belonged to all in common and undivided, as if all men had one patrimony. In memory of this precedent it was decreed that during the Saturnalia, by a leveling of all men's rights, slaves should sit down at banquets with their masters indiscriminately.[25]

Upon the Saturnalia, Lucian wrote in the next century, "there shall be equal honor to all, both slaves and free, both poor and rich." [26] This memorialization of the Golden Age by means of a festival underscored the original Greek view of the myth as "irrelevant to man's life as it now is . . ." The Golden Age, so the accepted interpretation ran,

was enjoyed by a different breed of mortals, in a different condition of the world and (in one version) under different gods, and no practical moral could therefore consistently be drawn from it for the guidance of the present race. It was by implication irrecoverable, at least by men's own efforts.[27]

Apart from its memorialization, the Golden Age myth was made to serve at least two other functions. After Virgil's precedent, it became a literary convention invoking a return of primitive bliss whenever a new reign was inaugurated. For the Cynics and Stoics it played a more meaningful role, serving as the basis of a critique of civilized life in the name of the virtues of nature. But neither the Cynics nor the Stoics envisioned a restoration of the primitive condition for society as a whole. The effort of the Stoics was "not to establish a new social order but to persuade individuals to return to the life of nature, as individuals." [28] Seneca drew a portrait of the Golden Age rich in detail and pregnant with didactic commentary on human weakness and virtue, but, as Norman Cohn has pointed out,

Seneca was convinced that the old egalitarian order was not only lost but necessarily lost. As time passed, men had become vicious; and once that happened, institutions such as private property, coercive government, differentiation of status, even slavery were not only inevitable but also needful; not only consequences of but also remedies for the corruption of human nature.[29]

Plato had indicated still another, but not a fundamentally different, application of the Golden Age myth when he declared communism to be an impractical ideal for society as a whole but appropriate for the elite of an ideal society. Medieval monasticism followed a similar pattern, integrating a communism of the elite with the generally hierarchical organization of the church and society.

Apostolic Christianity maintained the prevailing dualism by announcing a doctrine of equality relevant to man and society only in terms of eschatological promise. Insofar as the Christian community is an eschatological congregation it is "withdrawn from the world," and "this world's distinctions have lost their meaning" in this context. The message of Paul (Galatians 3:28), "There is neither Jew nor Greek, there is neither slave nor free, there is neither male nor female; for you are all one in Christ Jesus," is no call to revolt. Men are counselled to remain in whatever earthly station they find themselves because, as Bultmann puts it, "the negation of worldly differentiations does not mean a sociological program within this world; rather it is an eschatological occurrence which takes place only within the Eschatological congregation." [30] Whether the eschatological community is identical with the church is a question which has agitated Christendom for many centuries. Clearly, however, there is suggested in Apostolic Christianity a distinction between existing conditions, in which inequality is the rule, and the ideal condition, which is egalitarian but which is associated only with the expectation of redemption. As the eschatological impulse of Christianity recedes and the church comes into being, the ideal of equality comes to be associated with a vision of paradise lost rather than with an eschatological hope. Only the monastics and often heretical sectarian movements seek to fulfill the ideal in practice. The passing of Apostolic Christianity brought a shift in the discussion of equality from eschatological longing to acceptance of present corruption. In the patristic literature, especially of the later period, it was commonly held that inequality was not intended by God but that, as a result of the fall, inegalitarian institutions were indispensable. St. Cyprian, St. Zeno of Verona, and St. Ambrose, the latter citing the Stoa as well as Genesis, all declared equality of property to be the condition of innocence,[31] no longer possible after the fall.

It was Augustine, however, who provided the most general and most influential statement of this dualistic position. God had intended that men have dominion over "irrational creation"; thus "the righteous men in primitive times were made shepherds of cattle rather than kings of men, God intending thus to teach us what the relative position of the creatures is, and what the desert of sin . . ." Slavery and other forms of inequality such as now exist are "the result of sin." [32] No man falls under the domination of another but by the just punishment of God. The inequality of the earthly world is ordained by God, and because it is, slaves are to remain in subjection, not in "crafty fear but in faithful love, until all unrighteousness pass away, and all principality and every human power be brought to nothing, and God be all in all." [33] Equality is thus regarded as the original condition of mankind, no longer applicable to the world until redemption is complete. In the meantime the ideal is suspended and the justification of inequality becomes the justification of all temporal authority. The difference between the Christian citizen and the pagan, however, is that the pagan regards the city of man as an end in itself, whereas the Christian suffers its iniquities as a punishment for his sin and therefore lives "like a captive and a stranger in the earthly city." [34]

Just as constant a theme in premodern egalitarianism is the description of the ideal state in terms of a communism which is notable for its disdain of material goods. The Golden Age myth appeared in two opposed versions, one regarding the original state as a time of plenty and enjoyment, the other regarding it as a time of simple needs and no luxuries. The latter view is aptly described by Lovejoy and Boas as "hard primitivism." "Enough of the oak tree!" was the way one classical commentator described the attitude that must have propelled men out of their primitive condition.[35] The Cynics and Stoics idealize the simplicity of the primitive natural state, but their call for a return to the ways of nature is less an advocacy of the community of goods than an attack upon superfluous possessions. The man of wealth was to be pitied, not pillaged. The communism of Plato's guardians is designed to prevent them from developing attachments to material things. They are to be paid a sum sufficient only for their necessities. The patristic views of paradise are informed by a similar eulogy of simplicity and a condemnation of luxury as a temptation to sin. The monastic orders and the sectarian communist groups display an equally severe attitude toward worldly goods. Consistent with this attitude is another characteristic: the egalitarian condition is identified with the absence of work, with leisure, and with contemplation. In the Golden Age men's needs are provided for by spontaneous production. In the Christian paradise it was unnecessary for man to work until his expulsion. The Cynics actually glorify laziness and leisure.[36] Plato's guardians are to perform no labor save that of the mind. The monks devote themselves to contemplation; they work only as they must to subsist.

Whatever differences there are among the various expressions of equality characteristic of ancient and medieval times, the continuity of thought among them all is surely remarkable, especially when the general tendencies are contrasted with the characteristics of egalitarian thought from the Reformation onward. On virtually every point, the several forms of modern egalitarianism break sharply with these traditional views.

CHAPTER THREE

Equality in the Reformation

HE MODERN discussion of equality departs from the classical
precedents in the first place by a tendency to treat the
issue in terms that are operative as well as ultimate. For
moral philosophy in general and egalitarianism in particular, what
defines the modern experience is, if not the end of the classical
dualism, at least a constant chafing at it.

This movement of egalitarian thought from the plane of remote
ideals to that of immediate objectives, like other profound changes
also associated with the same historical designations, is not so
dramatic and visible as the terms "Renaissance" and "Reformation" might suggest. The revival of classical learning at first contributed only to the restatement of Stoic values in humanistic
ethics and to egalitarian utopias such as those of More and
Campanella. In effect Renaissance humanism reinforced tendencies already evident in the more visionary productions of the
millenarian sects, in which the oppressed and the impatient sought
to lead the promised life in communities of the perfect withdrawn
from the corrupt world (and usually from the corrupt church as
well). Ordinarily the sectarian movements did not exhort believers to act upon their beliefs in society. All these developments merely gave active renewal to the classical dualism according to which equality was a remote ideal of the past or future or a
condition toward which only the few best might aspire, but never

a proper goal for the whole of mankind in present conditions. In putting place for time, the Renaissance utopias may well have portended more radical developments, but in themselves they were no great departure from the same dualistic tradition.

The Reformation had a more pronounced role in bringing about a breach with this tradition. Many early critics of the papacy like Marsilius of Padua and William of Occam anticipated particular arguments of the Reformers, but it is in the writings of three prominent Protestant spokesmen that we may first discern systematic statements of egalitarian doctrines shortly to emerge in explicit political terms. From the start the note is unmistakably new, even though Luther, Calvin, and Müntzer were no less indebted to the theological tradition than the secular humanists were to the dormant legacy of classical philosophy. The single most important difference, perhaps, is that the Reformers incurred their debts in a deliberate effort to reform, to reorient, Christian society. The religious Reformers are united by a sense of the need to make the ultimate beliefs of the Christian immediate standards for understanding and conduct. Under the stimulus of this practical concern equality becomes a pressing issue. It can no longer be assigned to heaven, or to a primitive Eden, or even to some indwelling soul-stuff. For tactical as well as creedal reasons, the Reformers were driven to argue against the justification of inequality that sustained church and society alike, even though some were concerned to deny the implications of their doctrines which seemed to promote more far-reaching effects than they themselves had in mind.

LUTHER: THE SPIRITUAL EQUALITY OF CHRISTIANS

In Luther's attack upon certain of the accepted interpretations of fundamental Christian doctrines concerning the character of man, the conduct of life, and the organization of church and society, a conception of equality emerges which in a number of important respects foreshadows and contributes to the development of Liberal political egalitarianism. The key to this contribution is Luther's theological restatement of the Christian conception of spiritual existence in the world. This theological principle, in

the novel formulation it receives in much of Luther's work, underlies his denial of the superiority of the religious over the secular
estate, his advocacy of the equal authority of all believers in
spiritual matters, and his notion of life as a competition in virtue
challenging every Christian, no matter what his office or station,
to perform his vocation in a spiritual manner.

Luther's conception of spiritual existence was never completely
detached from its medieval antecedents. Especially when he was
confronted by practical consequences of his innovations which
threatened the success of the Reform movement as a whole,
Luther tended to revert to the older conception of spirituality.
This is particularly evident in his response to the assertion of
temporal authority against the doctrines of the Reformers and in
his rebuke of the rebellious peasants. Luther may well have feared
that the application of his doctrine to politics would jeopardize
the prospects for a reformation of the church. Nevertheless, the
logic of the Lutheran position leads as directly into politics as it
does into religion.

Sometimes Luther's demand for an end to the division between
the secular and the religious realms is made perfectly clear. In his
letter to the German nobility, Luther called upon the temporal
lords to direct the reform of the church themselves because

there is really no difference between laymen and priests, princes and
bishops, "spirituals" and "temporals," as they call them, except that
of office and work, but not of "estate," for they are all of the same
estate . . . though they are not engaged in the same work . . .[1]

And again:

it is intolerable that in the canon law so much importance is attached
to the freedom, life and property of the clergy, as though the laity
were not also as spiritual and as good Christians as they, or did not
belong to the Church. . . We are all alike Christians, and have baptism,
faith, Spirit, and all things alike. If a priest is killed, the land is laid
under interdict—why not when a peasant is killed? Whence comes
this great distinction between those who are equally Christians? Only
from human laws and inventions![2]

Luther knew perfectly well that these "human laws and inventions" were not offhand abuses or superficial errors. Centuries
of effort on the part of apologists for papal power had gone into

establishing the difference between the two estates and claiming superiority for the spiritual, not only in its own limited sphere but also in that infinitely extensible area in which the spiritual authorities were to guide the use of the temporal sword. In Luther's view, the distinction between spiritual and temporal, *sacerdotium* and *imperium*, *ecclesia* and *civitas*, had been fabricated into an instrument of papal power which could be and had been exercised in ways not in accord with the spiritual mission of the church. "What is the use in Christendom of those people who are called the Cardinals?" he asked. Were they, as ranking members of the spiritual estate, vicars of Christ and shepherds of his sheep? Not at all; their only "duty" was to lay hold of the wealth of Italy and Germany for the augmentation of the papal treasury.[3]

In the first instance Luther's attack thus took the form of an exposure of the doctrine of spiritual supremacy as the rationalization of a desire for power. He was compelled, however, to go further because, like the canonists who had constructed it, he recognized that this doctrine was only the top layer of a many-tiered theological argument. Just underneath the distinction between spiritual and temporal estates, which established a hierarchy of persons, lay the distinction between those vocations which were sacred and those which were carnal. Deeper still was the distinction between soul and body, for it was upon the interpretation of this relation that the entire edifice was erected. As Walter Ullmann has pointed out, the canonists in particular thought of the conflict between pope and emperor as the political aspect of the antagonism between soul and body. They argued that "just as the soul is superior to the body, in the same way the pope is superior to the emperor."[4] By the same analogy the entire clergy was superior to the laity.[5] Given this system of analogies, the canonists concluded, it is against nature to consider everyone equal. Indeed, as they argued, the entire universe could not exist except upon the presupposition of inequality expressed in the social hierarchy.[6]

Luther's attack upon this justification of inequality did not stop at the superstructural level which defined the relations between pope and emperor, clergy and laity. It went straight to the premises of the canonists' argument. Luther would hardly have denied the existence, indeed the supremely crucial importance, of an antagonism between soul and body. But he understood this antagonism in a way that precluded any attempt to use it to justify social hierarchy. Luther denied both of the related conclusions that the canonists had reached: that certain vocations were spiritual, others carnal, and that the men who performed them were "spirituals" and "carnals." For Luther the conflict between soul and body was a problem *for all Christians* in *every calling* they pursued. When Paul told the Galatians, "Walk in the Spirit and ye shall not fulfill the lust of the flesh," he gave this counsel "not only unto hermits and monks, which lead a single life, but unto all Christians . . . we should not err with the Papists, which dreamed that this commandment belongeth only to their clergymen." Nor is the meaning of "fleshly lust" confined to sexuality or to bodily desires, for it applies just as much to "spiritual" temptations. Paul warned the faithful "not only to bridle the gross motions of the flesh, as carnal lust, wrath, impatiency and suchlike; but also the spiritual motions, as doubting, idolatry, contempt and hatred of God, etc." Thus it is impossible, according to Luther, to base a distinction of vocations upon the antagonism of body and soul, since the category of "sins of the flesh" applies to "spiritual" as well as "bodily" activities.[7]

It is upon this reworking of Christian theology that Luther argues against the distinction between the temporal and spiritual estates. The injunctions of the law do not apply exclusively to particular callings; prince and priest, all who are Christians, face an identical challenge. "So let every man in his calling walk in the Spirit, and he shall not fulfil either his carnal lust or any of the works of the flesh."[8] Hence "they [the Papists] are madmen, not understanding what the Spirit or what the flesh is. The Spirit is whatsoever is done in us according to the Spirit . . . Wherefore all the duties of a Christian man, as to love his wife, to bring up his children, to govern his family, honour his parents, obey the magistrate, &c. (which unto them are worldly and carnal) are the fruits of the Spirit."[9]

To go from Luther's critique of church doctrine and organization to the reforms he proposed is merely to restate the same beliefs in other terms. The idea that all vocations are alike in presenting an opportunity for spiritual conduct and that all Christians are equally capable of spiritual existence expresses itself in Luther's celebrated advocacy of "the priesthood of [all] believers." [10] Luther did not conceive of the equality of Christians as a merely inner condition, or as a remote eventuality, in the manner of Augustine, but as an existential imperative, at least in the organization of the church:

Through baptism all of us are consecrated to the priesthood . . . [W]hen the bishop consecrates it is the same thing as if he, in the place and stead of the whole congregation, all of whom have like power, were to take one out of their number and charge him to use this power for the others, just as though ten brothers, all king's sons and equal heirs, were to choose one of themselves to rule the inheritance for them all—they would all be kings and equal in power, though one of them would be charged with the duty of ruling.[11]

The priests should be "ministers chosen from among us, who do all that they do in our name." [12] No one may make use of the priestly power "except by the consent of the community or by the call of a superior. For what is the common property of all, no individual may arrogate to himself, unless he be called." [13] In the church there is no authority accorded individuals save what is conferred by the congregation, and all authority granted is subject to revocation:

No one must put himself forward and undertake, without our consent and election, to do what is in the power of all of us. For what is common to all, no one dare take upon himself without the will and the command of the community; and should it happen that one chosen for such an office were deposed for malfeasance he would then be just what he was before he held office . . .[14]

The equality of believers applies not only to the election of ministers, but also to the interpretation of Scripture:

It may well happen that the pope and his followers are wicked men, and no true Christians, not taught of God, not having true understanding. On the other hand, an ordinary man may have true understanding; why then should we not follow him?

. . . although they allege that this power [to interpret Scripture] was given to Peter when the keys were given to him, it is plain enough that the keys were not given to Peter alone, but to the whole community . . . [I]f we are all priests . . . and all have one faith, one Gospel, one sacrament, why should we not also have the power to test and judge what is correct or incorrect in matters of faith? [15]

If Luther had carried his egalitarianism nowhere else than to the church, the importance of his reform to political history and to the history of political thought would be great enough. To suggest that the spiritual equality of Christians was at all applicable to social institutions, even if only to the church, was to question seriously not only the distinction between earthly servitude and ideal equality, upon which both ecclesiastical and secular hierarchy had found firm support, but also the later medieval attempt to justify both civil and ecclesiastical hierarchy by analogy with the hierarchy of the heavens.[16] If the papal doctrine of apostolic succession was invalid, monarchic succession and aristocracy of birth could not remain outside the shadow of doubt. If it became established that the head of the church could claim no exclusive right to interpret divine law, would not the right of his secular counterpart to declare the law of nature undergo similar critical scrutiny? In these momentous respects Luther's ecclesiastical reform points in the direction of the Liberal revolt against inequality in political authority.

Far-reaching as are the political implications of this limited view of Luther's doctrines, it remains to be seen whether they are really only implications and extensions, or whether they are not actually included, from a theoretical point of view, in the doctrines themselves. Luther was fond of citing the saying of Peter (I:2:9), "Ye are a chosen generation, a royal priesthood and a priestly kingdom," [17] and he referred to it in the *Treatise on Christian Liberty* when he announced, "We are all priests and kings in Christ, as many as believe in Christ." He was careful to guard against misinterpretation by explicitly denying that Christian liberty is to be understood as giving every Christian dominion over earthly things; it gives him a spiritual "dominion" over the sufferings caused by earthly oppression and human weakness.[18]

If Luther intended the same reservations to apply to spiritual equality, he certainly departed from the earlier trend of his thought. If there is no such thing as a temporal calling, if all vocations are spiritual, whether governmental, ecclesiastical, or economic, how should one calling entitle its holder to possess *authority* over other Christians? Luther denied that the bishops or the pope had any authority, by virtue of their calling, over "laymen." He sought the help of the princes in overthrowing the usurped authority of the Roman Church, "especially since now they also are fellow-Christians, fellow-priests, 'fellow-spirituals,' fellow-lords over all things . . ." [19] If the vocation of other "fellow-spirituals" whose province was the ministry did not give them *authority* over other Christians, how could those whose province was government claim any exemption? Under the medieval formula they could claim authority on the basis of a distinction between spiritual and temporal realms; but now that their concerns were made spiritual, and all Christians declared spirituals, what ground could there be for prescribing obedience to temporal officeholders? Luther had already demonstrated that the mere articulation of callings into an organic division of functions had no bearing on the question of authority, at least not church authority. How then could those who ministered to the bodily concerns of society, themselves as much spiritual servants of God as any priest, claim authority on the basis of their function?

Luther never resolved the knotty political questions his doctrines raised. When he was confronted with disagreeable inferences he simply left his own position and retreated to traditional lines of defense. In 1523, after he had been condemned by the Diet of Worms, Luther was in no mood to argue for the right of princes to interfere in religious matters, on any basis. His treatise on the limits of secular authority therefore cuts the ground from under his earlier appeal to the nobility by raising again the issue of the two distinct realms, secular and spiritual, and denying that secular authorities are fit to judge spiritual issues. Luther here resumes the Augustinian cloak in no uncertain terms. "If all the world were composed of real Christians . . . no prince, king, lord or sword would be needed," but few are really Christians, so it is impossible that a society could exist with nothing other than the Sermon on the Mount to guide it.[20] Secular government is ordained by God as a necessary means of controlling a sinful world. Even though the world cannot dispense with the sword, princes have no warrant for interfering in spiritual matters. They are after all only "God's jailers and hangmen." [21] It is up to the bishops to guard true doctrine and punish heretics; besides, "heresy can never be prevented by force," which is the only instrument belonging to the princes.[22] "[H]ow dare the senseless secular power judge and control such a secret, spiritual, hidden matter as faith?"[23] Luther heaps disparaging remarks upon the secular authorities: it is well known, he observes, that a prince is a rare bird in heaven.[24] The realm of Christ is another matter, and "these two kingdoms must be sharply distinguished." There is no such authority among Christians "but Christ Himself, and Christ alone. And what kind of authority can there be where all are equal and have the same right, power, possession, and honor, and no one desires to be the other's superior, but each the other's inferior?" [25]

This treatise can be read as a refinement of Luther's earlier position. It retains the attack on ecclesiastical hierarchy, but now contends for a temporal authority which does not reside in the whole community. The difficulty with such a reading is that it must ignore the degree to which Luther has retreated from his earlier radical position to conventional grounds. Luther's distinction of two realms reverts to the distinction at the heart of the accepted medieval theory. In this respect alone, the argument of the treatise runs against the general trend of Lutheran thought away from the separation between church and society and toward their reunification in a world in which all callings would be considered spiritual. This, at any rate, is what is novel in Luther's attitude. Luther's disparaging references to the temporal authorities are reminiscent of nothing so much as Augustine's characterization of the rulers of the Roman *civitas* as a "band of robbers." When Luther had previously described them as "now fellow-spirituals," surely he must have had in mind something a good deal different. And regardless of what he had in mind, the implications of his theory lead inexorably to an extension to the "temporal realm" of the attack upon ecclesiastical inequality. Once Luther had begun to distinguish between true Christians, of which for purposes of temporal authority there are few, and nominal Christians, who compose the bulk of society, what becomes of his attempt to break down the medieval grades of perfection and the differential system of religious obligations? The canonists would surely have agreed with Luther as far as he took the argument. And they would have gone on to point out that, given his premises and given the fact that secular government has an effect upon the conditions of faith, it was essential that the church be made superior. But on this road there would lie no reformation.

A similar reversion to medieval thinking is exemplified in Luther's admonitions to the rebellious peasants. Here, even more explicitly than in his treatise on *Secular Authority*, he argues for the very distinction between spiritual and carnal which he had earlier denied and, consequently, for a distinction between carnal and spiritual vocations.

If, according to Luther, the works of the world were to be sanctified as the service of God, it followed that the conditions of labor were no longer exempt from spiritual regulation. This was the plain implication the peasants drew from his doctrines. In the moving *Twelve Articles* the peasants of Swabia demanded to know why, if all men were equally spiritual, they should be kept in serfdom.[26] They addressed a letter to Luther, asking him to comment on their arguments. Luther took pains to restrain his anger. He was deeply disturbed by the peasant agitation, partly because he sympathized with the peasantry and partly because, if the Reform movement should be held responsible, Luther and his followers would make even more enemies among the powerful than they already had. Luther's answer to the peasants was that for the most part they were wrong and had been misled by such false prophets as the "satan of Allstedt,"[27] Thomas Müntzer. Luther reminds them that Abraham had slaves and that Paul commands servants to obey their masters, because Christian freedom is not something carnal. The argument of the peasants

would make all men equal and turn the spiritual kingdom of Christ into a worldly, external kingdom; and that is impossible. For a worldly kingdom cannot stand unless there is in it an inequality of persons, so that some are free, some imprisoned, some lords, some subjects.[28]

The peasants have no right to resist the lord, Luther insists, even if he suppresses the Gospel. In such a case the peasants are advised simply to leave and seek the Gospel elsewhere. In this, as in temporal matters, it is not for the common man to judge for himself whether or not a ruler is wicked. Princes may only be judged and punished by others who hold the sword by God's authority. For the peasants to arrogate this power to themselves, because they consider themselves wronged by a lord, would make them judges in their own case, which, Luther urges, is both intolerable and against the law of nature. For, "if your enterprise were right, then any man might become judge over another, and there would remain in the world neither authority, nor government, nor order, nor land, but there would be only murder and bloodshed."[29]

Here too Luther overrides his own precedents. He had himself avoided a similar charge of promoting anarchy in the church by assigning authority to the community and to the officers chosen by the community. Now he feels compelled to make even this argument a dead letter as far as the peasants are concerned. The peasants demanded the right to choose their own pastor[30] and to support him with the tithes which they paid to the lord, traditionally taken for the support of the church. Luther did not contest the right of the peasants to choose their pastor, all other things being equal. What he denied was that they had any right to dispose of the tithes as they chose, because to do so would amount to robbing the lord. If they could not support a pastor from "their own" resources, they must request the lord to appoint a pastor. Here Luther was met with the practical aspects of the relations between the spiritual and temporal, and in effect chose to maintain the superiority of the princes over even the reformed congregations. In addition he exposed his own late attempt to separate them as at least suspiciously opportunistic. Even as opportunism, it seems a principle ill-fitted to serve a reformation in view of the considerable extent of church-owned land worked by serfs. To put himself in so awkward a position, Luther must have felt himself quite at the mercy of immediate pressures.

These pressures were real and important. In the effort to separate what is new in Luther's doctrine from what is old and antagonistic to it, it would be a mistake not to recognize that Luther went through a development influenced by arguments raised against him, by a regard for the reception of his message, and in general by a concern for the manifold problems of a reform movement. Karl Holl has concluded that, despite Luther's attempts to delineate two distinct realms, it was ultimately his own doctrines which led to the state supervision of the Lutheran church.[31] And Max Weber has demonstrated that, despite Luther's strictures against preoccupation with wealth and the goods of the earth, his own teachings readily served to inspire acquisitive habits.[32]

These anomalous outcomes had a common origin in Luther's over-all effort to level all the walls separating spiritual and temporal. The spiritualization of previously temporal callings acted as a spur to dormant ambitions and opened the way to eminence to individuals and groups long excluded from respectability. Even the emphasis upon faith rather than works as the means to salvation made it possible for later generations to regard economic behavior as ethically indifferent. Luther did not intend all these consequences. His image of society was organic and functional, not atomistic and acquisitive. Since men ought to conduct their lives as servants of God in Christian brotherhood, not as rivals for power and wealth, their economic relations would surely need to be regulated by ethical norms. Nevertheless, the impact of Luther's position in many respects indicates a movement toward Liberalism in economics as well as politics. The equal spirituality of all men and all callings conferred certain rights with critical political implications. Every Christian now had the right to interpret the Bible for himself; not that all interpretations were correct, but only the community could decide which to accept, and no belief could be enforced by coercion. The frequent efforts of Reformers to settle their doctrinal differences by persuasion, or, when discussion was of no avail, their inclination either to abide by the will of a given community or to leave and found a new one, soon found echoes in democratic politics.

Luther certainly anticipated the economic individualism which arose as a counterpart of political Liberalism. It is in Luther's discussion of labor in one's calling that the first inkling of the Liberal doctrine of competitive equality can be seen. It was Luther, not some latter-day *laissez-faire* Liberal, who wrote:

He who wishes to be poor should not be rich; and if he wishes to be rich, let him put his hand to the plow and seek his riches in the earth! It is enough if the poor are decently cared for, so that they do not die of hunger or of cold. It is not fitting that one man should live

in idleness on another's labor, or be rich and live comfortably at the
cost of another's discomfort, according to the present perverted custom . . . God has not decreed that any man shall live from another's
goods save only the priests, who rule and preach, and these because
of their spiritual labor . . .[33]

Luther's emphasis on the positive value of labor as an aspect of
the calling was in itself an important contribution to the emergence
of modern egalitarianism. In classical times aristocracy, leisure, and
a disdain for labor often went together. Aristotle and Plato provided philosophic justification for this attitude by treating labor
as no more than a necessary condition of existence to be performed
by those not fitted for the higher ends of life; leisure (scholé) was
identified, or at least associated, with meditation or the philosophic
life, the highest human end.[34] Medieval Catholicism carried classical aristocracy into the organization of the church not only in the
form of a hierarchy of offices, but in the form of grades of perfection. The perfect religious life was the one most divorced from
physical labor, not of course in the negative sense of idleness but
in the positive sense of meditation. The philosophic counterpart
of this attitude was the elevation of the spirit over the flesh.
Luther's reinterpretation of this antagonism coincides with his
new attitude toward labor. The critique of monasticism implies
the critique of the notion of grades of perfection in vocations. For
Luther the act of glorifying God was not to be performed apart
from life, in meditation, but through one's calling, whatever it
might be, and in the attempt to bridle the natural man, the "old
Adam." To avoid such an engagement by denying the flesh altogether and by not laboring in a calling was to act contrary to
nature and to encourage those very excesses of fleshly desire which
it was intended to prevent. "A man cannot be idle," Luther
warned, "because the need of his body drives him and he is compelled to do many good works to reduce it to subjection."[35]
Monkhood and mendicancy were both condemned as dangerous
to the spiritual life.

Luther's identification of labor with "good works" is worth
noting. He had a very low estimation of the value of such "good
works" as were represented by religious feast-days, and in at least
one place contrasts them to labor, which he finds truly holy. "The

holy days are not holy and the working days are holy . . . they [the priests] would be doing a far better work if they honored the saint by turning a saint's-day into a working day." To the common man these festivals are injurious, because he spends too much, neglects his work, and is so sapped of his strength that he "weakens his body and unfits it for work." [36]

Luther's attitude toward commerce is in some ways even more radical for his time. He did not advocate free trade; like many of his contemporaries he was in favor of municipal mercantilism, but he strongly attacked the tendencies toward monopoly which were developing in the late feudal economy. He denounced the trading companies and the joint stock companies, condemning both as monopolies.[37] He opposed them for two reasons: monopolies drive out competition by unfair methods, and it is immoral to make a profit by simply investing money for a guaranteed return. If one uses one's own money in the effort to make a profit, there is always the risk of loss and therefore, according to Luther, the enterprise is a moral one.[38] Investing in stock, even though the profit envisioned be moderate, is immoral because this risk is avoided. Just as monkhood was immoral because it avoided the perils of life, or sought to avoid them, so the effort to attain easy financial security was not the mark of a true Christian. Economics, like the other aspects of life, was for Luther the context for a fraternal competition in virtue, a virtue not to be practiced apart from the world in the mortification of the flesh, but in precisely those places and those activities where the devil is closest to the touch.

At its inception such an attitude toward life was fully as revolutionary as any of those espoused in the Reformation. From a later point of view, it appears as an attempt to steer a middle course between the romanticism of pietistic despair and the romanticism of chiliastic enthusiasm. Unlike Calvin, Luther did not so emphasize human wickedness as to strip earthly activities of any inherent virtue. On the contrary, by emphasizing human spirituality he encouraged a limited individual pride and responsibility. Luther therefore did not conclude with Calvin that men had best abandon all pretensions and surrender themselves in faith to a God whose power was absolute and whose will was unfathomable. Calvin regarded the emancipation from the Law as a proof of man's incorrigible sinfulness, whereas Luther saw it as the gift of freedom. Luther's God made it clear to all who would read His revelation with the aid of the Spirit what they were obliged to do for His glorification and their salvation. The chasm between man and God was not disabling: through faith man partook of God's spirituality; the will of God was not entirely hidden; the tension between good and evil was within man; he was not to seek absolute tranquillity, but to labor in that tension to prove the firmness of his belief.

CALVIN: EQUAL DEPRAVITY

As an ecclesiastical reformer Calvin made a notable but not unique contribution to the rise of egalitarian institutions. His attack upon the hierarchical organization of the Roman Church for the most part merely followed the lead of Luther and the other moderate Reformers who preceded him. He too denied that papal supremacy and hierarchy could be justified either by Biblical injunction or by the example of the primitive church. Nor did he accept the Catholic view that Christ had conferred supreme ecclesiastical authority upon Peter in the first place. In fact, Calvin argued, Christ gave no more authority to Peter than he did to the other apostles, and Peter was considered by them as "one of twelve, their equal and colleague, not their master." [39] Peter himself, in his letters to pastors, "does not command authoritatively as a superior, but makes them his colleagues, and courteously advises as equals are wont to do . . ." [40] Far from supporting hierarchical order, the example of the primitive church, which is confirmed by Scriptural doctrine, indicates that all authority resides in the community of believers and should be delegated to qualified members of the community elected to their offices by the congregation. Once elected, the presbyters of the early congregations met together and designated one of their number bishop, "lest, as usually happens, from equality dissension should arise." This election, however, did not confer upon the bishop any arbitrary authority; he was to rule only as "president in an assembly." [41] For "in every meeting, though all are equal in power, there should be one as a kind of moderator to whom the others should look up."[42] In the practice of the Roman Church the "whole right" of election "has been taken from the people" and "has been given to the canons alone." As a result it has become the custom that a candidate for ecclesiastical office is held up "to be adored, not examined" by the people.[43]

Like Luther, Calvin proposed to reform the organization of the church by extending authority to the members of the congregation. But his assault on the Roman hierarchy did not lead him to advocate direct democracy in the church. Since he had no confidence that decisions made by a crowd would be wise,[44] Calvin preferred a system of indirect popular government in which each congregation would elect its own officers from a list of nominees drawn up by a select committee. Calvin certainly intended that the populace play a significant role in the formation of policy. He had nothing but indignation for the suppression of the popular study of the Bible by the Roman Church:

Lest anyone should long for greater light, an idea had been instilled into the minds of all, that the investigation of that hidden celestial philosophy was better delegated to a few, whom the others might consult as oracles—that the highest knowledge befitting plebeian minds was to subdue themselves into obedience to the church.[45]

Doubtless Calvin had no intention of suggesting that a popular interpretation of Biblical doctrine would have greater validity than one made by a limited group. For that matter, he denied that the decisions of councils of learned and godly men would necessarily be correct. For Calvin the only guarantee of a correct interpretation is the special illumination of spirit with which God assists his elect.[46] Precisely how the doctrine of spiritual illumination was to be incorporated with the organization of authority in the church is a question he left unanswered.

Calvin's political doctrines are a good deal more ambiguous than his church reforms. Although his teachings fostered much that was novel and subversive of existing political principles, Calvin himself, again tracing a Lutheran pattern, reverted to accepted positions when faced with some of the political inferences drawn from his religious thought. On the one hand he seemed to be advocating, in his conception of the "holy community," an integration of politics and religion; on the other hand he could write that "the spiritual kingdom of Christ and civil government are things very widely separated." [47] Spiritual liberty is therefore perfectly compatible with civil servitude. That "there is neither Jew nor Greek . . . neither bond nor free . . . neither male nor female," should be taken to mean only "that it matters not what your condition is among men, nor under what laws you live, since in them the Kingdom of Christ does not at all consist." [48] Yet at the same time he could make it a function of government to constitute and safeguard true religion, to curb the wicked in behalf of divine law; [49] and he could describe magistracy as "the most sacred, and by far the most honourable, of all stations in mortal life." [50] In practice Calvin certainly made no great effort to separate church and state in Geneva, as later generations of Calvinist theocrats justly observed.

There is a similar ambiguity in Calvin's discussion of the right of resistance. He begins his discussion of resistance in the chapter on civil government in the *Institutes* by arguing that Christians ought not to resist the most unjust, the most "impious" prince, but ought to obey him because all power is of God, and if power is abused and made unduly coercive it must be that God desires to punish the king's subjects.[51] He then modifies this denial of the right of resistance by distinguishing between private individuals, who are said to have no right to resist, and public authorities, such as the Spartan *Ephori* and the estates, which may indeed have such a right.[52] Finally, on the very last page of the *Institutes*, he introduces another modification which opens the door to the complete reversal of his position. Christians are not bound to obey their sovereign, he asserts, in contravention of God's word.[53] This is of course precisely the platform upon which a host of later Calvinists, notably Althusius, Hotman, Knox, Buchanan, and the author of the *Vindiciae contra tyrannos*, constructed their case for civil disobedience and constitutionalism.

If Calvin was not unique in sponsoring an egalitarian reform of the church, and if he stopped short of extending these reforms to politics clearly and decisively, he was at the same time the author of a set of theological doctrines containing a novel theoretical view of equality with important political implications. As sharply as their positions in regard to church reform coincided, the Lutheran and the Calvinian conceptions of equality were widely divergent. Whereas Luther had fashioned a theory of equality upon an assumed universal human capacity for spiritual understanding and conduct, Calvin founded his theory of equality on the assumption of an incorrigible depravity. And whereas Luther's theory had Liberal political implications, Calvin's was profoundly Conservative.

Although the elements of this theory had been expressed before him, Calvin brought them together in rather a new order. Prior to Calvin the Conservative theory of equality had been employed either as a critique of equality or as a justification of inequality. Plato offered the classic example of the first position: the egalitarian stage of history is the final stage of degeneration, a stage in which the appetites gain total control over the nobler parts of the soul. For Plato the levelling spirit and the base passions which Calvin designates as man's concupiscence [54] were intimately associated. Augustine had offered the other classic model of the Conservative theory as a justification of inequality: the fall from grace had suspended the equality which God had originally intended until redemption; meanwhile inequality was to be accepted as an expression of God's punishment for human wickedness.

Even as Calvin continually expressed his debt to Augustine (who is cited more often than anyone else in the *Institutes*), he proceeded to revise the Augustinian view of equality in a most radical way. For Calvin the fall from grace was such a determining condition of earthly existence that it overrode completely the eschatological vision retained by Augustine from Apostolic Christian thought of a redemption to be accomplished on earth. For Calvin the tension between the fallen condition and the promised redemption takes the form of an opposition between earthly life and heavenly life. The result is, with respect to equality, exactly the reverse of what it was for Augustine. On earth, according to Calvin, men are equal in that they are all creatures of depravity. In the judgment of God, however—a judgment which is not definitely made known to men on earth—they are unequal: some are to be saved and others damned. In the eyes of God, "all are not created on equal terms, but some are preordained to eternal life, others to eternal damnation." [55]

Even this inequality, however, is of a quite peculiar kind. As Karl Holl has observed, it would be foolish to consider Calvin's elect as an *Edelrasse* in the ordinary sense of an aristocracy, either of blood or merit, because election has nothing whatever to do with the qualities of man as man: "the predestined is no more worthy of grace than he whom God has condemned." [56]

Calvin had difficulty maintaining the doctrine of predestination because it was argued against him that he was denying that God held out any invitation to repentance. In his reply to Westphal, who had objected that Calvin's doctrine of predestination in effect denied the efficacy of baptism, he seems to have wavered somewhat, or at least to have softened the emphasis on predestination. Calvin answered by denying that he had ever taught that "we ought to begin with predestination in seeking assurance of salvation." He even contends that "secret election was mentioned by me in passing . . ." He had argued for predestination not to close pious minds to God's invitation, but only because, according to God's word, the sacraments provide the final seal of election upon those whom God has already chosen.

I only said that the Spirit of God does not work indiscriminately in all, but as he enlightens the elect only unto faith, so he also provides that they do not use the sacraments in vain. Should I say that the promises are common to all, and that eternal salvation is offered in common to all, but that the ratification of them is the special gift of the Spirit, who seals the offered grace in the elect, would Westphal say that the word is removed from its place?

Having thus explained his position Calvin sums it up succinctly: "while God invites all by the word, he inwardly gives an effectual call only to those whom he has chosen." [57] The fact that a man receives the sacraments does not necessarily mean, therefore, that he receives the full benefit of them. God is simply not promiscuous with His love, although why He chooses one man rather than another is a mystery to man. The fact that He does so is evident, Calvin argues, from the choice of Israel and from the selection of individuals even within the covenanted people. "The covenant of life," the evidence indicated to Calvin, "is not preached equally to all . . ." [58]

Nevertheless, although men are ultimately distinguished according to whether they are predestined to salvation or not, it is impossible to know for certain who has been chosen. No one, therefore, can claim any superiority over anyone else. Indeed, as far as human nature itself is concerned, there are no great distinctions among men. They are all equally depraved, equally perverse. The Spirit of God declares that

> every imagination of man's heart from infancy is evil . . . that there is none righteous, none that understandeth, none that seek after God . . . but that all are useless, corrupt, void of the fear of God, full of fraud, bitterness, and all kinds of iniquity . . . that the carnal mind is enmity against God, and does not even leave us the power of thinking a good thought.[59]

Originally man was created in the image of God, endowed not only with natural aptitudes but with a divine spirit. Through sin mankind has lost the image of God entirely and is left only with natural gifts. These natural gifts are so corrupted that they are of no use to man in his most vital concerns.[60] His reason is so perverted that he is blind to God's word. Those who hold that salvation is available to all who profess, by their own act of will, a belief in the word of God, ignore this pervasive corruption of the natural faculties.[61] In order for man in his fallen state to attain belief, his understanding must be enlightened by a new divine gift. The truth is that "when men are judged by their natural endowments, not an iota of good will be found from the crown of the head to the sole of the foot . . ." [62] Nor can salvation be attained by the performance of good works. This too would require that man be considered capable of attaining his salvation by acts of his own will, a view which fails to appreciate the total character of human depravity. Those who hold that works are necessary to salvation

> [n]o doubt . . . agree with us in holding the doctrine of original sin, but they afterwards modify its effects, maintaining that the powers of man are only weakened, not wholly depraved. Their view, accordingly, is, that man, being tainted with original corruption, is, in consequence of the weakening of his powers, unable to act aright; but that, being

aided by the grace of God, he has something of his own, and from himself, which he is able to contribute. We, again, though we deny not that man acts spontaneously, and of free will, when he is guided by the Holy Spirit, maintain that his whole nature is so imbued with depravity, that of himself he possesses no ability whatever to act aright.[63]

Man is not only incapable of influencing his salvation by his own will; he is so depraved that he fails to perform his most elementary obligations toward his creator. God created humanity in order that He might be glorified by intelligent beings. Instead men seek only their own self-glorification. In their self-pride they do not recognize their common depravity:

For so blindly do we all rush in the direction of self-love, that everyone thinks he has a good reason for exalting himself and despising all others in comparison . . . Hence the insolence with which each, as if exempted from the common lot, seeks to exalt himself above his neighbour, confidently and proudly despising others, or at least looking down upon them as his inferiors. The poor man yields to the rich, the plebeian to the noble, the servant to the master, the unlearned to the learned, and yet everyone inwardly cherishes some idea of his own superiority. Thus each flattering himself, sets up a kind of kingdom in his breast . . .[64]

This blind refusal to recognize their own equality complements the rejection of God's dominion over His creation. The consequence is perpetual anxiety. "This life," Calvin somberly declares, "estimated in itself, is restless, troubled and in numberless ways wretched, and plainly in no respect happy . . . what are esteemed its blessings are uncertain, fleeting, vain, and vitiated by a great admixture of evil." [65] On the one hand man is driven by his passions to pursue all manner of carnal gratifications; on the other hand he is a creature of fear and restless anxiety:

We have a frenzied desire, an infinite eagerness, to pursue wealth and honour, intrigue for power, accumulate riches, and collect all those frivolities which seem conducive to luxury and splendour. On the other hand, we have a remarkable dread, a remarkable hatred of poverty, mean birth and a humble condition . . . Hence in regard to those who frame their life after their own counsels, we see how restless they are in mind.[66]

The insistence on human depravity is intended to have a didactic effect even as it also serves simply to state the plain truth about the human condition.

We bid a man begin by examining himself, and this not in a superficial and perfunctory manner, but to si[f]t his conscience before the tribunal of God, and when sufficiently convinced of his iniquity, to reflect on the strictness of the sentence pronounced upon all sinners. Thus confounded and amazed at his misery, he is prostrated and humbled before God; and, casting away all self-confidence, groans as if given up to final perdition.

Then the sinner is shown that his only resort is to throw himself on the mercy of God.[67] "We lay him completely prostrate, that he may become sensible of his utter insufficiency in regard to spiritual righteousness, and learn to seek it, not partially, but wholly from God . . . [B]y convincing man of his poverty and powerlessness, we train him more effectually to true humility, leading him to renounce all self-confidence, and throw himself entirely upon God . . ." [68] The Christian who recognizes his depravity and accepts the authority of God "will bear his humble lot with greater equanimity and moderation . . . for he has a solace in which he can rest more tranquilly than at the very summit of wealth and power." [69]

Calvin's belief in equal depravity may logically issue in a certain institutional egalitarianism and, in fact, has sometimes been cited as the rationale for democratic government. If all men are fallible and seekers after power, no one ought to have more authority than can be safely entrusted to a man known to be corrupt. On the other hand, this doctrine of equality, in view of the intractable character of the human nature it describes, might well be used to argue against any institutional reform. Calvin himself was far from advocating social revolution. "Let every one then live in his own station, poorly or moderately, or in splendour . . . [but] let them regard it as the law of Christian liberty, to learn with Paul in whatever state they are, 'therewith to be content' . . ." [70]

The ambiguity of Calvin's egalitarianism made itself evident as soon as the substantive tenets of his anthropology and of his theory of the government of God were transposed from a religious to a secular dimension. Two different attitudes emerged from the restatement of Calvin's theology in political terms, neither of which accurately reflects his thought in its original form. By shifting the emphasis and engaging in outright modifications Calvinists reshaped Calvinian theology to promote both limited democracy and unlimited oligarchy.

Calvin himself gave some hint of the democratic direction his thought might be made to take when he indicated his preference for government by an aristocracy of merit tempered by popular control. The argument he offered in support of his preference is important because it joins his theology to a political position:

Owing, therefore, to the vices or defects of men, it is safer and more tolerable when several bear rule, that they may thus mutually assist, instruct and admonish each other, and should any one be disposed to go too far, the others are censors and masters to curb his excess.[71]

In this way the argument from depravity could be made to serve democracy, especially if it is used in the first place to deny the possibility of identifying the elect aristocracy. When the notion of religious liberty which Calvinists outside Geneva often found indispensable to their continued existence was extended to include other individual rights, the Calvinist position could veer in the same direction as Liberalism. This tendency was further supported by the affinity, in practical effect, of Calvin's theory of vocational stewardship and the belief in the pursuit of happiness. Similarly, the Calvinian indifference to inequalities of wealth could also be assimilated to the belief of Liberals in a reward proportionate to industry.

Despite these similarities, it was necessary for Calvinists who took this democratic line to suppress certain of the implications of Calvin's theology and to qualify severely certain other points of doctrine. Sovereignty had to be attributed to the community under law rather than to a secular agent of God. Self-interest had to be recognized as a legitimate principle, and the human capacity for reason had to be given a validity equal to that of the assumption of depravity. In England and America this restatement of Calvinian theology was gradually blended with Liberalism by advocates of limited government, but what survived could often be ascribed to Calvin only as a remote inheritance.

The theocrats of Puritan England and the Massachusetts Bay

Colony took a quite different course in the same effort to apply Calvinian theology to politics. Their restatement was based upon the fundamental modification of Calvin's theology to permit the identification of the elect on earth.[72] Given this serious modification it was possible to limit membership in the active political community to "saints." In this case the transposition of theology into politics was made even easier by the identification of church and state. At the same time, since the elect considered themselves superior to the unregenerate sinners in the eyes of God, they could reason that it was their duty to act as God's agents in keeping a watchful eye on the unredeemed. The attitude ascribed to Jonathan Edwards is typical of this development: "Although original sin starts men on a common level, the level of infinite unworthiness is one on which no man can contentedly remain. Sooner or later all men strong enough to accept the doctrine of utter depravity escaped from it, like Edwards, through faith in their own election." From this it was a short step to the conviction that "if God rules autocratically over the elect and the damned," the elect should "rule in his name on earth . . ." [73]

Neither of these two Calvinist positions restates Calvin's theological doctrines in political terms with anything approaching the comprehensiveness or fidelity with which Calvin's thought is mirrored in a political philosophy—expressed by Thomas Hobbes —which he did not directly inspire and which he might well have found thoroughly abhorrent. This paradox may be easier to accept if we imagine a translation of Calvin's theology into politics, with all the key terms retained in the form of secular analogues. As a descriptive theory a political version of Calvin's theology would assert that men are equal only in the sense that they are all equally driven by their base passions. Left to their own resources they are unable to secure either the ultimate goal of salvation or the more limited goal of tranquillity. When they recognize their depravity and their inability to live by their own resources with any degree of success, they covenant among themselves to obey the dictates of a single, absolute sovereign. The covenant affirms their surrender of self-pride and their agreement to obey the sovereign. The Calvinian covenant is a "free" covenant in the sense that it is a promise of salvation by God which does not bind

God to the observance of the promise.[74] As a sovereign, God himself was under no law; his actions, however, could only be just.[75] The equality of all men under the absolute authority of the sovereign would not confer an equality in rights or possessions, except as the sovereign decides. Like the quest for tranquillity which generates the relationship, the result is an intangible psychological equality. This psychological equality is accompanied by another psychological relation to the sovereign himself. As man exists truly only in God, so, the political analogue would run, his true secular existence is his participation in sovereignty, not in the ordinary sense of political representation, but in the psychological sense of an identification with the sovereign. In all these ways Calvin's theological reflections on equality state the essential elements of the modern Conservative view, clearly foreshadowing the explicitly political reflections of later exponents, notably of Hobbes.

Calvin's stress on equal depravity presents a clear contrast with the Lutheran emphasis on the equal capacity for spiritual activity. But these two versions of equality do not exhaust the range of alternatives produced in the Reformation. To complete the picture we must also include a spokesman for those whose belief in equality took the form of communism—a communism not only of possessions but, more importantly, of the spirit.

MÜNTZER: THE COMMUNITY OF THE PERFECT

A cross, a sword, and a rainbow: these were the symbols adopted by the Allstedt *Bund*,[76] the militant miners, journeymen, and peasants who waged war against the Catholic Church and the temporal powers of Saxony during the Peasant War of 1524-25, with the ideological inspiration of Thomas Müntzer. Müntzer began his career as a convert to Lutheranism. He proved to be a gifted student of the Bible and of church historians.[77] He remained a Lutheran, however, only until he came in contact with the "Zwickau prophets," a group led by Nicholas Storch and strongly influenced both by Anabaptism and the chiliasm of the Bohemian Taborites. Müntzer combined the social radicalism of the Taborites with the mysticism of Tauler, Seuse, and Joachim of Flora.[78]

He broke with Luther over the issue (as he conceived it) of whether faith was to be achieved as a direct gift of God or through the Word of the Bible, taking an extreme position against Biblicism and for direct revelation. Müntzer preached in several towns, incurring the wrath of the authorities and gathering a devoted following. Pressed to give an accounting of himself to various secular authorities, Müntzer responded by urging them to join him in destroying the "godless," including not only the Catholic clergy but also the "learned-in-Scripture" (*die Schriftgelehrten*)[79] led by the lying Luther (*Doktor Lügner*),[80] who were deceiving Christendom with their false preachings. When Luther succeeded in turning the princes against him as a "rebellious spirit" (*aufruhrischen Geist*),[81] Müntzer turned to the peasants and townspeople, exhorting them to overthrow all the godless, the princes included, and re-establish the original equality of early Christianity. Müntzer was captured when the nobility massed four thousand men and besieged the town of Frankenhausen in which he and Heinrich Pfeiffer, his practical revolutionary counterpart, were leading the rebellious peasants. He confessed under duress to having advocated communism of property and the overthrow of authority.[82] A contemporary work, attributed until recently to Luther's associate, Philip Melanchthon, reported of him that, in addition to fallacious theology,

he also taught that all goods should be common, as it is written in Acts 4:32 that the Apostles made goods common. With this he made the mob so mischievous that they no longer wanted to work, instead, if anyone was in need of wheat or cloth he went to someone rich wherever he chose, demanding it as his Christian right, since Christ wished that all should share with the needy: Matth. 19:21. Wherever any magistrate did not give willingly, it was taken from him by force. This was done by many, including those who lived near Thomas . . . Thomas led such mischief and increased it daily and threatened all princes in the neighboring area . . .[83]

There is little direct discussion in Müntzer's own writings of communism in property and of equality in political authority; and what little there is occurs in those writings which appeared just before and during the open conflict. In 1524 Müntzer addressed his *Explicit Unmasking of the False Beliefs of a Faithless World* not to the temporal authorities but to "poor, miserable

Christendom."[84] Later in the same year he addressed his *Highly Provoked Defense and Answer to the Unspiritual, Soft-living Flesh in Wittenberg* to "His most serene highness, the firstborn Prince and omnipotent Lord Jesus Christ, the good King of all Kings, the valiant Duke of all believers, my most gracious Lord and faithful protector, and to his only sorrowing bride, poor Christendom."[85] In this tract Müntzer exposed the princes and their temporal apologists as impious thieves of what properly belonged to all. They teach, "Thou shalt not steal," and they insist only that the law be applied literally, even though they know full well that people rob only because the princes have taken for themselves what God gave to all in common. First they take "the fish in the water, the fowl in the air and all that grows on the earth" for their own property, and then they tell the poor: "God has commanded you not to steal." To this, *"Doktor Lügner* says Amen."[86]

Despite the paucity of his references to communism, Müntzer has come to be regarded, particularly by Marxists, as a forerunner of modern Socialists. Engels' appreciative treatment of Müntzer in his study of the Peasant War[87] has been followed by a number of studies in the present century which proclaim him as a proto-Bolshevik. A recent work by a Soviet historian pays considerable attention to Müntzer's theological roots and doctrines but concludes that the drift of his thought, though neither specifically proletarian nor *bauerlich,* was generally communistic.[88] "The hazy theological form obscured the revolutionary nature of Müntzer's doctrine, but this form was conditioned by the character of the epoch."[89]

Students of theology and church history have come to regard Müntzer's social radicalism as an aspect of what George H. Williams accurately and concisely describes as his "Revolutionary, or charismatic, Spiritualism." For Müntzer, Spirit is a force transforming its possessors into prophets charged with the active restoration of God's kingdom and the annihilation of the "ungodly." As Williams points out, Müntzer thus straddled the camps of both the Contemplative Anabaptists, like John Denck, and the Revolutionary Anabaptists of Münster.[90] A number of studies by German historians of the church and theology, stimulated by Karl

Holl's "Luther and the Enthusiasts,"[91] have elucidated the peculiar characteristics of Müntzer's theology by comparing it with Luther's. The differences go a long way toward accounting for their contradictory attitudes toward the reform of church and society.[92]

The most recent commentator, employing psychoanalytic criteria, considers Müntzer one of the precursors of modern totalitarianism. "Perhaps after all," he concludes his study of Müntzer, "it is a sound instinct that has led Marxists to claim him for their own." [93] Ernst Troeltsch, however, in his brief consideration of Müntzer in *The Social Teaching of the Christian Churches*, dismissed his doctrine as a typological accident. Müntzer, Troeltsch wrote,

represents a reawakening of mystical ideas combined with fanatical Hussite and Taborite revolutionary ideas. This combination, however, was merely accidental; it did not represent a real fusion of these various elements. It can be explained only by the character and destiny of this restless man, who was always eager for peculiar and spectacular activities.[94]

Troeltsch's dismissal of Müntzer as an accident of personality derives less from an objective appreciation of Müntzer than it does from Troeltsch's inability to fit Müntzer into the typological categories which he proposed. Müntzer's position could hardly be classified under the "church type," which is "overwhelmingly conservative," a defender of the *status quo* with universalist ambitions.[95] Neither could it be cited as a good example of the "sect type," which emphasizes

lay Christianity, personal achievement in ethics and religion, the radical fellowship of love, religious equality and brotherly love, indifference towards the authority of the State and the ruling classes, dislike of technical law and the oath, the separation of the religious from the economic struggle by means of the ideal of poverty and frugality, or occasionally in a charity which becomes communism, the directness of the religious relationship, criticism of official guides and theologians, the appeal to the New Testament and to the Primitive Church . . .[96]

The difficulty, however, is not that Müntzer is so peculiar but that Troeltsch's categories are built out of an early twentieth century Liberal view of the world which did not as yet appreciate the difference between the sect and the movement. Troeltsch, like Max Weber, found the crucial modern political dilemma posed in the degeneration of the pacifistic, charismatic, voluntaristic sect into the coercive, oligarchic, and bureaucratic church. From this perspective he could not appreciate Müntzer's relation to militant Socialism and to totalitarian movements generally. Indeed, it is tempting to write off the other images of Müntzer as equally bound to the *Zeitgeist* and to the commitments of the various scholars who advance them. Nevertheless, if we examine Müntzer's doctrine in the light of the development of egalitarianism and in contrast to the doctrines of the sectarians and Luther, it becomes reasonably clear both that Müntzer belongs to the Socialist tradition and that he advances certain ideas which, while not exclusively attached to Socialism, have figured in its totalitarian expressions.

Müntzer was by no means the first in the Christian tradition to call for the restoration of primitive equality, but he did so in such a way as to break sharply with the various strands in traditional Christian communism. The Anabaptists of his day, with whom he was friendly but with whom he ought not to be confused, only gave expression to a new version of older Christian communism. The crucial distinction is that the Anabaptists retained the classical belief that Socialist equality was capable of serving as a way of life only for communities of the perfect, not for all the world. Like the communism of Plato's guardians and of the Catholic monastic orders, the Anabaptist belief in the community of property and the abolition of all distinctions is coupled with the requirement that the practitioners be those exceptional men capable of extraordinary discipline, asceticism, and dedication. Prior to the difficulties with the Spiritual Franciscans, the Roman Church was able to integrate such egalitarian communities into the general hierarchical order of the church precisely because of the separatist and perfectionist character of the monastic doctrines. The Anabaptists' position is therefore more significant for Protestant church history than it is for the history of egalitarianism. Their yearning for the unambiguous restoration of Apostolic Christianity[97] led them to withdraw from the wider Protestant community, and aroused the antagonism of those reform groups who wished to retain the catholicity of the Roman

Church without its diversity and without its distinctions between spirituals and carnals. But because the Anabaptists were satisfied to confine their efforts at restoration to the establishment of communities of the elect, there to await God's final disposition, their doctrines of Socialist equality remain within the classical framework. This is apparent if we contrast the writings of one of the Moravian Hutterite Anabaptists, Ulrich Stadler, with those of Müntzer. The ideal of the Hutterite community is that

One, common, builds the Lord's house and is pure; but mine, thine, his, own divides the Lord's house and is impure. Therefore where there is ownership and one has it, and it is his, and one does not wish to be one with Christ and his own in living and dying, he is outside of Christ and his communion and thus has no Father in heaven.[98]

This should be the rule for the entire world, "but the wickedness of men has spoiled everything." The goods of the world were given by God and should be held in common: "whoever appropriates them for himself and encloses them is a thief and steals what is not his." Communism is not practiced, because "of such thieves the whole world is full." Significantly Stadler adds here only a prayer: "May God guard his own from them."[99]

In Stadler's view there is a division of mankind into the saints who follow God's will and the carnals who disobey God's law. It is impossible for the latter to live the life of community. "Indeed, for such unmortified, carnal, natural men without the Spirit, it certainly is a heavy, bitter, unbearable life. Such persons seek freedom only to dwell some place unto themselves in order that they might live pleasantly according to the flesh and unto their corruption."[100] The elect of God are the outcasts, "poor, miserable, small, and rejected of the world."[101] They should not allow themselves merely to be trodden down, but should "group themselves and hold together here in misery after they have been driven out in the worst sort of way."[102] For "in this time a place has been given to the bride of the Lamb in which to dwell amid the wasteland of this world . . . to await the Lord until he leads her after him here in tribulation and afterward receives her with eternal joy."[103] At least in this community it can be brought to pass that "property, that is, his, mine, thine, will not be disclosed in the house of the Lord, but rather equal love, equal care and distribution, and true community in all the goods of the Father according to his will." [104]

Müntzer's position is quite different. In advocating the restoration of equality, Müntzer was no spokesman for sectarian withdrawal, pacifism, or ascetic sufferance of persecution. Müntzer at once sums up many of the tendencies of sectarian communism, in its millennialist and ascetic formulations, and points forward to the later appearance of militant secular Socialist movements which would seek to transform the world by the violent overthrow of the forces of domination. As Norman Cohn has pointed out, it is only in the later Middle Ages that the myth of original equality becomes the basis of an activist effort to overthrow domination and restore the original state. Numerous individuals and groups foreshadow particular elements of the expression Müntzer gave to this reorientation of Socialist thought: the Flagellants, with their belief in extreme suffering as the way to redemption; the Free Spirits, in their doctrine that true Christian existence was only possible in an identification with God; Joachim of Flora, with his portrait of historical progress toward the age of the Holy Spirit; Tauler and the other mystical theologians with their doctrines of direct revelation and the divinization of man. [105] Müntzer combined all of these elements and forged them into a programmatic doctrine of revolution. With Müntzer the Christian eschatological underground emerged into the open as a major historical force.

Müntzer shared the communist ideals of Stadler and also believed that the elect of God were, in Stadler's phrase, the "fighters and heralds" [106] of the restoration. But he believed that the restoration would not be accomplished through a withdrawal from the world but only by universal, active transformation. Müntzer's elect were to serve as a kind of vanguard of the millennium. Directed by the Spirit, his followers were not to shrink from the use of violence against the enemies of God. In a few years Müntzer passed from the advocacy of a reconstruction from above— guided by the secular authorities—to revolution from below to be undertaken by an armed community of prophets.

An important element in this reshaping of the traditional egalitarian ideal into a revolutionary doctrine is the notion of spiritual

understanding and existence developed by Müntzer. To ordinary
sectarian chiliasm Müntzer added his own version of mystical
theology, redefined to support revolutionary activism. Müntzer's
mysticism substituted action for contemplation and the community of prophets for the isolated mystic.[107] The elect would
enter into a direct relation with God, without any separation or
any mediation, and through this process they would become equal
with God and among themselves in the possession of the identical
Spirit.

The conflict between Luther and Müntzer in theology went to
the root of the issue of the meaning of spiritual existence and
understanding. The mature Luther retained the youthful influence
of Tauler and the *Theologica Germania,* but he tried to integrate
mystical theology with a doctrine emphasizing the revelation of
the Word in the Bible. Luther did not believe that the Bible could
be understood simply by being read; as the Scripture is the work
of the Spirit it can only be understood by someone who experi-
ences the same Spirit. "For," as Luther explained, "no one can
understand God according to God's Word correctly unless he
has it, without mediation, from the Holy Spirit." But even as he
thus recognized the interdependence of Word and Spirit, Luther
held that the Word was the sole vehicle of Spirit.[108] It was on
this point that Müntzer disagreed most emphatically. Müntzer
took the extreme position that spiritual understanding could only
be achieved in direct transaction with God. A man might therefore attain the experience of the inner light without ever having
read a page of the Bible. A pagan might sooner be called to the
ranks of the elect than the most ardent Biblicist.[109] Müntzer is
said to have summed up his position in a characteristically bold
expression: *"Was Bibel, bubel, babel! Mann muss auf Winkel
kriechen und mit Gott reden."* [110]

In order for a man to cast off his carnal condition he must
"experience" true belief. This could not take place in the gulf
between man and God opened in Lutheran justification by faith.
No one could become a true Christian except by identifying himself with God and Christ through the experience of suffering.
Then he would become, in Tauler's phrase, *vergottet* (divin-
ized).[111] Müntzer exhorts his followers continually to strive to be

Gottformig (Godlike) and *Christformig* [112] (Christlike). In order
to achieve this identification it is necessary for men to imitate
the experience of Christ. Every man must suffer the passion of
Christ; every man must experience not simply the "half-Christ,"
the "sweet Christ" who is soft and beautiful and speaks honeyed
words, but the "bitter Christ" as well, the Christ of affliction
whose experience is beyond words.[113] The sweet Christ is the
Christ of comfort and solace and therefore of Luther, whom
Müntzer refers to as "Brother Soft-Living."[114] Luther would
divert men from their mission in the service of God by keeping
them from the path of active religious experience. Luther shouts
"Believe! Believe!" and thinks he can make men true Christians.
But the only way to God is the way of suffering, not comfort,
not of dependence upon Christ but of identification with Christ.
"No one can believe in Christ [unless] he first becomes equal to
Him,"[115] asserts Müntzer in his gloss of Matthew 16:24, and
"Who does not die with Christ cannot be born again with
him,"[116] in his gloss of Romans 5:8.

Unlike Luther, Müntzer rejects any and all forms of mediation
between God and man. Neither sacramental nor Scriptural grace
can stand between them. Spirit is to be transmitted directly from
God in the experience of revelation. In this respect also, however,
Müntzer's mysticism departs radically from traditional mystical
theology. His argument for the "experience" of revelation, which
he opposes to "unexperienced belief" *(unerfahrene Glaube)*,[117]
all but overthrows the attempt of the mystics to confront God in
the purity of contemplation by withdrawing entirely from the
active life. The peculiar character of Müntzer's theology is well
illustrated by his understanding of baptism. According to Müntzer, baptism is to be understood as a "movement" *(Bewegung)*
in the soul. In the Bible, he points out, wherever baptism is performed, whether by water or wine or without liquid, it is always
a "movement of the heart."[118] The Anabaptists held an entirely
different view. For them baptism presupposed belief and hence
was invalid if administered to children. To this proposition Müntzer agreed, but not because he held the Anabaptist view of belief
as a rational persuasion. As belief was properly only experienced
belief, so baptism could only be an active experience.

This theological activism was reinforced by the social character of Müntzer's mysticism. The mystical experience was to be achieved not by solitary individuals but in a group of adherents. Luther had called for a priesthood of believers; Müntzer called for a community of prophets. "A true preacher," he declared, "must be a prophet when the world appears so shameful. The whole world must be prophetic in order that it may discern the true prophets."[119] The society of true prophets was an organization of God's elect realized in the covenant or *Bund* of Allstedt. This covenant was the expression of Müntzer's direct revelation. All those who shared the bond of an immediate revelation would stand together in a union of the elect. The covenant of the elect served Müntzer as a bridge between the mystical doctrine of direct revelation and the political activity in which the *Bund* engaged under his direction. "Nothing can help Christianity unless the elect are made known by active desire, work and unceasing diligence."[120] What was necessary was not the passive suffering of self-abnegation and self-mortification, but an active striving to do the work of God where there was the *risk* of suffering.

The first act of the *Bund* was the destruction of a chapel which Müntzer had described as the abode of the devil. Called to account for their conduct, Müntzer and his followers responded that they were acting as avengers of the Lord who had himself said that he did not come to bring peace but a sword. The godless must be exterminated by the elect; if on this account "violence should be done by us, the world and especially the pious elect will know why we suffer and that we become identical with Jesus Christ . . ."[121] The possession of the Holy Spirit made the elect "amoral supermen,"[122] released from all obligation to support the Law, from all propensities to sin attaching to carnal creatures. "Who has received (*entphehet*) the Holy Spirit, whatever he does (*wie er soll*), he can never again be cast down."[123] For the perfect, violence was a sacred mission. Even the Bible, Müntzer asserts, justifies violence against the godless. He therefore urged the Saxon princes to participate in the activities of the *Bund*, warning them that if they failed to join him, the sword would be taken away from them by the elect of God. Later, when Luther succeeded in definitely turning the princes against him, Müntzer took the position that since princely authority was only valid as a consequence of the fall, it was due to be overthrown in the restoration of original equality. Unlike Luther, Müntzer does not associate the use of violence with the fall from grace; violence is sanctified as an instrument of God's wrath to be wielded by those who become one with him.

Müntzer did not dwell upon the image of the primitive community or of the coming millennium. He was more concerned with the process of restoration. He said only that in the original Christian community God was sole Lord and all men were equal before him. The fall from grace was a fall from the immediacy of this relation, a fall to the level of creature from the level of spirit. In his *Sermon Before the Princes*, Müntzer pictures the course of the world as a history of increasing domination and at the same time of the growing power of the Spirit. Both will converge in the final apocalyptic struggle between the elect of God and the servants of the devil. He pictures God and Christ as a stone, a cornerstone which grows larger through history but is continually trampled upon by the godless. He draws upon the seventh book of Daniel to foretell the ending of this devilish kingdom, adding a fifth stage to the four described by Daniel. The stone which is Christ has become great and will smash the clay kingdom. The princes had better step boldly on the cornerstone as St. Peter did. "A new Daniel must arise and interpret for you your vision and this [prophet] . . . must go in front of the army."[124] The sword of the rulers is given to the princes for the punishment of the wicked and the protection of the pious. God alone can accomplish his will, but the princes can serve as God's servants. Only the hypocritical will refuse to do the work of the Lord on the ground that Christ killed none; "the godless have no right to live except as the elect wish to grant it to them."[125] From this exhortation to the princes it was an easy step to the agitation of the masses. In his call to rebellion, issued from Mulhausen in April 1525, Müntzer urged the members of the Allstedt *Bund:* "On, while the fire is hot! Don't let your sword get cold! . . . Smite cling-clang upon the anvil of Nimrod. Throw his tower to the ground!"[126]

In Müntzer's steady evolution toward Revolutionary Spiritualism, Socialist egalitarianism began to cast off its associations with sectarian withdrawal, pacifism, and ordinary asceticism and acquired a mystical identification with universal purpose, an activistic code of behavior, and an eschatological view of history. The ideal of communism came less and less to be identified either with the remote past or with the special and separate community of the perfect. Ascetic suffering was transformed into the dangerous practice of revolutionary violence against the powers of domination. History came to be regarded as a dual process in which oppression would grow ever more burdensome and at the same time the forces of God, represented by Spirit, would reach their fruition. The poor, as the elect of God, would arise against the devilish powers and, guided by Spirit, restore original equality. Having vanquished the godless by extermination and expulsion, the elect would presumably be equal among themselves.

Müntzer's vision of a community of the perfect, at once human and divine, spiritual and active, realizing itself as an achieved destiny in the world, completes the spectrum of egalitarian expression in the Reformation. The new values announced in theology by Luther, Calvin, and Müntzer remain to be given secular restatement and application, but in principle the breach with classical dualism has been made. Equality now stands as the ultimate and immediate goal of modern Western man. The nature and implications of this new goal, however, are already a matter over which there is radical disagreement. Is the call for equality a plea on behalf of the right of all men to decide in common the rules of mutual accommodation and, at the same time, a declaration of the duty of every individual to demonstrate his virtue by performing the works of the world? Is it a common condition of incapacity which men are called upon to recognize and which they may only overcome through submission to an omnipotent authority? Is it a mode of emancipation in which they are to be lifted above the disabilities of human nature and the limitations of ethical rules in order that they may abolish all the inequities of the social order? In posing these questions the Reformers stated with powerful clarity the choices that were to confront their intellectual descendants for many generations.

From Theology to Politics

⟋⟋⟍⟍⟍⟍⟍

W HEN THE Reformation came to England the egalitarian
principles espoused by the continental Reformers took
on explicit relevance to secular affairs. Earlier Protestant
spokesmen, preoccupied with the work of religious renovation,
had been inhibited from making too probing an appraisal of the
social order by the need to secure support from secular authorities. In England, where the religious reformation became a political and social revolution, the secular implications of the doctrines
of reform were drawn quickly and concretely.

Virtually all the parties to the Puritan[1] Revolution were identified both with varying attitudes toward religion and the church
and with varying conceptions of the social order. The "holy
community" may have been their common goal, but each group
had a different idea of what such a community must entail—and
with these views went different conceptions of equality. The
Levellers took a position similar to Luther's, while the Presbyterians drew upon elements of Calvin's doctrine. The Diggers,
Fifth Monarchy Men, Anabaptists, and other enthusiast sects
envisioned a communistic equality such as Müntzer had earlier
described. The Independents shied from doctrinal identification
and made alliances with different groups at different times.

Precisely how the Puritan groups drew political implications
from religious premises is not altogether clear. A. S. P. Wood-

house contends that all the Puritan groups began from common moral and religious principles but diverged in applying them to society. All espoused the "priesthood of believers" and therefore opposed ecclesiastical hierachy and any distinction between clergy and laity. All agreed at first that the doctrine of election had no bearing on worldly rank. But when the same principles were extended to society, differences arose. Presbyterians and Independents maintained that believers are equal among themselves but superior to others. Millenarians claimed that the Saints are equal among themselves but superior to others inasmuch as they are not bound by the restraints intended for carnal men. Other groups, including the Levellers and Diggers, did not make equality in the church a basis of superiority in society but stood instead for social equality by analogy with the equality of believers.[2]

Woodhouse's explanation takes no account of the differences of theology which divided the Puritans as much as continental Protestants. These differences were not trivial, however, and they certainly go some of the way toward explaining the differences of application which Woodhouse finds a way to account for on nontheological grounds. The Presbyterians, for example, would surely have arrived at the same egalitarian conclusion as other Calvinists had they followed Calvin's insistence that the elect could not be known on earth. The Presbyterian Samuel Rutherford, in fact, did draw a politically radical conclusion from fundamental Calvinian doctrine. In Lex, Rex (1644) Rutherford argues that

he who is supposed to be the man born free from subjection politic, even the king born a king, is under the same state of sin, and so by reason of sin, of which he hath a share equally with all other men by nature . . . [N]one are by nature kings, because none have by nature these things which essentially constitute kings, for they have neither by nature the calling of God, nor gifts for the throne, nor the free election of the people, nor conquest. And if there be none a king by nature, there can be none a subject by nature.

Government, he concludes, is only legitimate if established by consent.[3] That Rutherford could arrive at political equality from the premise of equal depravity indicates that, without any modification of Calvin's position to permit the distinction of the elect from the damned, it is at the very least logically possible to reach democratic conclusions from Calvinist assumptions. Because many Presbyterians did modify Calvin's argument, they could arrive at a quite opposite conclusion. Their understanding of the equality of believers as an equality of oligarchs may be credited not only to an integration of the church with politics, as Woodhouse suggests,[4] but also to a logically prior modification of Calvin's theology.

Much the same case can be made out for the Levellers. Did the Levellers hold an egalitarian position in politics because they "segregated" church and state and drew an analogy between them, or because they were able, quite logically, to infer political equality from their belief in spiritual equality? Luther had already brought the same principle to bear on church organization.[5] The Levellers may be said to have brought it to bear on the social order.

The Levellers and Diggers provide clear illustrations of the appearance of two of the modern concepts of equality in transition from religion to politics. The Presbyterians, because they adapted Calvin's doctrines to suit the needs of oligarchy, do not provide as good an example of the restatement of a Conservative concept of equality as can be found outside Puritan ranks in the political thought of Thomas Hobbes. Writing to the questions raised by the Puritan Revolution, Hobbes expounded in secular terms a view of equality remarkably similar to the one Calvin had put forward in the cause of religious renovation.[6]

THE LEVELLERS: EQUALITY AND LIBERTY

The Levellers believed that men had been created equal in the sense that all were capable of knowing the dictates of virtue and of conducting themselves in accordance with those dictates. The fall had threatened to alter this double capability, but the intervention of Christ, "the Restorer and Repairer of mans losse and Fall," freely performed by a merciful God, had removed the curse of sin and opened anew the way to salvation for all. The fall could therefore provide no excuse for subjection. In creating man, God "made him not Lord . . . over the individuals of Mankind, no further then by free consent, or agreement, by giving up their power each to other, for their better being . . ." As he gives no such authority to Adam, neither is it inherited by "any of Adam's Posterity." [7] For the Levellers it followed that no government could be legitimate unless it was established by the consent of the governed. As Lilburne puts it, men are

by nature all equal and alike in power, dignity, authority, and majesty, none of them having by nature any authority, dominion, or magisterial power one over or above another; neither have they, or can they exercise any, but merely by institution or donation, that is to say, by mutual agreement or consent, given, derived or assumed . . . for the good benefit and comfort each of other, and not for the mischief, hurt, or damage of any; it being unnatural, irrational . . . wicked and unjust, for any man or men whatsoever to part with so much of their power as shall enable any of their Parliament-men, commissioners, trustees, deputies . . . or servants, to destroy and undo them therewith. [8]

For the Levellers, men were spiritually equal in terms of their capacity to know virtue because God had created them all in His own image and endowed them with reason and understanding. God, says Walwyn, made man "naturally a rationall creature, judging rightly of all things and desiring only what was necessary." [9] The Word of the Scripture is so plain that "the meanest capacity is fully capable of a right understanding." [10] This divinely directed faculty of reason is assisted by another inborn asset, the law of nature inscribed in the heart of every man. For the Levellers the law of nature provides the ethical direction of the understanding which Spirit-and-Scripture provide for Luther. While these conceptions are by no means identical, they are similar in that they locate mediation between God and man in the individual faculty of understanding, which is believed to be governed, or at least to be capable of being governed, by a divinely implanted ethical impulse. This human understanding is believed to be fully capable of comprehending Scriptural injunctions and individual self-interest without the aid of scholarly glosses or ecclesiastical interpretation. "Let me prevaile with you," Walwyn urges, "to free yourselves from this bondage [to authority], and to trust to your own considerations in anything that is useful for your understandings and consciences." [11] Luther located the moral law in Scripture but insisted that it could only be properly understood with the aid of Spirit. The Levellers located the moral law both in the Scripture and in the human soul.[12] Those whose understanding was not guided by the ethical impulse, they believed, would indulge in intellectual conceit.

Like Luther, the Levellers derive from the premise of human spiritual equality a belief in equal authority, but not a belief in the equalization of the rewards of industry. The Levellers rejected communism because they understood equality as a guarantee of liberty for all, and they supported free competition because it provided equal opportunity. This policy may well have reflected the class interest of the fairly homogeneous group of small tradesmen and apprentices from whom the Levellers drew support.[13] But their advocacy of free trade and their attack on monopoly, in particular on the Merchant Adventurers' Company, also reflect a set of beliefs not so obviously related to their economic interest as to be considered mere rationalizations. The Levellers had a kind of stewardship theory of human talents which played an important part in their political and economic thinking. A Leveller pamphlet propounded the theory vividly:

God hath given no man a talent to be wrapt up in a Napkin and not improved, but the meanest vassal in the eye of the Lord is equally oblieged and accomptable to God with the greatest Prince or Commander . . . in & for the use of that talent betrusted unto him.[14]

The leading Leveller spokesman in the Putney debates, Colonel Thomas Rainborough, made use of this theory in arguing for the extension of the suffrage without regard to wealth or property:

I do hear nothing at all that can convince me, why any man that is born in England ought not to have his voice in election of burgesses. It is said that if a man have not a permanent interest, he can have no claim; and [that] we must be no freer than the laws will let us be . . . I do think that the main cause why Almighty God gave man reason, it was that they should make use of that reason, and that they should improve it for that end and purpose that God gave it them . . . there is nothing that God hath given a man that any [one] else can take from him. And therefore I say, that either it must be the Law of God or the law of man that must prohibit the meanest man in the kingdom to have this benefit as well as the greatest. I do not find anything in

FROM THEOLOGY TO POLITICS 65

the Law of God, that a lord shall choose twenty burgesses, and a gentleman but two, or a poor man shall choose none.[15]

Implicit in the Leveller economic doctrines is a form of the same principle. To hinder individual economic activity would be to restrain the opportunity for all men to express their natural talents. To make property common would presumably have the same effect. In addition, it might revive the medieval disdain for the works of the world and direct men's natural capacities for creative industry into the vain, idle, and unnatural alleys of speculation and intrigue. Economic activity was for the Levellers, as for Luther, a concrete field of battle in which the divine gifts could be made operative, not for the sake of wealth, but as a competition in virtue. When God's intention is known and acted upon, Walwyn assures his readers, "you will no longer value men and women according to their wealth, or outward shewes, but according to their vertue, & as the love of God appeareth in them." [16] This belief in the duty to foster the expression of natural talents has a claim more impressive than any Napoleonic decree to be considered the ancestor of the modern belief in equality of opportunity.

Sometimes the Levellers put forward beliefs that might well have served as the starting point for more elaborate discussion. Overton wrote that

by natural birth all men are equal . . . born to like propriety, liberty and freedom, and as we are delivered of God by the hand of nature into this world, every one with a natural innate freedom and propriety . . . even so we are to live, every one equally . . . to enjoy his birthright and privilege, even all whereof God by nature hath made him free . . . Every man by nature being a king, priest, prophet in his own natural circuit and compass, whereof no second may partake but by deputation, commission and free consent from him whose right and freedom it is.[17]

Ordinarily, however, they were more concerned with pressing for specific reforms than with producing systematic political philosophy. Moreover, they were deeply imbued, as were others in the Puritan camp, with a typical "sectarian distrust of finespun rationalizations." [18] It was left to Locke and other Whigs, when the turbulence of the century finally entered its descending arc, to codify the Leveller program and to articulate their demands with a political philosophy.[19] The elements of that philosophy are already present in the Leveller tracts advocating an "agreement of the people" as the foundation of legitimate government; a widely extended suffrage; the right of equal justice; freedom of thought; religious toleration; and the right to private property. All these specific points of the Leveller program reverberate with remarkable fidelity in the later systematic doctrines of Locke, Sydney, Milton, and Harrington.

But the relation of the Levellers to Luther on the one hand and to these political philosophers on the other goes deeper than particular points of agreement. The Levellers share with them a common bond of ethical aspiration. Like Luther, the Levellers did not so emphasize the effect of the fall as to make it the permanent and unalterable condition of social organization. Neither did they believe, on the other hand, that redemption restored the state of innocence in perfect purity. Christ's intervention only rekindled the godly spark nearly extinguished by the fall. It was upon the fall that the divine moral law was imposed as a way of regulating sinful men.[20] Social regeneration means that men live according to the principles which govern the state of innocence, but in the new, artificial context of a social order based upon mutual covenant and regulated governmental institutions designed to implement and enforce the moral law. This formulation is quite similar, at least formally, to the Lockean theory of the advance from the state of nature to civil society. Because of the emphasis on law, however, it diverges from the theological view of Luther, although the Mosaic religion of law which Luther saw superseded by the gospel of Christianity is characterized as a burden imposed upon man from outside himself. The attainment of Christian freedom releases man from bondage to the law in that Christ reigns in his conscience and his conscience directs him to virtuous activity.[21] The law which the Levellers advocate is at once self-imposed and implanted in conscience. The covenant assumes at least a partial regeneration of mankind, sufficient to move all men to recognize and act upon the dictates of conscience. The Leveller's political covenant is therefore in keeping with Lutheran doctrine even though the covenantal form derives more from

Calvin than from Luther. For the Levellers, men do not enter into the covenant in order to recognize the power and authority of an omnipotent sovereign, but in order to create a legitimate government as a fiduciary instrument of the authority which resides only in the community governed by the moral law. Luther's view of the organization of the church expresses a similar principle. Authority resides in the community of Christians, which establishes articles of faith in keeping with God's will, and delegates its authority to elected officers for the implementation of the articles of faith.

The Leveller attitude toward the regeneration of society is also indicated in their attitude toward suffrage. In the Putney debates Rainborough, Wildman, and Petty argued with great force in favor of universal suffrage without regard to social and economic distinctions, on the ground that all men are by nature equal in authority. Rainborough put the case in a justly celebrated declaration:

For really I think that the poorest he that is in England hath a life to live, as the greatest he; and therefore truly, sir, I think it's clear, that every man that is to live under a government ought first by his own consent to put himself under that government; and I do think that the poorest man in England is not at all bound in a strict sense to that government that he hath not had a voice to put himself under.[22]

The right to vote ought not to be made contingent upon the extent of a man's material wealth, but upon the capacity to reason which is conferred upon all men equally.[23] From this statement of principle to the provisions of the second and third "Agreement of the People" (1648), in which the interpretation of universal suffrage is spelled out in detail, significant qualifications are introduced. In addition to excluding Royalists from the suffrage for seven years, in the second Agreement, and for ten in the third, both versions deny the vote to persons who are servants or receive alms. The second version also excludes wage earners.[24] These restrictions may well indicate that the Levellers were concerned with their own prospects for power under the proposed arrangement, even though they disclaimed such motives. At the same time the restrictions are also accounted for on grounds of principle. In the Putney debates, Petty justified the limited suffrage of the first Agreement on the ground that those who are excluded "depend upon the will of other men and should be afraid to displease them." The Levellers were not so moved by the principle of natural equality as to demand the total and universal restoration of the rights conferred by nature. They were content to make conditions of servitude and dependence a limitation of natural freedom and to recognize this limitation by restricting the suffrage.

The Levellers' interest in only a modified restoration of innocence is also indicated in their general approach to social reform. In *A Manifestation* (1646), of which Walwyn is reputed to be the author,[25] their aim in establishing government is described as "having bin all along to reduce it as near as might be to perfection," while recognizing that "the pravity and corruption of mans heart is such that there could be no living without it." [26] Walwyn had previously asserted that because of human depravity the state of innocence, in which men were concerned only with the procurement of necessities, had been superseded by the pursuit of superfluous luxuries.[27] Now he argues that unless consent is unanimous, property may not be made common by legislative action. Otherwise the right of property is to be assumed to be an individual right not alienated to the society. In effect the Levellers seem to have agreed with the argument of Henry Ireton and his supporters in the Putney debates that to make the suffrage universal would endanger property,[28] but they sought to avoid this possibility not by restricting the suffrage to the propertied but by removing property from legislative authority. Walwyn is equally suspicious of the tendency of authority to corrupt its possessors.

We confess indeed, that the experimentall defections of so many men as have succeeded in Authority, and the exceeding difference we have hitherto found in the same men in a low, and in an exalted condition, makes us even mistrust our own hearts, and hardly beleeve our own Resolutions of the contrary.

For this reason they have proposed "such an Establishment, as supposing men to be too flexible and yeelding to worldly Temptations, they should not have a means or opportunity either to injure particulars, or prejudice the Publick, without extreme hazard, and apparent danger to themselves." [29]

It is in this attempt to balance natural aspirations against the temptations of self-interest that the Levellers come closest to the attitudes which were to guide Locke. The principles of nature are to govern the organization of society. Natural freedom is to be respected and expressed in the decision-making process. At the same time, institutional restraints are to be constructed to prevent the abuse of the ideals so realized. This similarity exists on both a general and a specific plane. As Locke was to argue against Filmer's use of tradition as a source of legitimacy, Overton wrote that reason alone "is the fountaine of all just precedents."[30] Neither Locke nor the Levellers believed that reason was so powerful a force in social deliberation as to make external restraints unnecessary. Overton's *Appeale* undertakes to establish as the foundation of government the equality and the liberty of all, and to preserve that foundation by the construction upon it of safeguards against experienced human shortcomings. In first principles, individual liberty and equality are supreme:

For to every individuall in nature, is given an individuall propriety by nature, not to be invaded or usurped by any . . . for every one as he is himselfe hath a selfe propriety, else could not be himselfe, and on this no second may presume without consent; and by naturall birth all men are equall and alike borne to like propriety and freedome, every man by naturall instinct aiming at his owne safety and weale.[31]

From this basic principle of nature proceeds that compact of each with others by which government is established. The compactors elect deputies whose authority is limited to the province allotted them by the electors. "The transgression of our weal by our trustees is an utter forfeiture of their trust, and cessation of their power." [32] When that occurs, power reverts to the constituent community. "All betrusted powers if forfeit, fall into the hands of the betrusters." Ultimate authority resides in "the fundamentall originall, rise and situation" of government, "which is the people, the body represented." [33] If, because of the confusion attendant upon such occasions, it is impossible for the people to elect alternative authorities to supersede those who have betrayed their trust, it is the right of any man or group of men to overthrow such a corrupt government on behalf of the people, if the people are in danger of "imminent ruine and destruction."[34] Such action is no less than an obligation of nature, just as the purpose of government is the natural desire for security. Magistracy is "an Ordinance amongst men and for men, that all men may have an humane subsistence and safety to live as men amongst men, none to be excepted from this humane subsistence, but the unnaturall and the inhumane, it is not for this opinion, or that faction, this Sect or that sort, but equally and alike indifferent for all men that are not degenerated from humanity and humane civility." [35]

The idea of equality expounded in this view of government expresses the Leveller belief in the possibility of human redemption. Original innocence and purity cannot be entirely recaptured, but reason is still strong enough in most men for people to be trusted to govern themselves properly. In this state men are to be regarded as discrete individuals, each with a right to dispose of himself and his talents as he chooses, so long as this exercise does not violate the laws of God and nature or impair the basic general welfare of the community. The competitive exercise of all the talents in human nature which promote individual and social welfare is to be sanctioned as the highest form of social morality. In these essentials, Leveller egalitarianism carries Luther's religious doctrines into politics and prepares the way for the integral philosophy of Liberal equality.

HOBBES: EQUALITY AND SECURITY

The question who is the better man, has no place in the condition of meer Nature; where . . . all men are equall. The inequallity that now is, has bin introduced by the Lawes civill. I know that *Aristotle* in the first booke of his Politiques, for a foundation of his doctrine, maketh men by Nature, some more worthy to Command, meaning the wiser sort (such as he thought himselfe to be for his Philosophy;) others to Serve, (meaning those that had strong bodies, but were not Philosophers as he;) as if Master and Servant were not introduced by consent of men, but by difference of Wit: which is not only against reason; but also against experience. For there are very few so foolish, that had not rather governe themselves, than be governed by others: Nor when the wise in their own conceit, contend by force, with them who distrust their owne wisdome, do they alwaies, or often, or almost at any time, get the Victory. If Nature therefore have made men equall, that equalitie is to be acknowledged: or if Nature have made men unequall; yet because men that think themselves equall, will not enter into conditions of Peace, but upon Equall termes, such equalitie must be admitted. And therefore for the ninth law of Nature, I put this, *That every man acknowledge other for his Equall by Nature.* The breach of this Precept is *Pride.*[36]

If the Levellers extended Lutheran egalitarianism into politics, it remained for Hobbes to expound a political version of Calvin's conception. He did so, however, in the process of a restatement of political philosophy intended to supplant religion and theology. This restatement consisted of an attempt to formulate a science of politics using the "clear and exact method" [37] of geometric logic and a philosophic justification of authority and obedience founded on a purely secularist, "natural" set of values. As Raymond Polin has suggested, Hobbes "seems to be one of the first philosophers, like Machiavelli, to conceive a politics with the clear intention of excluding the divine from its principles, and the influence of religions and churches from its practice." [38] Indeed, perhaps the most profound motive of Hobbes's work is the desire to sever political philosophy and political science from theology and the church and to anchor them instead in the methods of seventeenth century natural science and the institutions of civil society.

In view of this underlying motivation it is interesting that Hobbes should have retained at least the rhetoric of theology, even while he was introducing into political philosophy the mechanistic imagery of the science of his day. The Leviathan is described both as an "Artificiall Man" [39] and as a *"Mortall God"*;[40] and the sovereign is designated, in a metaphor compounded of both styles of thought, as the "Artificiall *Soul*" of the commonwealth.[41] It is easy to imagine why Hobbes did not discard the rhetoric of theology along with the theological mode of analysis and the conception of society as an expression of a divinely ordered universe. To those as yet unaccustomed to thinking about politics "scientifically," the message of his philosophy could be broached in more familiar terms. Even later in the century Locke apparently felt it necessary to argue the Bible with Filmer before setting forth a discourse on civil government composed upon deistic and rationalistic principles. As a clever polemicist, Hobbes also must have recognized that the surest way to cut the ground out from under his theological opponents was to turn their own sources against them, even if this tactic required tortuous exegesis, to say the least.

To dismiss Hobbes's use of theological rhetoric on these grounds, however, is to risk ignoring an even more significant tactical possibility. Like Hobbes, Machiavelli faced a similar problem in his effort to replace Christian values by an ethic of secular survival and fulfillment. It is therefore instructive for the understanding of Hobbes's use of theological rhetoric to note that Machiavelli employed classical props such as the glory of the Roman past and the Roman conception of *virtù* as a substitute for the emotional symbols of religion. For Hobbes theological rhetoric serves a similar purpose. By retaining the rhetoric but infusing it with an entirely different set of values, Hobbes could hope to transfer to his secularist philosophy the sense of importance and the will and dedication which were ordinarily invested in religion. It could not have been without some deliberation of this sort that Hobbes drew his description of government from the Book of Job, described the sovereign as the "Mortall God," and sought in numerous other ways to hang the trappings of religion on his political philosophy.

Ironically enough, even though Hobbes himself intended to manipulate theology for his own subversive purposes, the relation of his thought to Christian theology turns out upon examination to be a good deal more substantial than his superficial rhetorical adoptions would seem to indicate. The really striking feature of Hobbesian thought in this connection is its similarity both to Calvin's anthropology and to his understanding of authority and obedience. It would be patently erroneous to hold Calvin responsible for Hobbism or to identify Calvin with the motives and values of Hobbes. Two theorists could scarcely be farther apart in their conceptions of the purpose of human life. The recognition of the similarity in their theories provides an excellent fulcrum for a comparison of the uses to which their common theory of human nature can be put. There is certainly more than a superficial resemblance between Calvin's understanding of human nature and the portrait Hobbes paints of man as a creature trapped in a jungle of passions. Calvin had argued that, because of human depravity, life on earth was bound to be afflicted with anxiety and insecurity so long as man attempted to live by his own resources. Since he could no longer hope to merit salvation, all that man could realistically strive to achieve by his own efforts was an inner tranquillity in the face of the torments of the world. To secure tranquillity it was necessary to surrender all pride, to forego all claims of self-sufficiency, and to become the obedient servant of an omnipotent divine authority the justice of whose ways man could not understand.

Upon all these points Hobbes recapitulates the argument of Calvin in political terms, except that he makes several substitutions. For inner tranquillity he substitutes physical and psychological security. For the omnipotent authority of the creator God, he substitutes the power of an earthly protector. For Christian eschatology he substitutes an equation of earthly security with salvation and of civil order with the kingdom of God. Thus secularized, the conceptions of human nature which had served Calvin in the effort to exalt God and remind man of his humble station become for Hobbes the basis of a civil authoritarianism. For Hobbes, however, obedience is no mere surrender. The recognition of depravity is now designed to lead to a kind of redemption by man of himself. The creation of order by mankind, through a universal submission to the "King of the Proud," who is "made so as not to be afraid," [42] is the symbol and manifest of this human self-redemption.

Hobbes set forth his dialectic of depravity and redemption both in philosophical form and in his analysis of Scripture. The appearance of human depravity is confirmed both in the Scriptural account of the fall from grace and in the fall from innocence described in pagan mythology. In the De Cive he alludes to an age of innocence when "it was peace and a golden age." In this golden age men were not equal in authority: some held power and others obeyed. There was no disorder because the right of the rulers to command went unchallenged. In this presumably idyllic state "princes kept their empires entire, not by arguments, but by punishing the wicked and protecting the good." Men were kept in peace "not by disputations, but by power and authority," and the "science of justice" was "wrapped up in fables" rather than "openly exposed to disputation." [43] It was inevitable, however, that this dubious bliss should end, because man is the only one of the creatures endowed with the faculty of speech. He would begin by assigning names to things and would advance from this simple but momentous step to the very heights of philosophy; for reason, according to Hobbes, is precisely the establishment of logical relationships among named objects.[44] Out of this development of reason as an instrument of desire must have arisen that dramatic and revolutionary phenomenon, the private judgment of good and evil.

The theological parallel is here obvious and intended. God gave Adam the power to name all the things of the earth. Adam was bound to use this power, once he had learned to employ it in reasoning, to question the myths which governed Paradise. In raising his questions he committed an act of disobedience, expressing a will to raise himself to the level of God. In eating the fruit of the forbidden tree Adam asserted the right of each man to make his own private judgment of good and evil, thus denying God's sovereignty in favor of the equal sovereignty of men. As a result of his sinful disobedience, man fell from the state of grace to the state of nature and lost the immortality God had promised him. Not all men remained in this state of nature. The Jewish nation, through its patriarch, Abraham, made a covenant with God and thereby established itself as a civil society under the sovereignty of God, with the patriarchs and the high priests acting as his agents. The relations of Paradise were thus in a manner re-established. The sovereignty of God was again rejected in the time of Samuel, when the people demanded a human king, and was restored only with the advent of Christ. Hobbes interprets the Scriptural passage, "My kingdom is not of this world," to mean that God's kingdom on earth was not re-established *until* the founding of Christianity. "This world," according to Hobbes, refers only to the period between the anointment of the first human king and the establishment of Christianity. The Christian king then becomes the vicar of Christ on earth, or as Hobbes also calls him, "God's lieutenant." [45] The immortality lost upon the fall is reinstated along with the permanent restoration of civil society; but this immortality is now not granted to men as individuals but to society as a whole through the succession of its rulers, which Hobbes designates an "Artificiall Eternity." [46]

Hobbes redefines traditional Christian eschatology to make the advent of Christ a final restoration of primitive innocence and immortality on earth. By redeeming the sins of man, Christ gained a "Victory over death" [47] and established the "Kingdom of God . . . on earth." This kingdom is the civil commonwealth in which God "reigneth by his Vicar, or Lieutenant," the civil sovereign.[48] As the commonwealth is the kingdom of God, salvation is the participation in this commonwealth. Salvation is achieved not in an afterlife but on earth whenever there is order and security. "To be saved, is to be secured, either respectively, against speciall Evills, or absolutely, against all Evill, comprehending Want, Sicknesse, and Death it self." Hobbes admits to difficulty in establishing from Scripture the place in which salvation is to be located, but it seems to him that because the kingdom of God is "an estate ordained by men for their perpetuall security against enemies and want . . . this Salvation should be on Earth."[49]

In expounding his mechanistic theory of political psychology Hobbes presents essentially the same case in other terms. Through the use of the resolutive-compositive method he dissolves the relations of civil society into the elements of human nature, and "constructs" civil society out of these elements as he observes them. Formally this provides two intellectual models—the state of nature and the state of civil society. All actual historical social relations fit into either one or the other category. In nature, as distinguished from civil society, men follow not only their own private judgment but their own immediate self-interest. In this respect they are all alike: each strives as best he is able to maximize his satisfactions. Moreover, they are all endowed by nature with roughly the same advantages. "Nature," Hobbes writes,

hath made men so equall, in the faculties of the body, and mind . . . [that] the difference between man, and man, is not so considerable, as that any one man can thereupon claim to himselfe any benefit, to which another may not pretend, as well as he.

Strength of body in some is balanced by the "secret machination" or confederacy of others physically weaker.[50] Men are equal not only in their ability to work their will, but also in being driven by the same passion for power. All of their actions can be accounted for as expressions of the motions of desire and aversion. For Hobbes the role of the passions is so important that he associates desire with life itself: "for as to have no Desire, is to be Dead." [51] Reason has no role but that of an instrument of the passions; unlike the theological right reason, which Hobbes rejects as entirely subjective,[52] it does not contribute to the creation of value, but only to the fulfillment of desire. Human values are determined by the passions: that for which we have a desire is esteemed good; that toward which we feel aversion is evil. The function of reason is to indicate a way of fulfillment to the passions, or to check the expression of a less intense passion for the sake of a more intense passion whenever there is conflict. This kind of reason, which is the reason that is operative in society, is common to all men:

Prudence, is but Experience; which equall time, equally bestowes on all men, in those things they equally apply themselves unto. That which may perhaps make such equality incredible, is but a vain conceipt of ones owne wisdome.[53]

Men do not admit their natural equality precisely because they are all given up to self-love. All the pleasures sought by natural man express his supreme evaluation of the exercise of power over others. Beauty and "general reputation amongst those of the other sex" are considered honorable because they are signs of "power generative." Physical strength is honorable as a sign of "power motive" ("*et à avoir tué son homme*");[54] the ability to persuade is honorable because persuasion is accomplished by "a certain violence of the mind";[55] riches are a sign of "the power that acquired them"; nobility shows "signs of power in the ancestors." Humility is the fear of power, laughter the result of a sudden recognition of our own pre-eminence, as weeping is the result of a "sudden conception of defect." Lust is not only an appetite for sexual pleasure, but a desire to be recognized as the possessor of a power "so much to please." Charity is the greatest of virtues because it is the greatest "argument to a man of his own power" to find himself "able, not only to accomplish his own desires, but also to assist other men in theirs."[56]

Thus men are naturally equal in two respects. They are all driven by the same passion for self-glorification, and in the pursuit of this goal they are all equipped with roughly the same abilities to attain it. The life of man can be compared to a race which "we must suppose to have no other goal, no other garland, but being foremost; and in it . . . Continually to out-go the next before, is felicity. And to forsake the course, is to die." [57] From the equality of desire and ability there arises a competition among men which threatens the overthrow of equality and the ultimate destruction of the competitors. "There is no way for any man to secure himself" so that he may pursue his desires in peace except "to master the persons of all men he can, so long till he sees no other power great enough to endanger him." Indeed some men set out to dominate others without the ulterior motive of security simply because they take pleasure in contemplating their own power.[58] Success in such a competition is out of the question, because no man can tolerate signs that another undervalues him, and because wherever any particular good is in scarce supply contention and strife are bound to arise. As a result the life of man in the state of nature is bound to be a life of perpetual fear and insecurity.

If Hobbes's description of the natural condition is very similar to Calvin's, so is his notion of the way out of the state of nature. Only if all rights to act according to private judgment are surrendered and transferred to a common authority can the burden of fear and insecurity be laid aside. In the state of civil society a new artificial equality replaces the equality of nature. In nature men are equal in their common addiction to the pursuit of power and in their possession of an identical ability to achieve power. In society they are equal because they are all equally powerless and because they have recognized this new equality in making the covenant. Given Hobbes's description of human nature it is remarkable that he should consider it possible for mankind to achieve a renunciation of the quest for personal power. Indeed Hobbes does not expect that this renunciation will be maintained by the force of promises alone. There are, in human nature, "two imaginable helps to strength" the keeping of covenants:

either a Feare of the consequences of breaking their word; or a Glory, or Pride in appearing not to need to breake it. This later is a Gener-

osity too rarely found to be presumed on, especially in the pursuers
of Wealth, Command, or sensuall Pleasure; which are the greatest
part of Mankind.[59]

To the covenant, therefore, must be added the power of the
sword. But there is a sense in which Hobbes attempts to compensate subjects for their renunciation of personal power. Hobbes's
theory of representation permits the citizen to ignore his actual
inferiority to the sovereign in favor of a psychological identification with him. As the universal *persona* the sovereign is the pro-
jection of every member of society.[60] Whereas in the state of
nature each individual had seen himself as the only sovereign, in
civil society he would be able to bask in the reflected glory of an
omnipotent ruler, participating, like all the other citizens, in the
power and freedom from restraint enjoyed by the sovereign.
Through this identification with the sovereign the citizen would
consider himself the source of command and the recipient of
obedience. Representation provides a benign psychological satisfaction of the desire for power in lieu of the destructive outlets
available in the state of nature. The original frontispiece of the
Leviathan captures the peculiar character of Hobbesian political
representation in portraying the sovereign as a giant man holding
in either hand a sword and a sceptre; inscribed in his body, like
so many homunculi, are the smaller figures of the citizens.

On the one hand, then, Hobbes wished to come to terms with
the passions by providing them with a limited but secure opportunity for gratification. On the other hand, as his theory of representation indicates, he was also anxious to forge an identification
of the citizen with his society beyond self-interest. Surely it is not
simply an inability to follow his own logic which leads Hobbes to
conclude that a soldier may not refuse to go to war on behalf of
his sovereign, even though no man can be compelled to forfeit his
life.[61] For Hobbes as for Machiavelli, the establishment and preservation of a stable and strong society is an achievement of the
highest order and not merely a utilitarian alternative to the anarchy of complete individual autonomy. Stability in civil society
represents the ability of an admittedly depraved species to overcome its own inherent weaknesses sufficiently to exercise a con-
tinuous control over itself. Hobbes was quite conscious of this

motive in undertaking to develop a civil science. To understand the causes of social antagonism, he declared, it was not necessary to seek the help of transcendental knowledge, "because we make the commonwealth ourselves." [62] If it was to be made to last and to act with vigor, the raw material of human nature expressed in the will to power would somehow have to be transformed into an instrument of peace. The Hobbesian sovereign, recognized and obeyed, is the depravity of man made legitimate and constructive.

The equality of the Hobbesian civil society is in this sense an equality of domination, which is sustained, at least in part, by an identification of those dominated with the holder of authority. It is this psychological relation which is the major expression of social equality. With Hobbes the Conservative theory of equality, which in its classical formulation had associated equality with tyranny, is made into an advocacy of psychological equality as the counterpart of actual domination. It is a matter of indifference, from the point of view of this Conservative egalitarianism, in what proportions property is distributed. The sovereign is to decide the division of *meum* and *tuum* in whatever way he believes best suited to the preservation of society.[63] Because the sovereign is the personification of the citizens, they all are considered to be equally the authors of any such distinction.

Measured by Liberal or Socialist standards, such a conception of equality is neither valid nor truly egalitarian. Given the assumptions of Hobbes and Calvin concerning human nature, however, equality can take only two forms: either an equality of depravity, which produces insecurity, or a psychological equality made effective by actual domination, which provides security. Insofar as security is valued, the Conservative theory of equality becomes an instrument for construction as well as a critique of human failings.

WINSTANLEY: EQUALITY AND COMMUNITY

. . . we justifie our act of digging upon that hill, to make the earth a common treasurie. First, because the earth was made by Almighty God to be a common treasury of livelihood for whole mankind in all his branches, without respect of persons; and not that any one according to the Word of God (which is love) the pure Law of Righteousness, ought to be Lord or landlord over another, but whole mankind was made equall, and knit into one body by one spirit of love, which is Christ in you, the hope of glory.[64]

Into the political issues confronting the Reformation of the seventeenth century Gerrard Winstanley carried the same combination of activistic mysticism with chiliastic prophecy which Müntzer had introduced over a century before to announce a restoration of communistic equality. The refinements which Winstanley introduced within this context raise a number of the problems which have remained important to later exponents of the Socialist conception of equality. Winstanley's innovations point forward to the thinking of the young Hegel and of Marx as much as his similarities to Müntzer indicate his links to the earliest expressions of the doctrine. Is the identification in love of Socialist equality compatible with the methods of violent overthrow? If not, can it be expected to be brought about by patience and labor, in the confidence that Spirit is the master of history? Winstanley began from the premise that the millennium could not be introduced by violence, but he ended by advocating a transitional use of domination and coercion, restrained by checks against the abuse of power. Before he came to this practical compromise, Winstanley introduced a number of other ideas which, like this development in his thought, were to be reproduced in later Socialism.

The common term linking Winstanley not only to Müntzer, but at the same time to the young Hegel and to Marx, is the notion of Spirit as a form of understanding, a description of purpose in history, a behavioral norm, and a statement of the essential identity of men with one another and with God. Like Müntzer, Winstanley believed that the restoration of original equality would be the work of Spirit incarnate in history. Winstanley identifies Spirit with "reason," freedom, and love. He sees it as the seed of purpose in history, hidden since the fall brought antagonism and avarice to mankind, but becoming increasingly manifest in the course of history. Spirit "hath layne hid under the flesh, like a corn of wheat . . . under the clods of earth," but now it is "sprung out, and begins to grow up a fruitfull vine which shall never decay, but it shall encrease, till he hath filled the earth . . . This is the graine of mustard seed, which is little in the beginning, but shall become a mighty tree." [65] "The time approaches when the Spirit will begin to appear in the flesh." [66]

For Winstanley, as for Hegel after him, the age of Spirit would be the age of love and the age of freedom as well, for the two terms are aspects of the same vision. Where there is domination there is neither love nor freedom. Until "every one shall look upon each other as equall in the Creation" no man can be free; the pride which rules the master and the envy which rules the servant make both slaves of covetousness. [67] The age of the Spirit will see a return of the "innocency, light and purity of mankind." For every man this restoration will mean that the "Spirit of universal Love lives in him, and he lives in Love, enjoying the sweet Union and communion of Spirit, each with other." [68] Hegel was to conceive of this age of Love, the age of Spirit, as an era of "mutual recognition."

Winstanley even went to the point of proposing that this spiritualization would occur through what Hegel would describe as a dialectical separation and reunion of man and Spirit. Now, Winstanley writes, "the living soul and the creating spirit are not one, but divided, the one looking after a Kingdome without him, the other drawing him to looke and wait for a Kingdome within him." [69] This is the state of separation. In Hegelian terms it is the condition in which man is alienated from his essence, which is Spirit, and Spirit is alienated from man and his life on earth. The final term of the historical process is the reunion of the separated. "Then," as Winstanley puts it, "man is drawne up into himselfe again, or new *Jerusalem* . . . comes down to Earth, to fetch Earth up to live in that life, that is a life above objects." [70] The belief in a superterrestrial heaven, not to be experienced in mortal life, is thus an ideology of that phase of history in which Spirit and man are not yet reunited. "If any one say: The glory of Jerusalem is to be seen hereafter, after the body is laid in the dust; it matters not to me what they say, they speak their imagination." [71] To Winstanley it is only a "strange conceit" which suffers men to seek the New Jerusalem "above the skies." [72] This ideology of separation is superseded by the utopia of reunion, in which the New Jerusalem is to be established on earth and salvation is therefore to be understood as "Liberty and Peace" [73] enjoyed in the present life.

Spirit is also to be understood as Reason. "The Spirit or Father," Winstanley writes, is "pure reason." [74] He speaks of "the Spirit Reason, which I call God," as "that spirituall power, that guids all mens reasoning in right order, and to a right end." But this "Spirit Reason" is not to be confused with natural reason, which is for the most part blinded "by the imagination of the flesh." [75] Reason is spiritual only when it is experienced as a revelation from God. Ordinary sense experience and deduction are of no avail until

the spirit Reason . . . break forth out of the Clouds of your heart, and manifest himself within you. This is to cast off the shadow of Learning, and to reject covetous, subtile proud flesh that deceives all the world by their hearsay, and traditional preaching of words, letters, and sillables, without the spirit: And to make choyce of the Lord, the true Teacher of every one in their own inward experience; The mysterie of the spirit. [76]

The difference between spiritual reason and ordinary sense perception is illustrated by Winstanley in an allusion to the eating of the fruit of the two trees in Paradise. It is "unexperienced Imagination," that is, reason unaided by Spirit, which eats of the tree of knowledge of good and evil. Only "when mankind by experience," that is, through direct revelation, eats of the tree of life does it gain true understanding. [77] Indeed in one place Winstanley confesses that he began to use the term reason as a description of spiritual understanding only because the opponents of mystical direct revelation attacked enthusiasm as a denial of reason. "I am made to change the name from God to Reason; because I have been held under darknesse by that word, as I see many people are." [78]

Winstanley followed the example of Müntzer in condemning those who conceived of spiritual understanding merely as sincere belief. It is not the belief in Christ which brings salvation but the presence within man of the power of Spirit. [79] Only the modern Pharisees worship God at a distance and call it blasphemy "to say Christ is in you." [80] The Gospels were written by the "experimentall hand" of shepherds and fishermen who had experienced

God's revelation even though they belonged to no learned profession. As Müntzer railed against the *Schriftgelehrten,* Winstanley complained that "the university learned ones have got these mens writings; and flourishes their plaine language over with their darke interpretation, and glosses, as if it were too hard for ordinary men now to understand them." [81]

Winstanley also follows Müntzer in revising the traditional association of spiritual understanding with contemplation. Instead he makes the "experience" of mysticism into an activity. All abstract speculation is sinful, for it leads either to idleness or to the exercise of cunning in the attempt to discover ways of advancing one's own self-interest. There are five fountains of knowledge, all of them practical. "Traditional knowledge, which is attained by reading, or by the instruction of others," is "not practical, but leads to an idle life, and this is not good." Speculative, "imaginary" inquiry is "an idle, lazy contemplation the Scholars would call knowledg"; actually, it is a mere show of knowledge, a parroting of words without understanding. Anyone who indulges in it "will not set his hand to work," as is evident from the example of lawyers and clergymen. In order "to prevent idleness and the danger of Machivilian cheats," [82] it is wise to educate children in trades rather than in arts and letters.

Spiritual existence, like spiritual knowledge, is not to be attained in contemplation but in activity. Müntzer had expressed his activistic mysticism in the form of violence involving the risk of suffering. For Winstanley the substitution of action for contemplation took another form, the more specifically Socialist form of labor. The Diggers went to St. George Hill to plow the commons when a voice declared to them in a trance: "Work together, Eate Bread together, Declare this all abroad." The voice was heard three times, which the Diggers took to mean that they should declare the message by word of mouth first, then in writing, and finally by deed.

We have now begun to declare it by Action, in Diging up the Common Land, and casting in Seed, that we may eat our Bread together in righteousness. And every one that comes to work, shall eate the Fruit of their own labours, one having as much Freedom in the Fruit of the Earth as another.[83]

Through common labor the Diggers "joyne hands with Christ, to lift up the Creation from Bondage, and restore all things from the Curse." For it is God's plan that none should own the land, but all should labor upon it together and enjoy its fruits in common. The blessing of creation is to have "peace in our hearts, and quiet rejoycing in our work . . . though we have but a dish of roots and bread for our food." [84] In the realization of the vision "all poor People by their righteous Labours shall be relieved, and freed from Poverty and Straits." [85]

It is significant that Winstanley's activistic modification of mysticism takes the form of labor rather than revolutionary violence, as it had for Müntzer. Formally both are in agreement in regarding Spirit as the secret inspirational power of redemption in history, revealing itself to man through an experience in which he becomes identified with God. Winstanley carried the belief in the divinization of man quite as far as Müntzer. "Every Saint," according to Winstanley, "is a true Heaven, because God dwells in him and he in God." [86] "When the second Adam rises up in the heart, he makes a man to judge all things that are below him." [87] No man can call the Father his God until "he feels and sees, by experience, that the spirit, which made the flesh, doth governe and rule King in his flesh." [88] The difference is that Winstanley attaches a specific ethical character to spiritual existence, whereas Müntzer defines as spiritual whatever the elect choose to do in God's name. Müntzer's spiritual man is released from bondage to the law in the sense that he is free to commit acts of violence against the godless without sin. Winstanley's understanding of Spirit precludes any such exemption from ethical mandates because for him Spirit in behavior must express freedom in love. Violence is forbidden to the spiritual man because Spirit is in its nature the antithesis of separation and antagonism between men. Because he conceived of Spirit as a kind of *élan vital* providing an unlimited sanction for those who possess it, Müntzer could urge his followers to revolutionary violence against the holders of power and wealth in the belief that violence was the fulfillment of spiritual inspiration. Winstanley fully recognized the disparity between the methods of love and the methods of domination and at first believed quite firmly that the instruments of domination could not successfully be used on behalf of love. Contrary to Müntzer's advocacy of a revolution led by the spiritual elite, Winstanley denied that the restoration could be accomplished "by the hands of a few" charged with the Spirit. It would only come about "by the universall spreading of the divine power, which is Christ in mankind." [89] Neither the violent overthrow of authority nor forcible expropriation could serve this purpose. Whatever the power of the first Adam to make men unwilling to relinquish their property and authority,[90] they were not to be forced to do so by the use of violence. Instead "every one is to wait, till the Lord Christ do spread himself in multiplicities of bodies, making them all of one heart and one mind." [91] When this is accomplished, the possessors of wealth and authority will voluntarily surrender their rights and the earth will once again become a common treasury. Otherwise no attempt at restoration could possibly be successful; for to employ violence is merely to replace one form of domination by another:

> We abhor fighting for Freedom, it is acting of the Curse and lifting him up higher; and do thou uphold it by the Sword, we will not; we will conquer by Love and Patience, or else we count it no Freedom: Freedom gotten by the Sword is an established Bondage to some part or other of the Creation . . . Victory that is gotten by the Sword is a victory that slaves get one over another; and hereby *men of the basest spirit* (saith Daniel) *are set to Rule.*[92]

For all the pacifism and patience of Winstanley's theoretical position, however, it is also significant that Winstanley lost his patience. When he turned to the practical task of reforming the existing order, he took a rather different attitude. Instead of waiting for the Spirit to make itself known to all men as it had manifested itself to the Diggers, Winstanley appealed to the holders of power to begin the work of restoration. It was to Oliver Cromwell that Winstanley addressed the program he designated *The Law of Freedom in a Platform*. In this program, he announced, "is the Original Righteousness and Peace in the Earth." He cautioned the "friendly and unbyassed reader" not to take this platform for the final manifestation of God's kingdom, but to "despise it not while it is small," [93] indicating that he conceived of it as a beginning of the restoration which might be managed by human effort with God's help. Cromwell, he explained, had already been the instrument of God in leading Englishmen to freedom from the kingly yoke. But all Englishmen had participated in this effort of liberation and only a few had profited from it. The common people, Winstanley urged, ought not to be deprived of the fruits of victory. To what avail would their sacrifices have been if the king were removed and the laws of monarchic tyranny maintained? Parliament, he complained, had done nothing to turn the crown lands, and the lands granted by royalty to the nobles, back to the people, from whom the Norman overlords had originally stolen them. Nor was there any sign that the people were to be permitted to partake of political freedom. An hereditary parliament, Winstanley pointedly remarked to Cromwell, is even more offensive against justice than an hereditary monarchy.[94]

What then should be done? Earlier Winstanley had counseled patience and faith in the inevitable triumph of Spirit. Now he appealed to established authority to begin the work of reform. "I have set the candle at your door," he wrote to Cromwell, "for you have power in your hand . . . to Act for Common Freedom if you will; I have no power." [95] Winstanley did not go so far from his original position as to suggest that this authority should be used to force a reform upon those who would not agree to it. "I do not say, nor desire, that every one shall be compelled to practise this *Commonwealths Government;* for the spirits of some will be Enemies at first." [96] It is sufficient that a beginning be made affecting only the common lands and those who will voluntarily adhere to the new scheme.

The new order which Winstanley proposes, despite the voluntarism which supports its initiation, has a number of features which are distinctly coercive. As in ancient Israel there will be no beggars in the new society,[97] but Winstanley apparently did not expect that full employment would be achieved without coercion. "Idle persons and beggars," he asserts, "will be made to work." [98] The establishment of communism in production and consumption, in place of buying and selling, would eliminate many but not all evils. It would not change human character to such an extent that all would be able and willing to support the new law (to which, presumably, they would all initially have agreed) without compulsion. The new order would have to take account of differences in character. "Some are wise, some are foolish, some idle, some laborious, some rash, some milde, some loving and free to others, some envyous and covetous." [99] To cope with those who would upset order, law and government will remain necessary. Offenders against the law are to be punished severely, by penalties ranging from whipping to death; idlers are to be enslaved until they are adjudged ready to work. Nor would status distinctions disappear in this effort to achieve "Common Freedom." Distinctions would be conferred in recognition not only of age but of industry and office. Government is to be based upon the assumption that the old Adam remains very much alive. Earlier Winstanley had written of unredeemed mankind:

everyone that gets an authority into his hands, tyrannizes over others; as many husbands, parents, masters, magistrates, that lives after the flesh, doe carry themselves like oppressing Lords over such as are under them; not knowing that their wives, children, servants, subjects are their fellow creatures, and hath as equall priviledge to share with them in the blessing of liberty.[100]

Now, in his program he advises annual election so that officials will carry out their duties in the knowledge that their activities will be scrutinized by the next set of officials and so that the hope of honor will spur men to virtue.[101] The right to hold office is not to be extended to all, especially not to "all uncivil livers, as drunkards, quarrelers, fearful ignorant men who dare not speak truth, lest they anger other men; likewise all who are wholly given to pleasure and sports, or men who are full of talk."[102] Among the officers to be appointed is a taskmaster who is to oversee those who are sentenced to lose their freedom for stubborn refusal to behave peaceably or to work. Such criminals are to be assigned tasks, and given food and clothing only if they perform their assignments. If they should prove "desperate, wanton, or idle, and will not quietly submit to the Law, the Task-master is to feed them with short dyet, and to whip them, *for a rod is prepared for the fools back*, till such time as their proud hearts do bend to the Law."[103]

Thus, while Winstanley begins with a vision of perfect harmony and peace to be attained by patience and labor, he ends as an advocate of "revolution from above" as an approach to the attainment of the millennium. In this final stage of his thought he comes to accept the need for the instruments of domination and coercion as agents of spiritual transformation. Presumably the establishment of the institutions of communism, aided by a new scheme of education and by a system of rewards and penalties, would promote the transformation of character he had previously believed could only be the work of the Spirit. It remained for Marx to combine Winstanley's belief in the attainment of spiritual consciousness through labor with Müntzer's view of the elect as a militant vanguard of the millennium, and to make legitimate the use of the instruments of domination and coercion in the transitional period by a militant workers' movement governing by a dictatorship of the proletariat. Well before Marx, Winstanley recognized the obstacles to the achievement of communism, but he too seems to have believed that these obstacles and the methods they would make necessary would not last beyond the period of transition.

Winstanley's religious Socialism completes the spectrum of egalitarian expression in the seventeenth century. While the mode of expression is in transition from theology to philosophy, the questions asked remain substantially the same as those first posed in the Reformation: Should the social order be designed to nurture and protect individual liberty? Must it, on the contrary, be designed to force submission from a depraved species, incapable of self-government? Or will it find its proper and highest form only when individualism is transcended by a sense of community and depravity is educated out of human character?

CHAPTER FIVE

Equality and Enlightenment

⚜

THE PHILOSOPHIC champions of enlightenment in the eighteenth century were for the most part less anxious to propose equality than to denounce extreme inequalities. They deplored the privileges and power of the nobility and clergy but took the side of the princes against the *canaille*. They argued that sovereignty belonged to the people as a matter of principle, but added that it was delegated to the monarch on condition that he adhere to the laws of the state and the law of nature. The problem of politics, as many of the philosophers understood it, was not to restore authority to the people or distribute and limit power, but to direct the attention of the ruler to the great goals of civilization: the furtherance of enlightenment, toleration, and human welfare.[1] For all of them the problem of philosophy was to clear away the shadows surrounding the natural origins of society so that the contrast between nature and convention would be too vivid to be ignored completely; for some it was also to establish ethical, psychological, and educational principles which would serve the cause of some future reform.

The attitude of the typical Enlightenment philosopher toward equality was therefore as ambivalent as that of the Stoic philosophers who had played a similarly catalytic role in classical times. The difference is that the attitude of the typical *philosophe* had a critical bite characteristic of the eighteenth century, with none

of the Stoic's anxious wish to detach himself from the pathos of
everyday existence. Equality, the *philosophe* was inclined to
argue, was undoubtedly a correct assumption for the state of
nature, but society was not nature, and equality was quite "chimerical" anywhere but in the state of nature. "Natural equality,"
said the article on the subject in the *Encyclopedia*, "is that which
is among all men by the constitution of their nature alone." This
equality "is the principle and foundation of liberty," and all
slavery, all gross inequalities of wealth, were established in violation of this principle. But, the authority added, no one ought to
suppose that all rank, all distinctions, or all differences of condition ought therefore to be overthrown. Natural equality must not
be confused with the absurd "chimera of absolute equality."[2]
How then was the great principle of natural equality to be applied? On this the *Encyclopedia* was silent, but the implied answer was the same as had been given by the Stoics. Extremes of
inequality were unjust and pretensions of superiority unwarranted,
but the best that could be hoped for in society was a modification
of inequality out of respect for the natural principle of common
humanity.

Montesquieu, whose authority was great with the authors of
the *Encyclopedia*, and Voltaire, whose work often served as a
popular gloss on current moral theorizing, both held substantially
the same opinion. "In the state of nature, indeed," wrote Montesquieu, "all men are born equal, but they cannot continue in
this equality. Society makes them lose it, and they can recover it
only by the protection of the laws."[3] What did this recovery
entail? In the well-regulated democracy, Montesquieu observed,
men are equal as citizens but not in their civic or private capacities. Perfect equality in wealth and status would be hard to achieve
and even dangerous. "Though real equality be the soul of a democracy, it is so difficult to establish, that an extreme exactness in
this respect would not always be convenient." Much the best
policy in a democracy would be to reduce the differences, to
"level, as it were, the inequalities, by the duties laid upon the rich,
and by the ease afforded to the poor."[4]

Voltaire was still less in favor of any radical reform of society
in accordance with the principle of natural equality. Equality, he

laid down in his *Philosophical Dictionary*, must surely be the condition of nature, where men are as free and self-sufficient as the animals, but such a condition would not suit society. "On our miserable globe it is impossible for men living in society not to be divided into two classes, one the rich who command, the other the poor who serve." Things could not be otherwise, he explained, because everyone desires the same scarce goods and because men have grown too dependent upon one another's services. "Thus," Voltaire concluded on a note of perfect paradox, "equality is at once the most natural and at the same time the most chimerical of things." A cook may have the right to think "in his heart of hearts" that he is the equal of the cardinal he serves; it does not follow that the cook may order the cardinal to prepare him dinner. The cook may say to himself that if the Turks took Rome and he became a cardinal he would make the master his cook. "This whole speech is reasonable and right," Voltaire comments with a mixture of fairness and realism, "but while he waits for the Grand Turk to take Rome, the cook must do his duty, or human society is perverted."[5]

The principle of natural equality had a much greater systematic significance for Helvétius, who made it the cornerstone of his doctrine of man and of his influential belief in the educational effect of environment. "Quintilian, Locke and I say: Inequality among intellects is the result of a known cause and this cause is the difference in education."[6] As bold as is this statement and as radical and far-reaching its portent, Helvétius did not himself draw out its political implications. His great contribution to egalitarian thought is to have provided a fresh theory with which political doctrines would later be constructed. The hedonistic psychology and the belief in the possibility of altering character by education developed by Helvétius and others in the eighteenth century were later to provide indispensable support for the utilitarian moral and political doctrines of Bentham and the Philosophical Radicals. The Benthamites would argue that because human nature was governed by the quest for pleasure, and because behavior could be changed by laws and social conditions, laws should be designed to allow every individual to maximize his pleasure to the utmost, or according to the good of the greatest number.

Kant performed a function similar to that of Helvétius in trans-
posing the argument over freedom from the sphere of natural
right to that of a logical necessity inherent in the very concept of
society under law. The categorical imperative and the idea that
law must reflect and promote universal autonomy both have profound bearing on the issue of political equality, but Kant himself
was chiefly concerned with laying the foundations for a just
social order and a universal fellowship of mankind.

If some of the most astute philosophic minds were thus only
indirectly concerned with equality as a political problem, others
with more practical commitments were popularizing egalitarian
ideals in the conventional terms of natural right. The later decades
of the eighteenth century witnessed a discussion of equality inflamed by democratic revolution, but in the heat of this discussion
philosophy was seldom the gainer. The declarations of Paine,
Saint-Just, and Robespierre, as important as they are to the social
history of the period, contribute little if anything to the systematic
consideration of equality. Babeuf is no great exception, but in the
absence of a more systematic theorist his position is useful to
consider.

To observe again the appearance of the three concepts of
equality we must single out those writers who constructed political philosophies out of the psychological and ethical speculations
of the time. In this way we can observe the development of the
Liberal concept of equality from Hooker to Locke and Condorcet;
the use of the Conservative concept by Rousseau to warn of the
approach of an authoritarian mass society; and the slow development of the Socialist concept over the latter half of the eighteenth
century.

HOOKER, LOCKE, AND CONDORCET: MORAL AUTONOMY
AND COMPETITIVE EQUALITY

In Locke's understanding of equality, the two principles already
evident in the thought of Luther and the Levellers—the equal
capacity of all men to know the moral law and the belief in a
competition in virtue—assume cardinal importance. From the
equal ability to know the moral law Locke argues for an equal
moral autonomy, and from this premise he goes on to declare the

equal authority of all partners to the social compact. Locke differs from his predecessors in contending that the moral law can be known by natural reason, unaided by an inborn ethical impulse or the special gift of Spirit, and in locating this moral law in nature rather than in the Scriptures. In regard to the second principle his modifications are perhaps more radical. The competitive equality advocated by Locke in economics is not obviously identical with either the Lutheran or the Leveller conception of a competition in virtue in which each man is to be judged according to how well he applies his talents to the works of the world. For Locke economic activity is both a means and an end: it is an end insofar as freedom requires the unimpeded exercise of natural faculties, and a means as the principal agency in the pursuit of happiness. Property is both an expression of unique personality and a source of hedonistic material gratification. Nevertheless, the Lockean justification of unequal reward also rests on the assumption that economic activity is a competition in virtue: distinctions in wealth are signs of difference in virtue, a virtue which, like Lutheran spirituality, exalts individual diligence, industry, and enterprise. Nor can any man legitimately withdraw from nature more than he can himself use, or so much as to deprive another of his rightful share in nature's bounty: to do so would upset the identity of virtue and natural appetite.[7] With the important addition of hedonism, Lockean competitive equality thus maintains the religious belief in a competition in virtue.

Locke's modification of the belief in the equal capacity of all men to know the moral law may be traced through an intermediate stage. Before the spiritual equality of Christians could become the natural equality of mankind certain barriers between religion and naturalistic philosophy had to be removed; "the judicious Hooker" put them out of Locke's way. Far from providing Locke with a mask for Hobbism,[8] Richard Hooker performed two quite different services for him. Hooker's distrust of Puritan spiritual perception led him to conclude that natural reason is the only trustworthy mode of spiritual understanding. From this it was a short step to a revival of the belief in natural law as the object of rational understanding. By developing and popularizing these arguments Hooker prepared the way for Locke.

In combatting the enthusiasm which he thought to be the salient characteristic of Puritanism, Hooker did not simply reject spiritual understanding. Instead he sought to reinterpret it to mean the exercise of natural reason. He admitted that the divine Spirit might manifest itself in direct revelation, but he argued that it was too difficult to judge the validity of the claims of those who alleged that they received such a direct and inner message. The Puritans, he contended, did only harm by limiting the conception of spiritual understanding to revelation and by making the light of nature "hateful with men" as though "God had so accursed it, that it should never shine or give light in things concerning duty any way towards him."[9] The Puritans are deluded in thinking "the wisdom of man . . . debased either in comparison with that of God" or condemned in the Bible.[10] If they allege special revelation as the basis of their interpretation of God's will, the Puritans "must profess themselves to be all (even men, women, and children) Prophets," an assertion which may easily be suspected as an illusion born of conceit. The only sure way to test the validity of convictions and interpretations is to gauge "not . . . the fervent earnestness of their persuasion, but the soundness of those reasons whereupon the same is built." If a doctrine is reasonable, we may be certain that it has been "wrought by the Holy Ghost, and not by the fraud of that evil spirit which is even in his illusions strong."[11]

This argument arises in the context of a general discussion of Puritanism and concludes in a discussion of Aquinas' categories of law. Here again Hooker hammers the doctrine of spiritual understanding into the form of natural reason.

The operations of Spirit . . . are as we know things secret and undiscernible even to the very soul where they are, because their nature is of another and an higher kind than that which can be perceived in this life. Wherefore albeit the Spirit leads us into all truth and directs us in all goodness, yet because these workings of the Spirit in us are so privy and secret, we therefore stand on a plainer ground, when we gather by reason from the quality of things believed or done, that the Spirit of God hath directed us in both, than if we settle ourselves to believe or do any certain particular thing, as being moved thereto by the Spirit.[12]

Human laws, he concludes, are therefore "probably derived, and certainly ought to be derived, by those who promulgate them, from the laws of nature and God, by discourse of reason aided with the influence of divine grace." [13]

Although the conversion of spiritual understanding into natural reason and the revival of natural law led Hooker to reject arbitrary authority, he did not associate reason and natural law with equality but instead with a hierarchy of the wise. To the Puritans he pointed out that Calvin himself was not so foolish as to permit the welfare of the church to "hang still on so slender a thread as the liking of an ignorant multitude." [14] Before he would consent to guide the Genevan church, Calvin insisted that the authority of the ministers to frame laws for the community be first recognized. He "ripely considered how gross a thing it were for men of his quality, wise and grave men, to live with such a multitude, and to be tenants at will under them." [15] He insisted that authority be vested in a permanent ecclesiastical court. The fact that this consistory was composed of twice as many lay magistrates as ministers, annually elected, provided it only with a republicanism of form. In practice, the "pastors' learning would be at all times of sufficient force to over-persuade simple men, who knowing the time of their own presidentship to be but short would always stand in fear of their ministers' perpetual authority." [16] Even the ministers themselves, in view of Calvin's pre-eminence, were so likely to express their opinions in the shadow of a "kind of secret dependency and awe" that in effect the government of the church would be in the hands of one man, despite its formal organization. Indeed some of the laymen found the practice of the consistory so oppressive that they complained it was little better than "Popish tyranny." [17]

The Puritans, Hooker argued, would go to the other extreme from Calvin and deny both reason and hierarchy. Hooker admits that "if the guides of the people be blind, the common sort of men must not close up their own eyes and be led by the conduct of such," [18] but he insists that popular support is no argument for the validity of Puritan teachings. People adhere to the Puritan cause not because they are persuaded by arguments from Scripture, but because they know there are faults in existing church organization and are ready to impute them to the prevailing system of ecclesiastical government. Offered an alternative, the multitude readily accepts it because, having had no experience with any other system, the ordinary man does not realize that the same defects would arise again from human failings. When the Puritans claim that their reforms are correct because they are derived from Scripture with the "special illumination of the Holy Ghost" they reach the ultimate stage of irrational appeal.[19] Little wonder the Puritans are so successful with women, whose "judgments are commonly weakest,"[20] and with the multitude as a whole.

In proposing an alternative to enthusiasm Hooker provided some of the elements of a Liberal theory of government, even though he would not countenance equality. According to Hooker's theory, God is the author of a rational universe in which man is a participant.[21] Men have a natural inclination to society[22] and they are not entirely depraved: the laws must be framed so as to accommodate both the "sincere" desires and the depraved passions.[23] All men are in some degree capable of reason, but not all are in fact guided by reason, because of custom and self-interest.[24] Through education men are capable of attaining higher levels of understanding.[25] But education is not entirely to be relied upon. Even though they be wise enough to recognize the law of nature, some men are so wicked that "no means of instruction human or divine could prevent effusion of blood." For this reason, and for this reason only, it is advisable that all be required to give "their common consent all to be ordered by some whom they should agree upon." Consent is justified not because all men are equal in understanding but because, without consent, differences in reason would not be admitted and some men would not agree to be subordinated to the wiser. Without consent,

there were no reason that one man should take upon him to be lord or judge over another; because, although there be according to the opinion of some very great and judicious men a kind of natural right in the noble, wise, and virtuous, to govern them which are of servile disposition; nevertheless for manifestation of this their right, and men's more peaceable contentment on both sides, the assent of them who are to be governed seemeth necessary.

The requirement of consent does not extend beyond the making of the fundamental compact. The power of the governors should be limited, not in the course of its exercise, but in advance by the terms of the compact.[26] Contrary to the "strange, untrue, and unnatural conceits" of the *Vindiciae contra tyrannos*, the people once having given their consent can never withdraw their obedience.[27] The original compact binds future generations as well, because society is a corporation and corporations are immortal.[28]

It would be improper to extend equality beyond this equal authority in establishing government, because life in public society requires order, and wherever things or persons are ordered "they are distinguished by degrees."[29] The order of estates is established by public authority in pursuance of a dictate of reason and nature. In the organization of the church "the first thing" required for its polity is "a difference of persons." Some must lead and others follow.[30] The Christian king, because he is ordained by God and agreed upon by the members of society, should have authority to create a civil and an ecclesiastical hierarchy. Individual men must be assumed to be self-interested, whereas government looks to the general welfare of the whole society. For the purpose of creating this government it is advisable to consider all men equals. Once the contract is made, however, this equality is superseded by "order," that is, inequality. This inequality, however, should not be erected on any basis other than differences in rationality. In the church the multitude is to be subordinated to the learned. In government all men are to be subject to law, in the making of which it is necessary that "none but wise men be admitted." Men are partial and self-interested, whatever their rank, but "the law doth speak with all indifferency."[31] This emphasis on government according to law qualifies the disavowal of a right of resistance in Hooker's denunciation of the *Vindiciae*. We are obliged to obey the laws of the public power "unless there be reason shewed which may necessarily enforce that the Law of Reason or of God doth enjoin the contrary."[32]

Locke followed Hooker in basing his political doctrine upon the rationality of man and upon natural law, breaking only gradually with the older tradition of natural-law thinking, represented by Hooker, to associate natural law with equality.[33] As early as

1669 Locke gave indications of the case he was to make against
Filmer's derivation of authority from the natural right of patri-
archy.[34] Against Samuel Parker, Locke argued that consent was
the only basis upon which any government could be considered
legitimate. The grounds for this assertion had been expounded by
Locke some years before in his *Essays on the Law of Nature*
(1660). Locke never published these essays, for reasons that
appear to relate to his interests in the philosophy of knowledge rather than to political philosophy. The conceptions of
natural law and legitimate government developed in the *Essays* are the parents of much that Locke set down later in the
Second Treatise.

Through the use of reason, Locke argues in the *Essays*, we can
know that God is the creator of the universe and we can discover
the plan according to which the universe is directed.[35] We are
obliged to obey this plan, the law of nature, because God is the
sovereign of the universe. Obedience "derives from the lordship
and command which any superior has over us,"[36] a power which
rests ultimately with God.[37] In order to know the natural law,
however, it is necessary to consult "not the majority of the people
. . . but those who are more rational and perceptive than the
rest."[38] Most people are guided less by reason than "by the example of others, or by traditional customs and the fashion of the
country, or finally by the authority of those whom they consider good and wise."[39] "Surely," Locke observes, "we have
been taught by a most unhappy lesson," the civil wars, that the
voice of the people is not to be confounded with the voice of
God.[40] Locke thus seems to follow the lines of Hooker's argument rather closely. He does not treat the question of the origin of
government, but it may reasonably be inferred that at this point
his argument for consent would have been on grounds of expediency. In another work devoted to the faculty of understanding,
Locke indicated clearly that he did not believe men were identical
in their faculties of reasoning.

There is, it is visible, great variety in men's understandings, and their
natural constitutions put so wide a difference between some men in
this respect, that art and industry would never be able to master, and
their very natures seem to want a foundation to raise on it that which

other men easily attain unto. Amongst men of equal education there is a great inequality of parts.[41]

In the *Second Treatise*, however, Locke seems to suggest that, in the state of nature, men are equal not only in their rational faculties but in other respects as well:

all the power and jurisdiction is reciprocal, no one having more than another; there being nothing more evident than that creatures of the same species and rank, promiscuously born to all the same advantages of nature and the use of the same faculties, should also be equal one amongst another without subordination or subjection.[42]

Since, as far as nature is concerned, there is no way of distinguishing the potentially wiser man, Locke may have reasoned, men must all be considered equal before education has a chance to show. Elsewhere in the *Second Treatise*, however, he explains natural equality more precisely: the reason that men are to be considered equal in nature is that, whatever their degrees of rationality, they are all *able* to know that God exists and what the law of nature is. "The freedom . . . of man, and liberty of acting according to his own will, is grounded on his having reason which is able to instruct him in that law he is to govern himself by."[43] Unlike Hooker, Locke grounds the requirement of consent in the formation of government upon the possession by all men of a minimum of reason enabling them to know the moral law and entitling them all to an equal voice in the making of the social compact. The political equality which the possession of reason ought to confer is not to be confused with other kinds of equality. By the statement, "All men are by nature equal," Locke asserts,

I cannot be supposed to understand all sorts of equality. Age or virtue may give men a just precedency; excellence of parts and merit may place others above the common level; birth may subject some, and alliance or benefits others, to pay an observance to those whom nature, gratitude, or other respects may have made it due; and yet all this consists with the equality which all men are in, in respect of jurisdiction or dominion one over another which was the equality I there spoke of as being proper to the business at hand, being that equal right that every man hath to his natural freedom, without being subjected to the will or authority of any other men.[44]

This equal right to natural freedom can only be realized in a society established by common consent and governed by the principles of the law of nature. "The end of the law is not to abolish or restrain but to preserve and enlarge freedom."[45] The "inconveniences" of a society without rules and mediators, regulated only by human selfishness, can be overcome through the establishment of government.

Because equality is conceived of by Locke as the equal right of all men to freedom, Lockean equality is not an instrument of levelling in any area other than the political. On the contrary, it is inseparable from a kind of individualism according to which each person is free to express his own personality in whatever way he chooses so long as he does not injure the common welfare or violate the law of nature. In areas outside of politics Lockean doctrine calls for competitive equality. Differences in wealth which result from men's employment of their rational faculties and their industry do not impair natural equality but actually fulfill the intention of nature to reward industry. Although the earth was given to men in common, God did not intend that it should remain common and uncultivated. "He gave it to the use of the industrious and the rational—and labour was to be his title to it."[46] This "natural" justification of unequal reward is qualified considerably by the development of a money economy. In nature the only limitation on acquisition is the stipulation that a man may not extract more than he can use before it spoils. This limitation is abrogated as it becomes possible, with the introduction of money, to convert a surplus into symbolic value. As a result, unequal industry begets considerable inequalities in wealth. Locke considers these inequalities justified not only because they derive from different degrees of industry, but also because the introduction of money can only have been contrived by tacit consent. This consent, he makes sure to add, is given outside the social contract and therefore cannot be set aside either by the terms of the contract or by governmental legislation, which may only regulate private contracts entered into under the tacit contract which establishes a money economy.[47] Competitive equality is thus by no means an ethical barrier to great disparities of wealth in society. On the other hand, it ought not to lead to exploitation and poverty, Locke seems to believe, because land is abundant and every man has the same ability to attain wealth, or at least sustenance, by exerting himself in agricultural labor. Locke seems further to assume that differences in rational capacity or even in education do not affect men's chances in the pursuit of happiness as much as does their willingness to apply a capacity for industry with which they are all equally endowed. If the diversity of social advantages or of natural talents counted as much as sheer industriousness, the ethical justification of property erected by Locke would be gravely undermined.

His political philosophy seems to involve a similar distinction between nature and society. In nature men are equal in authority. They act on this equality when they compact to establish government and retain it as a civil right in all matters pertaining to the fundamental compact. In making the compact, however, they agree to subordinate themselves to common governors and to forego their previously equal authority in the making of political decisions. Government thus provides a practical instrument for promoting individual liberty without impairing equality.

Condorcet, a century later, saw unfolding in history much the same set of principles Locke had argued for on the basis of natural right. Condorcet acknowledged the important contribution of natural rights philosophy in establishing the "single truth" from which the rights of man derive: "man is a sentient being, capable of reasoning and acquiring moral ideas."[48] This principle and the declaration of social and political equality which followed from it had been announced by Sydney and Locke and refined by Rousseau until they had become truths "that it is no longer possible to forget or combat."[49] No longer could it be asserted that the social contract existed between a people and its lawgiver, or that a constitution once received could never be altered, or that different nations might prescribe different rights. Nor would men dare any longer

to divide humanity into two races, one fated to rule, the other to obey, one to deceive, the other to be deceived. They had to recognize that all men have an equal right to be informed on all that concerns them, and that none of the authorities established by men over themselves has the right to hide from them one single truth.[50]

This triumph of egalitarian ideas was due to the general progress of human knowledge. In the past inequality and ignorance had supported each other. The mass of men had first been placed in subjection by a priestly caste claiming a monopoly of knowledge and successful in foisting on others a belief that they enjoyed equality "even in slavery."[51] The priestly caste was joined by another elite which made use of certain initial advances in the art of warfare, requiring training and the possession of horse and armor, to turn an assumed inequality into a real one. But gunpowder put an end to the monopoly of the means of coercion by knights in armor,[52] as printing dealt a mortal blow to the monopoly of knowledge.[53]

Indeed virtually every great event in history seemed to forward the advance of equality. The absolute monarchs intended only to overcome opposition from clergy and nobility, but in the process they "imparted to the law a spirit of equality." [54] The great strides made in science and mathematics were making it possible to direct nature into paths beneficial to humanity. Explorations and discoveries had expanded the opportunities for commerce, even as they had also introduced the evils of imperialism. But imperialism was only another battle due to be won. Progress would only be complete when it was accepted that "men of all races are equally brothers by the wish of nature and have not been created to feed the vanity and greed of a few privileged nations." [55]

With the French Revolution, Condorcet declared, humanity had entered the final stage of evolution. The idea of the indefinite perfectibility of the human species, which had been introduced by Turgot, Price, and Priestley,[56] would now be proven beyond doubt. The triumph of real equality, "the final end of the social art," would bring it about that

even the effects of the natural differences between men will be mitigated and the only kind of inequality to persist will be that which is in the interest of all and which favours the progress of civilization, of education and of industry, without entailing either poverty, humiliation, or dependency.[57]

The remaining inequalities must be respected as "the result of natural and necessary causes which it would be altogether foolish and dangerous to eradicate."[58]

The egalitarian society envisaged by Condorcet was to be an association of self-reliant individuals, enlightened to the extent that they were fully capable of governing themselves and of providing for their own needs independently. The great question facing humanity, he declared, is this:

. . . will men approach a condition in which everyone will have the knowledge necessary to conduct himself in the ordinary affairs of life, according to the light of his own reason, to preserve his mind free from prejudice, to understand his rights and to exercise them in accordance with his conscience and his creed; in which everyone will become able, through the development of his faculties, to find the means of providing for his needs; and in which at last misery and folly will be the exception, and no longer the habitual lot of a section of society? [59]

In politics real equality meant popular government; in economics it meant free trade and competition. Economic freedom was essential because "the only right that the general will can legitimately exercise over the individual" is to guarantee to each man his natural rights.[60] Public authority ought to establish such necessary instruments of liberty as standards of weights and measures, and ought to undertake projects to advance economic progress and prevent natural disasters. Otherwise people "should be able to use their faculties, dispose of their wealth and provide for their needs in complete freedom." [61]

Condorcet recognized that there already existed a disparity between the equality the law permitted and the equality men actually enjoyed. The progress of equality was being retarded by three principal causes: inequality of wealth, resulting from differences of income; inequalities of wealth and status conferred by inheritance; and inequality in education.[62] All these barriers, he felt, would gradually be overcome. Governments could assist by establishing systems of social security for the citizenry, to be financed "partly by their own savings and partly by the savings of those who make the same outlay, but who die before they need to reap the reward." By applying the calculus to the probabilities of life and to investment, social and private institutions could provide programs of insurance and annuities.[63] Society must also establish institutions of credit to make industrial progress independent of the great capitalists.[64]

Condorcet was especially confident of the benefits of expanded education. He anticipated the objection that universal education might give rise to a new inequality by asserting that an enlightened man could never be enslaved, even by someone more enlightened. Differences of learning would remain but they would be differences "among upright men who know the value of learning without being dazzled by it." Men of common sense would respect talent and genius and appreciate the great benefactors of humanity.[65]

The obstacles to equality, he also believed, would be easier to overcome because of the combined force of all the tendencies working against them. "With great equality of education there will be greater equality in industry and social wealth; equality in wealth necessarily leads to equality in education; and equality between the nations and equality within a single nation are mutually dependent." [66] People throughout the world would gradually grow to hate war and would join in permanent confederations.[67] Economic abundance would reduce the likelihood of conflict.[68] The danger of overpopulation would be met by measures to control birth because enlightened people would prefer a limitation "rather than foolishly to encumber the world with useless and wretched beings." [69]

For all these reasons Condorcet could close the century on a note of ebullient optimism, confident in the prospects of Liberal egalitarianism:

> The time will therefore come when the sun will shine only on free men who know no other master but their reason; when tyrants and slaves, priests and their stupid or hypocritical instruments will exist only in works of history and on the stage; and when we shall think of them only to pity their victims and their dupes; to maintain ourselves in a state of vigilance by thinking on their excesses; and to learn how to recognize and so to destroy, by force of reason, the first seeds of tyranny and superstition, should they ever dare to reappear amongst us.[70]

Locke might well have rejected these words as irreligious and far too inflammatory, but the sentiments expressed in the prophecy of an age of rational independence would surely have been congenial to him. As yet these sentiments could be shared by all those committed to Enlightenment. In time they would become more exclusively associated with the cause of Liberalism.

ROUSSEAU: EQUALITY AND MASS SOCIETY

No less strenuously than Locke, Rousseau worked to formulate a political philosophy that would affirm the principles of natural right; and no less ardently than Condorcet he wished to see them fulfilled in history. But before he arrived at the practical solutions he offered in the *Social Contract* and in his constitutional projects, Rousseau wrestled unsuccessfully with the conflict between natural origins and social necessity. *The Discourse on the Origin of Inequality Among Men* bears the marks of this struggle. In it Rousseau felt compelled to take a Conservative view of equality in society and to predict the return of a primitive equality of slaves in the new conditions of a brutalized mass society.

Rousseau followed Locke in characterizing the state of nature in the *Discourse* as a condition of peace and innocence, but he leaned toward the view of Hobbes [71] and Calvin in adding that the loss of innocence had left men in the grip of vicious passions and a blinding vanity. He was therefore unable to see how the principles of natural equality could be applied in the artificial conditions of society. He was able to offer a Liberal countenance elsewhere only by exchanging this pessimism for the assumption that all men had a capacity to know and to behave according to the moral law —a capacity which could not be completely extinguished by the vices of society.

Even in the *Discourse,* however, it was only with great reluctance that Rousseau took a pessimistic attitude toward the prospects of social regeneration. He offered the essay to his contemporaries as a "panegyric on your first ancestors, a criticism of your contemporaries, and a terror to the unfortunates who will come after you." [72] For men like himself, he lamented, "whose passions have destroyed their original simplicity," [73] there was no turning back to the calm and virtuous dispositions of nature. The tone of the essay was not lost on the generation which read his alternately melancholy and impassioned critique and promptly erected barricades on the boulevards of Paris. [74]

Nor did Rousseau mask his contempt for philosophers who provided the privileged with a rationalization for inequality. In tracing the philosophic inquiry into natural right, Rousseau became

the first to study the history of egalitarian thought and the first
to contend that the justification of inequality rested upon a distortion and suppression of the truth of human nature. To form a true
idea of natural right, he contended, it is first necessary to recognize that, in its successive developments, reason "has been led
to suppress nature itself." [75] At first the errors of philosophy were
not so much mischievous as confused. The "ancient philosophers"
did their best to contradict each other in regard to equality. (Presumably Rousseau means that Plato and Aristotle distinguished
natural orders of men whereas the Stoics argued for natural
equality.) The Romans (presumably the lawyers who followed
Gaius) confused man with the animals because of their peculiar
understanding of natural law. The "moderns," against whom Rousseau directs the brunt of his attack, limit the natural law, and
therefore equality, to human beings, because natural law is conceived to be a moral law framed only for moral creatures.

By making man "moral" these modern philosophers mean that
he is to be distinguished from the animals by virtue of his reason,
which is thus considered prior to nature. Only by making this
faulty assumption, Rousseau asserts, can they posit the existence
of moral creatures as an original condition. Having made this false
start, they proceed to erect elaborate metaphysical systems which
can neither be understood nor verified by others not devoted to
the same principles. If man in his original state actually held to
such principles, he must have been endowed with a degree of
knowledge and a trained faculty for argument such as even now
is possessed by only a few philosophers. Much of the *Discourse* is
therefore dedicated to demonstrating that man as he originally
issued from the hands of nature was only potentially rational and
must have developed his understanding only gradually, with all
manner of difficulty.

But the most serious critique, from a moral point of view, which
Rousseau levels at the modern natural law theorists is that their
theories are really concocted out of a consideration of what is expedient to society. These philosophers are the intellectual lackeys
of the *status quo*, paid to provide spurious justification for others
who profit from the inequities of the social order. The possession of property is said to be a right, whereas in reality it is only

the result of brutal usurpation. Tyrannical government is made to appear a natural consequence of human needs and dispositions, whereas actually it is the result of the cunning imposition of domination upon the weak by those who had the largest stake in order. Artificial inequalities, in addition to those of power and wealth, which have nothing to do with the nature of man, are similarly traced to innate endowments and natural necessity. Rousseau's critique aims to unmask modern philosophy as an insult to nature as well as to the integrity of philosophy itself.[76]

In his sketch of the history of the philosophic discussion of equality, Rousseau omits mention of Christianity; but it is plain from a remark made elsewhere that he would include what he conceives to be the Christian conception of equality in the same indictment he makes of modern philosophy. He seems to want to indicate that he is aware of the Christian view, and that it too must be rejected, but he politely sets it outside the scope of his consideration:

Religion commands us to believe that God Himself having taken men out of a state of nature immediately after the creation, they are unequal only because it is His will they should be so: but it does not forbid us to form conjectures based solely on the nature of man, and the beings around him, concerning what might have become of the human race, had it been left to itself.[77]

This attempt to side-step the Christian—really the Augustinian— discussion of equality points up Rousseau's dilemma. Rousseau did believe that man had been left to himself, that is to say, that he had been installed by nature in a simple, idyllic condition with perfectly appropriate sets of responses, but with something else as well: the capacity for free choice. "It is not . . . so much the understanding that constitutes the specific difference between the man and the brute, as the human quality of free agency." [78] Rousseau found himself faced with a difficulty not unlike the free will problem in theology. Nature (God) provided man with an originally innocent character and with a freedom to impair his innocence. If man uses his freedom in this way, is nature to be held responsible for human depravity and misery? Thus Rousseau can speak of the "equality which nature has ordained between men, and the inequality they have introduced." [79] In the *Confessions* he recalls the message which he wanted the *Discourse* to carry: "Madmen who ceaselessly complain of Nature, learn that all of your misfortunes arise from yourselves!" [80] Like Calvin, who insisted that God could not be held responsible for man's fall, even though He is the ultimate source of all that is and all that happens, Rousseau attempts to exonerate nature from a similar blame, even as he is compelled to admit not only that nature has given man his freedom but also that the faculty for perfectibility and the "accidents" which stimulate this faculty to develop itself and to improve the conditions of existence are as natural as man's original innocence.

Rousseau never grapples with this paradox openly, for it would have required him to abandon any attempt to hold nature up as the unassailable standard of virtue. He even attempts, without much success, to confuse the issue by speaking at times not of perfectibility, which he otherwise admits to be a natural endowment, but of the "supernatural gifts" and "artificial faculties"[81] that man acquires in the course of development. How could man acquire these gifts unless he were prepared by nature in advance? The faculty of perfectibility, Rousseau explains, was "potentially" possessed by natural man, but it could never have developed without "the fortuitous concurrence of many foreign causes that might never arise." [82] These "causes," as he describes them, are hardly so improbable; moreover they are natural in origin. Challenges to human survival, such as the competition from animals, the height of food-bearing trees, and the variations of climate and soil, posed difficulties which demanded the exercise of human ingenuity, and man responded, drawing upon the resources with which nature had provided him. To such responses, Rousseau asserts, we owe the development of fishing and hunting in the earliest stages of development and more complex industry later. Some "lucky chance" may have acquainted man with fire, but he learned himself how to produce it artificially and turn it to good use.[83]

Try as he would, Rousseau could not disentangle nature from the chain of events leading away from innocence to depravity. At best nature was an accomplice, at worst the source of the decline. The natural perfectibility of man was one count against nature; the other was the vanity that lurked in every human breast.[84] Driven by a will to self-glorification, man would expand his mastery over animals and things only to prepare the way for inequalities among his own species. When he had tamed the animals, Rousseau observes, he could not restrain his pride. "At a time when he scarce knew how to distinguish the different orders of beings, by looking upon his species as of the highest order, he prepared the way for assuming pre-eminence as an individual." [85] The formation of ordered, civilized society was the result of a combination of achievements of technological mastery over environment and the exploitation of these achievements by human passions for the sake of selfishness and further aggrandizement. So long as men only undertook labors they could accomplish by themselves, their passions found infrequent expression. But as joint labor developed and as one man stood in need of another, the natural inequalities that had gone unrecognized in the condition of isolation gave rise to differences in advantage.[86] If this were the only inequality to result from joint labor, Rousseau seems to suggest, it would not be against nature.[87] In fact, however, the accumulation of surpluses, the fixing of boundaries to land, and the general acquisition of property all led to an entirely artificial mode of life in which everyone sought to distinguish himself, in a thousand different ways, by trickery and sham as well as by wearying labor.[88]

In the state of nature there could have been no inequality because the conditions of life were the same for all and no one could have profited from any natural superiority.[89] Even if it could be assumed that nature distributed her gifts with partiality,

what advantage would the greatest of her favourites derive from it, to the detriment of others, in a state that admits of hardly any kind of relation between them? Where there is no love, of what advantage is beauty? Of what use is wit to those who do not converse, or cunning to those who have no business with others?[90]

In the state of nature, men could not have had the foresight or the knowledge to acquire possessions; and without possessions there could be no domination. A man forced to do the bidding of another against his will would simply have run off at the first opportunity, free as he must have been of property of any kind.

Inequality must have arisen as soon as society became permanent. "The bonds of servitude are formed merely by the mutual dependence of men on one another and the reciprocal needs that unite them." [91] Inequality arises as soon as difference and comparison are possible. It was then, as Rousseau poignantly imagines, that

each one began to consider the rest, and to wish to be considered in turn; and thus a value came to be attached to public esteem. Whoever sang or danced best, whoever was the handsomest, the strongest, the most dexterous, or the most eloquent came to be of most consideration, and this was the first step towards inequality and at the same time towards vice.[92]

Government was contrived by the rich, who were the ones with most to lose in the scramble for property and preference which developed out of expanding productivity and the permanence of society. They did not foist authority upon the others by strength; instead they resorted to cunning. By persuading the others that it would be to the advantage of all equally to stabilize existing relations, they masked the fact that this would be mostly to their own advantage. "Let us join together," they must have suggested, to establish rules "subjecting equally the powerful and the weak to the observance of reciprocal obligations." In quest for liberty, "all ran headlong into their chains." [93]

All forms of government merely fix the reciprocal relations existing at the time of original establishment. Where one man is pre-eminent, monarchy is the form of government; where several are equally powerful, aristocracy is established; and where there is less disproportion in wealth, democracy arises. The history of government is marked by three stages of progressive advance toward total tyranny. At first, with the establishment of a government of laws recognizing and guaranteeing property rights, society is divided into rich and poor. When laws alone prove to be of no avail against usurpation by the rich and robbery by the poor, it becomes necessary to erect a power over society to enforce the laws. At this point society comes to be divided into the powerful and weak.[94] Finally this division develops into a relation of master and slave as the lower elements are thoroughly brutalized by those with power. Paradoxically, "the last term of inequality"

—the relation of master and slave—restores the original condition under new and sinister auspices. "All private persons return to their first equality, because they are nothing." [95] Society rests, as it did before the creation of political ties, on the rule of the stronger. Man degenerates to the lowest conceivable level. He becomes "proud of his slavery" and even pays court to the rich and the powerful whom he despises and envies.[96]

Like Calvin and Hobbes, but very much unlike Liberals and Socialists, the Rousseau of the second *Discourse* could not conceive of the possibility of an equality in society other than an equality of depravity. No aristocracy could be distinguished which would not be subject to the perverse will to power. Everyone, whether he possesses political power or wealthy estates or nothing at all, is driven by envy and vanity. The rich usurp, the poor rob; both are depraved specimens of humanity.[97] Even the philosophers, as Calvin and Hobbes had already said, were not exempted from the universal taint of corruption. Rousseau, however, did not join his Conservative predecessors in extolling this one conceivable outcome. He described the surrender of human freedom to an absolute power and the rationalization of this surrender in the notion of equal citizenship as a terrible fate which man seemed destined to suffer. He balked at assigning the responsibility for this fate to nature, because in that case he would have had to accept it not only as a necessity but also as a condition of right. Toward the end of the *Discourse*, in a footnote, he offers a mild and clearly inadequate hope that the worst effects of this equality might be mitigated if society would distribute advantages according to the services of each individual.[98] He does not elaborate upon this suggestion, and thereby avoids confronting it with his fundamental misgivings. The Genevans were to be praised, he wrote in his dedication, for having had the "profound wisdom" to blend elements of natural equality and social inequality in a happy combination[99] by electing those superior in mental qualities as governors and obeying them.[100] Rousseau did not anticipate that Geneva, whose good fortune he attributed to special circumstances, would serve as a model for other communities. Even after composing the *Social Contract* he insisted that he had no solutions to offer that would be of any avail to large highly civilized societies. In a late work of self-exoneration he has a defender explain his intentions in terms that leave no doubt of these reservations. Throughout his work, says "the Frenchman," Rousseau meant to point out

that nature made man happy and good, but society depraves him and makes him miserable . . . In his first writings, he was more concerned with destroying the prestige of illusion which gives us a dumb admiration of the agents of our miseries . . . Throughout he makes us see the human species better, wiser and happier in its primitive state; blind, miserable and wicked to the extent that it is removed from that state . . .

But human nature does not retrogress, and once one is removed from them, there can be no turning back toward the times of innocence and equality; this again is one of the principles upon which he insisted most. Thus his object could not have been to lead back numerous peoples or great states to their original simplicity, but only to arrest, if possible, the progress of those whose small size and situation have preserved them from too rapid a march toward the perfection of society and the deterioration of the species . . . He worked for his homeland and for the small states constituted like her. If his doctrine could be of some use to others, it would be in changing their objects of value and thereby perhaps retarding their decadence.[101]

Plainly Rousseau did not take a Conservative position willingly. If he was no advocate of revolution, neither was he content with the *status quo*. It was simply that, given his understanding of human nature and the march of events, he could only prescribe resignation.

MABLY, MORELLY, AND BABEUF: EQUALITY AND PROPERTY

Rousseau's concern with the origins and justification of inequality, and by implication, of equality, was shared by many other Enlightened spirits of his day. In countries where the Reformation succeeded, this concern rose to the surface in the religious ferment. In France it was only in the eighteenth century and in consequence of secular developments that the traditional understanding of equality came into question. Widespread acclaim for reason and science aroused skeptical inquiries into received "prejudices." Accounts of "primitive" savages by missionaries and explorers, celebrating the virtues of unspoiled innocence, seemed to offer objective proof that "civilization" was as corrupt as the cynical philosophers were saying. The contrast between primitive innocence and civilized corruption did not necessarily affront inherited ideas. While religious skeptics could draw support from the anthropological findings in their effort to construct a morality based solely upon nature, the same findings could easily be construed by adherents of Catholicism as reinforcement to their belief in the revealed account of original innocence.

Carl Becker has suggested that despite the novelty of their vocabulary and despite their deism and atheism, the philosophers were "less emancipated from the preconceptions of medieval Christian thought, than they quite realized or we have commonly supposed."[102] However true this may be for the dominant winds in the climate of opinion, it does not suit at least one current of thought in the latter part of the century. Socialist thought, at any rate, began from Augustinian premises already modified to permit a critique of inequality,[103] and emerged from the century almost completely purged of premodern associations.

As yet, of course, Socialism was more a sentiment than a set of ideas. Because the critique of civilization usually led the philosophers to decry great inequalities of wealth, to sympathize with the wretched condition of the poor, and to condemn the pretensions and privileges of the idle rich, virtually all of them have been named among the "precursors of Socialism." It makes the field only somewhat smaller to restrict the designation of Socialist to those more interested in the reform of society than in the attack upon superstition, or even to draw a distinction between those who criticized social conditions and those who either ignored or accepted them.[104] It is nevertheless possible to trace the development of a Socialist concept of equality through a kind of incubation in the work of Gabriel de Bonnot de Mably and of Morelly (about whom so little is known that he must remain without given name) until it emerges fully formed in the polemical writings and declarations of François-Noël (Gracchus) Babeuf. Although Babeuf was an agitator rather than a philosopher, he may be said to have summed up, at the end of the century, the contributions of Mably and Morelly, and also to have taken a number of important steps beyond them in the direction of the later, systematic Marxian formulation.

Mably made one of the earliest attempts to distinguish the Socialist position from the general tendency of social criticism and reform. In certain respects his criticism of the Physiocrat Mercier de la Rivière expressed the most important differences between the proto-Socialists and Liberals of the period. Mably chided the Physiocrats not because they advocated a society based upon private property but because they taught that private property is natural and therefore just.[105] Mercier had argued that private property must have arisen once it became necessary to cultivate land, because the spontaneous production of nature was no longer adequate. Mably denied that the land would have had to be divided in order to be worked productively.[106] On the contrary, he asserted, it would have been natural for the members of a given community to cultivate their land together and share the fruits equally. Property must have been introduced because of the corrupting influence of the passions.

Mably does not hold that mankind can divest itself of this corruption or that the Physiocrats are at fault for accepting things as they are. For the Physiocrats to be truthful, he observes, they need not advocate a restoration of original communism. "This sermon would be useless." The passions have become so powerful that "no human power can today attempt to reestablish equality without causing disorders as great as those which it would be attempting to avoid."[107] Nature herself can now only indict mankind for its departure from the path of benevolent harmony:

You are all my children and I love you all equally; I have given you all the same rights; I have imposed upon you all the same duties, the entire earth is the patrimony of each of you; you were equal when you left my hands; why have you left your condition? [108]

Nevertheless, philosophers are obliged to give a true picture of nature and to suggest remedies which will at least soften the effects of the degeneration from original goodness. "Once having made the mistake, are we condemned to be eternally the victims of it?"[109]

The Physiocrats do not regard the creation of private property as the result of human wickedness. They see it as the natural avenue to the productivity needed to sustain life. Against this view Mably contends that private property is not a natural incident of production, and he adds that to make it seem natural is to make a virtue out of human appetite. The Physiocrats say that "the greatest possible happiness for the social body consists in the greatest abundance of objects proper to our enjoyment and in the greatest possible liberty to profit from them." For Mably this is to make man no better than the wildest animal. All material wealth is corrupting, he responds. It breeds a taste for luxury and indolence and encourages all the other vices to which mankind is prone. If private property were unknown, avarice, vanity, and ambition would also be unknown, and the humblest man would be happier than the wealthiest is where property exists.[110]

Accompanying the ascetic substance of Mably's communism is an asceticism of form. Communism can only be sustained, given human tendencies toward sloth and avarice, by rigid discipline. The Socialist societies which he takes as exemplary models are those of Sparta and of the Jesuits in Paraguay. It was the genius of Lycurgus, who had the wisdom to vest the ownership of all property in the state, which made the Spartans both virtuous and powerful. Nor ought Lycurgus to be reproached for having made the Spartans warlike. How else could his society be defended in a world where the introduction of private property had peopled the earth with brigands?[111] Plato wisely prescribed communism for the guardians and warriors because he knew it would prevent the dissensions caused by avarice and ambition. The reason his republic decayed is not to be found in "judicial astrology" but in the restriction of communism to the ruling elite. Because the majority was deprived of the guidance of philosophy it succumbed to the vices of property and communicated these vices to the rulers.[112] The Quakers are well intentioned, but they will probably not be successful because their pacifism compels them always to seek protection from an outside source.[113] Calvin did much good for Geneva, especially by establishing rigid sumptuary laws, but he made the fatal mistake of not prohibiting the acquisition of private fortunes. The result was a promotion of avarice which in time destroyed not only the sumptuary laws but political equality as well.[114] Even as Mably argues for discipline, however, he is scandalized by the Physiocrats' praise of the government of China, which is the very symbol of tyranny.[115] He seems to approve rigid discipline only when it is required to preserve communism against corrupt human nature and external enemies.

Despite his emphasis on the need for discipline in communist societies, Mably did not believe that communism was now so alien to human nature that it could only be imposed by coercion. It would be quite possible for men to cultivate the earth together and enjoy its fruits in common if legislators would make proper use of the desire for glory. "Why should the love of distinctions, glory and consideration not produce greater effects than property itself?"[116] Mably has in mind a desire for glory more akin to a religious notion of good works than to some naturalistic desire for power. Indeed, it is the religious orders that provide him with examples of how the desire for glory may be turned to good effect in communist society. Are the lands of the religious poorly cultivated? Not at all, because the incentives of religion are greater than those of accumulation. Moreover, once they acquire property, men become lazy and unfit for work, whereas the attainment of glory presumably entails no corrupting effects.[117]

Mably is inconsistent in his theory of natural equality. In one place he declares that men are identical by nature in all respects: "Who can deny that we leave nature's hands perfectly equal? Were not the same organs, needs, reason given to all men?"[118] Elsewhere he admits that "physical and moral qualities are not equal in all individuals." Left to themselves the interplay of natural differences would create social inequalities.[119] But he argues that the diversity of inclination and talent is not so great that education does not account for most of the differences between men. Besides, in the natural state, men's needs would have been so simple and uniform that their inclinations must have been very similar. Even differences of strength would not have led to permanent inequality, because if one man sought to dominate others the rest would join against him.[120]

Mably does not put his argument for natural equality only or even chiefly on grounds of equal capacities for reason or equal strength. The basis of his argument—and what distinguishes the Socialist from the conventional Enlightenment assumptions—is that men are identical in their needs. Nature, as Mably puts it, "has given us all the same needs to make us continually aware of our equality."[121] To put such emphasis on the identity of need requires that reason be downgraded. Mably explicitly rejects the usual glorification of reason. The philosophers would make man an angel, he declares, when all experience indicates that he is anything but that.[122] The Physiocrats labor under the same delusion as the other philosophers when they advocate a government by a magistracy endowed with a knowledge of the laws of nature. This can only result in a "legal despotism" because, no less than others, the magistrates will be governed by their passions and not by innocent reason.[123] Indeed all notions of perfectibility which are founded upon reason must similarly be rejected.

Reason for Mably assumes a negative importance. Although need is the standard of Socialist ethics, a reconstruction of society on natural grounds is difficult precisely because human reason is corrupted and enslaved to passions and possessions. "Very frankly," an exposition of the true natural doctrine of equality "will not make any impression on their spirit."[124] The passions are "so eloquent . . . that they have no need of evidence to convince our reason or at least make it their accomplice."[125] The innocence of nature is so warped by the passions and property that even the oppressed become convinced that domination is legitimate. It is even doubtful that the poor would consent to the reduction of great fortunes, for they would feel repugnance, shame, and embarrassment at being made equal to their erstwhile betters. The people have become so vile and so convinced of their worthlessness that they are flattered to be allowed to approach the rich, to serve them, and to merit their regard.[126] Two centuries passed before the Roman plebs took advantage of the right they won to share in government with the patricians. The Puritans fought to make a republic and then experienced opposition even within their own ranks.[127]

Mably is therefore not at all optimistic about the prospect for re-establishing equality. The natural capacities for understanding and conduct have become permanently disabled. Once the natural state is abandoned, inequality is inevitable; private property cannot be fought, at least not openly. "In all states where property has once been established it is necessary to regard it as the foundation of order, peace, and public safety."[128] But the virtuous legislator should try to mitigate the evils of property by arranging institutions and laws in ways that will induce and compel the passions to follow virtuous paths. The legislator must become an expert on the subject of the passions and he must learn how to deal with them, even by ruse. The state should serve as an example to the citizens. It should seek to promote frugality, not luxury. "The art of the legislator consists in diminishing the needs of the state and not in augmenting its revenues to support its needs more easily."[129] The state should take charge of inheritance, disposing of the goods of each deceased person so as to make the shares of wealth less unequal.[130] The goal of state activities would not be the destruction of property but the maintenance of a just balance among the various estates. "That is today the only equality possible to establish and conserve among men."[131] Whatever distance among orders is desired must be allowed, but only so long as there is neither tyranny nor servitude and "the most uncontested rights of humanity are respected."[132]

Morelly does not resign himself to the evils against which Mably directs his bitterness. Natural communism and equality, he argues, are not so remote and irrecoverable that society must be based upon private property and distinctions of authority and only meliorated by a concern for the poor. Morelly criticizes all the moral philosophers, ancient and modern, who say either that man is naturally perverse or that the conditions in which he must live make it inevitable that he should be perverse.[133] He does not believe that natural *innocence* can be recaptured, but he insists that it is possible to create artificial conditions in which the natural goodness of man can express itself. The trouble is that moralists have not yet considered how "to find a situation in which it would be almost impossible that man should be depraved, or wicked, or at least *minima de malis*."[134] Once this situation is discovered it would only be necessary to enact laws to prevent human corruption from finding expression and to educate men to live according to their lost natural dispositions.

Morelly's portrait of natural man, while similar in many respects to Rousseau's, differs fundamentally in several particulars. Sociability is evident from the start. Nature has created men with weaknesses and a diversity of talents, Morelly holds, so that they will all recognize their insufficiency in isolation. We have a natural aversion to isolation and a desire for society.[135] Differences of talent do not engender individualism but, on the contrary, a recognition of the priority of the community. Nature distributes "forces" differentially not to promote inequality and domination but so that all men will perform different labors for the common good. In physical capacities men are neither identical nor equal: "By the diversity of force, of industry, of talents distributed over the different ages of our life or the conformation of our organs," nature "indicates our different employments."[136] But nature also makes men sensible, "by the parity of their sentiments and needs, of their equality of conditions and rights and of the necessity for common labor."[137] Nor are passions a source of competition. Because our needs and desires are varied and sometimes only momentary we do not contest with others for natural goods, since we do not all want the same things at the same time and we are willing to cede rights to our fellows without feeling any deprivation.[138] Even vanity would contribute to sociability, since esteem would only be conferred for services to general welfare. Ambition could only promote contributions to the good of society.

Although Morelly believed communism in production and ownership of property to have been the natural mode of existence, he did not think that differences of rank would be completely absent from natural society. But such distinctions would be conferred according to "degrees of zeal, of capacity, upon the utility of the services of each citizen."[139] There would be a respect for age, intelligence, and skill derived from the recognition that the diversity of talents and forces contributes to social welfare. "The point of honor which still exists among the savage neighbors of our colonies is not to believe oneself great except in the degree to which one is useful to one's fellows." In nature "one does not become respectable except by services."[140] The orders in natural society are "not chimerical dignities" but a reflection of the "natural authority which the benefactor will acquire over the one who receives the benefit." Such authority could not take the form of domination. Who would want to dominate another where there would be no private property to excite envy? Who would want to be a tyrant where authority could only mean heavier responsibilities toward the common welfare without extra compensation?[141] The moralists assert that inequality is necessary because it creates ties of reciprocity: as the rich strive to retain their goods and the poor to lift themselves up from misery, both perform the labor required by society. This argument is absurd, Morelly asserts, because it starts from the assumption that there is no *natural* basis for reciprocity and mutual dependence. What need would there have been to found reciprocity "upon the pernicious expedient of inequality of fortune, when nature gives so many others so simple and marvelous."[142] Men are "naturally lazy," in the sense that they seek repose and comfort, but they are willing to work to acquire comfort and to help others. Among the savages laziness would be condemned as infamous and hard work praised as glorious. It is only in society, where property is instituted for some, and work required of others, that men acquire an aversion to work.[143]

While Morelly celebrates nature and condemns the perversion of nature in society, he does not consider the process of degeneration from nature irreversible. Laws and institutions, as well as moral philosophy, have contributed to the degeneration of natural man. By changing them, men may bring themselves closer to nature, though not to their original innocence.[144] The moralists argue that each man should surrender to others the same rights to property he wants to enjoy himself. But this is to beg the question. If private property were not permitted, no one would have either the desire for individual rights to property or the need to yield rights to property to others.[145] The way to reconstruct society is to make property common again and to legislate restraints upon antisocial behavior. With such laws it will become evident to everyone that his private welfare depends upon the general welfare.[146] If he is lazy he will not be rewarded, but if he is industrious he will enjoy esteem and honor.

Unlike Mably, Morelly does not celebrate monastic equality. The monks have an equality which is built out of laziness, not out of productivity. Monasticism, as an equality only among a part of society, inspires disintegration and cabals. Equality should be the condition of the whole of the people, all of whom should participate in the same active way.[147]

In Morelly's ideal society, labor is to be assigned according to capacity and goods are to be distributed to everyone equally. If there is not enough of a common necessity, no one is to receive any until there is enough for all, or everyone is to receive a small amount.[148] Vocations and work are to be assigned by a central authority of the elders of each group, taking into account the talents and inclinations of individuals.[149] There is to be every encouragement for science of a practical kind, but no room for new moral philosophies or additions to the moral law of society.[150]

Morelly's plan for a communist society was a theoretical step beyond the tradition of utopian Socialism to which Mably belonged. Babeuf took still another step by synthesizing theory and practice, but at the same time he was quite conscious of belonging to a tradition of egalitarian thought. To the "citizen jurors" before whom he was defending himself against a charge of conspiracy to overthrow the republic, Babeuf observed that in trying him the republic was indicting his masters—Rousseau, Mably, Diderot (Morelly), and Helvétius—"the other levellers."[151] The trial of the "Conspiracy of the Equals" was in reality a trial of the apostles of the Revolution, of "all those whose ashes have been received into the *Panthéon*." The only difference between himself and these illustrious men, Babeuf charged, was that they had demonstrated the egalitarian character of nature, and he, Babeuf, had attempted to persuade the nation to accept this demonstration and adopt a scheme of natural justice.[152]

If this were the only difference it would still be significant enough, for unlike Babeuf none of his "masters" had suggested that the natural condition could be restored. But there are a number of other differences which Babeuf himself apparently did not recognize. Babeuf did not conceive of the restoration of communist equality as a return to an austere primitive standard of living. The goal of this restoration was not to take man back to the woods where he could rest quietly near a brook, but to provide him with four good meals a day, good housing, and whatever other amenities the progress of industry and agriculture could offer.[153] Babeuf also decried luxury, but only insofar as it was accompanied by proletarian misery. Nor was Babeuf the least bit ambiguous in condemning the notion that superiority in talent or greater industrial exertion should be the basis for higher rewards. Undoubtedly, he admitted, there are differences in natural aptitudes, but it is "absurd and unjust" to give a greater recompense to those whose work requires "a higher degree of intelligence and more application and tension of spirit." For "that does not extend the capacity of the stomach at all." [154] Nor does the fact that one man becomes a magistrate and another a tailor indicate a greater degree of application or painstaking on the part of the magistrate. It may be that one man will have more difficulty learning to be a tailor than someone else will have in becoming a magistrate.[155] Like Mably and Morelly, Babeuf adds to this admission of natural inequalities the qualification that education is responsible for most of the differences in attainments. But such considerations are beside the point. The argument for equality rests on the fact that men have equal needs. The effort of the egalitarian restoration is to make sure that no one will become "richer, more powerful, or more distinguished, by his unique knowledge (*lumières*), than any one of his equals." [156] In the new republic, "all useful estates (and there will be no other kind) will be equally honorable." [157] Is it the fault of a particular man "that he did not receive at birth more fortunate dispositions? Should he on that account enjoy fewer advantages?" [158] For Babeuf the answer is clear: equality can only mean that regardless of particular talents and aptitudes all men are to enjoy the fruits of their common labors without distinctions of any kind. In the future society, the only distinctions will be those of age and sex.

Babeuf borrowed from Condorcet the term *égalité réelle*, or, as he also puts it, *égalité de fait*, to distinguish between the equality of communism and the equality of rights before the law. The French

Revolution stated the ideal of equality but achieved only a limited equality before the law. For this reason the Revolution was only a prelude, an "advance messenger," of "another revolution, greater and even more solemn, which will be the last." In the *Manifesto of the Equals*, attributed principally to Babeuf's associate, Sylvain Maréchal, the basis of the egalitarian revolution is declared to be the common ownership of goods, not merely an equality of political rights. Equality must be put "under the roofs of our homes." In vain do the possessors of wealth and power seek to contain the masses by offering them legal equality. Equality requires the *"common good*, or *goods in common!"* The time has come when the "revolting distinctions of rich and poor, great and small, masters and valets, governors and governed" must be made to disappear. The evil is spread over the face of the earth and has grown intolerable. The moment has come to establish the "Republic of the Equals." A few thousand privileged supporters of the *status quo* cannot stand before the mass of the people.[159]

In the *Manifesto,* Maréchal and Babeuf also announced their disdain for the cultural concerns of the philosophers: "Let the arts perish, if necessary, so long as we may have real equality." [160] In his trial Babeuf defended this declaration against the charge that equality would destroy culture. Babeuf dismisses this criticism as ridiculous, arguing that a return to natural equality should not be confused with a return to the conditions of nature. The achievements of the arts and sciences in raising the cultural and material level of the general welfare are to be accepted and encouraged. At the same time Babeuf remarks that if the *beaux arts* were to disappear, the mass of the people would feel no deprivation, because they have been so brutalized that they are unable to enjoy them. Babeuf admits that the arts will undergo changes in the era of equality. Artists will no longer have to flatter their rich patrons and create the silly frills demanded by luxury. Under the aegis of equality, the arts will respond to the requirements of "general utility." They will be much improved over the arts of luxury and leisure, by the "sublime imprint" of the "great sentiments to which an association of happy people will necessarily give birth." [161] The progress of science will in no way be impeded by equality. In the first place, because the workday will be shorter, people will have more time in which to make great scientific discoveries. Secondly, since education will be universal, natural genius will have an opportunity to express itself wherever it is to be found.[162] Finally, it is "well proved" that the progress of science does not depend upon private property, but upon the love of glory. The egalitarian society will confer all honor upon the *bienfaiteur* who contributes to the progress of science, but it will remain ever mindful that, as knowledge is never the creation of a single man, the fruits of scientific discovery should belong to the entire society.[163]

Babeuf claimed in his defense that he sought only to persuade his fellow citizens of the desirability of advancing beyond the limited equality of the Revolution to the real equality of communism. His conspiratorial activities are well documented, and the tone of his manifesto is certainly such as to amount to an exhortation to overthrow the existing regime, given the revolutionary climate of the times. Indeed, as we have seen from the example of Müntzer, it is only a small step from the advocacy of a total restoration of innocence over the opposition of the existing Satanic authorities to the exhortation to violence by a proletarian movement in the cause of progress toward utopia. The *philosophes* in general, and Mably and Morelly in the Socialist tradition, sought to accomplish limited reforms through the agency of the wise legislator. Babeuf, with his vision of an immediate total restoration, could only address the proletarian masses. In adding this final touch to his restatement of Socialist egalitarianism, Babeuf comes the closest of any of the French Socialists, closer even than Saint-Simon and Fourier, to anticipating the Marxian position. Marx was to make precisely Babeuf's distinction between equality before the law (bourgeois equality) and an equality based upon identical need. He too was to advocate the total restoration of original equality in the context of the advance of productive techniques, a restoration to be effected by the consciousness and activity of the proletarian masses.

By the end of the eighteenth century, then, egalitarian thought was established upon thoroughly secular foundations, but the subdivision of the lines of inquiry remained unchanged. To some the prospect of equality portended individual moral autonomy and the right to compete fairly. To others it augured only a decline toward the new barbarism of mass society. Still others foresaw from it the development of a totally new man, restored to innocence and living in harmony with others, thanks to the destruction of the single most formidable barrier to social improvement, private property. It remained for philosophic minds of the next century to bring these points of view into mutual confrontation and indeed to experience this confrontation as the most significant fact of actual social experience.

The Liberal Crisis

꧁ ꧂

I N ENGLAND and America, where stable representative government was well-established, at least as a matter of principle, by the middle of the nineteenth century, Liberals were
turning their attention to the unfinished business of social reform. The antislavery and anticolonialist crusades, like the agitation for the emancipation of women and the extension of education, drew philosophic support from the Liberal conception
of equality. Experience with these social questions soon made
it apparent that the moral principles appropriate to government
and citizenship were not necessarily adequate to questions of
property and income. Liberalism, as many of its adherents realized full well, had come to serve as a rationalization of unjusti-
fied social inequalities. Poverty was ascribed, as a matter of
course, to indolence or imprudence, even though it was increasingly obvious, as John Stuart Mill put it, that "accident has
so much more to do than merit with enabling men to rise in the
world."[1]

At first, Liberals who were troubled by the discrepancy between their values and the reality about them sought to alter
the conditions of life so that artificial barriers and advantages
were removed or neutralized. They did not abandon belief in
individual initiative but only concentrated their energy upon
the effort to make it possible for the free play of individual tal-

ents actually to take place. Even this effort required a more realistic appraisal of social conditions than was provided by the Lockean image of a state of nature in which all men began upon the same footing. Locke's justification of unequal reward for unequal industry presupposed a simple agrarian economy where land was abundant and where labor was virtually the sole factor of production. The enclosure movement in England had been only the first of a series of blows to this justification. The rise of commerce and industry and the revelation of the economic importance of scarcity by the Classical Economists dealt out further blows almost fatal to the very premises of Lockean Liberalism. The modern economy, as Socialists were pointing out, presupposed a fundamental inequality in the separation of the workers from ownership of the means of production. Moreover, as the Liberals themselves realized, the chances for success of two men with unequal economic opportunities were quite different from what, in theory, they should have been in an agrarian economy.

In addition, the Liberal theory of society as a collection of individuals competing with one another in independence was being challenged by other developments engendered by economic change. The advance of technology and the spread of commercial-industrial organization and attitudes threatened to remake completely the relatively atomistic postfeudal society which had become fixed in the Liberal imagination. The most significant social relations were increasingly those described in such terms as "class" and "mass," and pressures toward conformity with public opinion seemed to make intellectual mediocrity a real if unacknowledged standard. Reluctantly, Liberals found themselves forced to concede that, so long as education continued to lag behind emancipation, the apprehensions of Tocqueville and other Conservative critics of democracy were justified. But this admission raised a serious question. Could Liberalism be adapted to these changed conditions, or was it simply obsolete?

Liberals who adopted the Utilitarian system of Bentham considered equality one of the four guiding principles of civil law, along with subsistence, abundance, and security. Bentham had said that the law could do nothing directly to achieve the economic goals of security and abundance, and he had also said that security should precede equality because the pain of frustrated expectations would generally exceed the pleasure of unexpected gratification.[2] The Philosophical Radicals nevertheless found a way to resolve the conflict between the two goods by proposing legislation abolishing the barriers to the distribution of property and providing for the division of property through inheritance.[3] Progressive taxation would accomplish the same purpose later, but this was a device less easily assimilated to the Benthamite theory. Bentham himself believed that to provide economic incentives, and thereby to promote a maximization of happiness, it was best that wealth be graduated in numerous degrees, "regular and insensible," between "the fortune of the least rich and that of the most rich." [4] Otherwise Utilitarianism was ill-equipped to provide an answer to the threat of a "tyranny of the majority" and to the debasement of standards, since it was itself considered a part of this very trend. From this point of view the very reforms the Utilitarians championed seemed likely only to make matters worse.

To these difficulties of Liberalism, John Stuart Mill brought a mind singularly well-equipped and a temperament as judicious and tolerant as liberal education has ever produced. By modifying Utilitarianism and by assimilating the objections of Socialists and Conservatives, Mill provided the basis for a fresh philosophy of Liberalism. Those who would not accept such revisionism found a champion in Herbert Spencer. In rejecting Utilitarianism and natural rights philosophy in favor of a theory of social evolution, Spencer managed to preserve the values of traditional Liberalism intact while abandoning the outmoded theories in which these values had been imbedded. The difference between the theories of Mill and Spencer announced a crisis in Liberalism which survives into the present. From this time forward the term Liberal was to acquire a double meaning, and the Liberal concept of equality was to be interpreted in two different and contradictory ways as a guide to social action. Particularly in its initial phase, however, the dispute was not so much a matter of ultimate values as a question of how those values were to be achieved. Mill and Spencer both conceived of equality as an expression of personal liberty, but they differed, as have generations since, over the areas in which this liberty was to be realized and over the kind and degree of collective authority it was advisable to use on behalf of the individual.

JOHN STUART MILL: THE MODIFICATION OF LIBERAL DOCTRINE

The argument advanced by Mill on behalf of female emancipation is typical, in its application of the traditional Liberal canons of justice, of the reasoning used by advocates of many other social reforms popular in his time. "As society was constituted until the last few generations, inequality was its very basis . . . two persons could hardly cooperate in anything, or meet in any amicable relation, without the law's appointing that one of them should be the superior of the other." Liberal reform had triumphed over feudal hierarchy with respect to most of the fundamental obstacles to emancipation, but until full civil equality was extended to women and to other groups excluded from the benefits of progress, liberty would remain a species of privilege. The doctrine of individual self-fulfillment demanded that everyone enjoy the same opportunity to express his or her distinctive talents.

. . . so long as competition is the general law of human life, it is tyranny to shut out one-half of the competitors. All who have attained the age of self-government have an equal claim to be permitted to sell whatever kind of useful labour they are capable of, for the price which it will bring.[5]

The inhibition of this competition is both an unjust deprivation of individual rights and an obstacle to the welfare and progress of society:

There need be no fear that women will take out of the hands of men any occupation which men perform better than they. Each individual will prove his or her capacities . . . by trial; and the world will have the benefit of the best faculties of its inhabitants. But to interfere beforehand by an arbitrary limit, and declare that whatever be the genius, talent, energy, or force of mind of an individual of a certain sex or class, those faculties shall not be exerted . . . is not only an injustice to the individual, and a detriment to society, which loses what it can ill spare, but is also the most effectual mode of providing that, in the sex or class so fettered, the qualities which are not permitted to be exercised shall not exist.[6]

As he observed the changes occurring in society, however, and as he considered the objections of others to the reformist beliefs he had absorbed in his youth, Mill came to recognize that traditional Liberalism was no longer viable. There is no more eloquent statement of the crisis of Liberalism and of Mill's effort to resolve it than the frank admission, in his *Autobiography*, of the two principal changes in his and Harriet Taylor's political and social thinking in their later years:

We were now much less democrats than I had been, because so long as education continues to be so wretchedly imperfect, we dreaded the ignorance and especially the selfishness and brutality of the masses; but our ideal of ultimate improvement went far beyond Democracy, and would class us decidedly under the general designation of Socialists. While we repudiated . . . that tyranny of society over the individual which most Socialist systems are supposed to involve, we yet looked forward to a time when society will no longer be divided into the idle and industrious; and when the rule that they who do not work shall not eat, will be applied not to paupers only, but impartially to all: when the division of the produce of labour, instead of depending, as in so great a degree it now does, on the accident of birth, will be made by concert on an acknowledged principle of justice; and when it will no longer either be, or be thought to be, impossible for human beings to exert themselves strenuously in procuring benefits which are not to be exclusively their own, but to be shared with the society they belong to. The social problem of the future we considered to be, how to unite the greatest individual liberty of action, with a common ownership in the raw materials of the globe, and an equal participation of all in the benefits of combined labour.[7]

As carefully drawn as this final statement is, it would probably be wrong to infer from it that Mill, and those Liberals for whom he may justly be considered a spokesman, abandoned Liberalism for Socialism and Conservatism. It is clear that Mill wished to preserve some form of individualism, perhaps an individualism which would be detached from selfish egoism and realized not in economic activities but in opinion and culture. In economics, however, the Liberal belief in competitive equality would have to yield to an altruistic, Socialist egalitarianism if society wished to retain its pretensions to justice. In politics and culture, Liberals would have to set themselves against any extension of equal power wherever such an extension would tend to give equal authority to the competent and the incompetent. Ideally, Liberals would join with the Socialists in seeking to level inequalities of wealth, and with the Conservatives in limiting the influence of numbers and irrationality in politics and culture. But Liberals were not to abandon their belief in the universal capacity for understanding as the basis of a society of rational individuals. They were to work toward that goal by fostering the expansion of education. In the meantime, they had no choice but to bear in mind the limitations of existing conditions.

As far as Mill went to accommodate Socialist and Conservative criticisms, he never fully accepted them without important Liberal amendments, exceptions, and qualifications. Mill's attitude toward the claims made on behalf of the working class is continually modified by his concern for individual liberty. In the early period of his political writing he was as suspicious of poor laws as the most hidebound *laissez-faire* Liberal, arguing that legislation which had the effect of restoring feudal, paternalistic relations between the workers and either industrialists or the state would produce more harm than good. An obligation to support the poor "never has existed . . . without, as a countervailing element, absolute power . . . over those entitled to receive it. Such a relation has never existed between human beings, without immediate degradation to the character of the dependent class."[8] As a still unreconstructed Liberal, Mill warned the radical apostles of the welfare state against the consequences of paternalism in social welfare. The radicals, he wrote,

cannot mean that the working class should combine the liberty of action of independent citizens, with the immunities of slaves. There are but two modes of social existence for human beings: they must be left to the natural consequences of their mistakes in life; or society must guard against the mistakes, by prevention or punishment. Which will the new philanthropists have?

Moreover, the claims of labor had to be weighed against the

Malthusian iron law of overpopulation. If the poor were to be coddled, this law would take effect and only worsen the situation for everyone. Why should the rich be compelled to make sacrifices merely to permit the working class to increase its rate of procreation and thereby spread misery and bring everyone down to the same unfortunate level? [9] At the same time, Mill defends the efforts of Louis Blanc and other French Socialists to fashion a *droit au travail* law similar to the Elizabethan Poor Law. It is one thing, according to Mill, to revive paternalism for the sake of relief and quite another to guarantee a decent subsistence to those unable to find work and to those who could work if given the opportunity to do so. Unlike the English poor law, the French legislation "gave no pledge that the State should find work for A or B . . . It relieved no individual from the responsibility of finding an employer, and proving his willingness to exert himself." [10]

The solution of the problem posed by the poverty of the working class—the Liberal solution—would have to entail respect for individual effort as well as for social welfare and a hardheaded coming to terms with Malthusian theory. In principle,

the earth belongs, first of all, to the inhabitants of it . . . every person alive ought to have a subsistence, before anyone has more . . . whosoever works at any useful thing, ought to be properly fed and clothed before anyone able to work is allowed to receive the bread of idleness.

But,

although every one of the living brotherhood of humankind has a moral claim to a place at the table provided by the collective exertions of the race, no one has the right to invite additional strangers . . . without the consent of the rest. [11]

The "additional strangers" could only be prevented from making their appearance if birth control (Mill apparently could not bring himself to use so direct a term) were practiced on a considerable scale. The *droit au travail* laws, in any form, "would be a fatal gift . . . unless some new restraint were placed upon the capacity of increase, equivalent to that which would be taken away." [12] The only way to help the poor, in the long run, is to educate them so that they will undergo "changes in their minds and habits as shall make them fit guardians of their own physical condition." [13] In this respect, as in others, education is the key to the improvement of the working class, for "all that is morally objectionable in the lowest class of the working people is nourished, if not engendered, by the low state of their understandings." [14] If the poor could be taught the need for birth control, and the rich the justice of sharing their wealth more equitably, a solution would be at hand. With education, class hatred would give way to "real attachment, a genuine feeling of subordination" which would be "the result of personal qualities." [15] Such harmonious cooperation in industry would be far more appropriate to an age of free individuals than a revival of feudal paternalism.

Insofar as Socialists accept the Liberal notion of reward according to merit, but protest that the existing system of distribution is not in accord with this principle, Mill is sympathetic to their position. The Socialism of Robert Owen and Blanc is "the modern form of the protest . . . against the unjust distribution of social advantages," [16] and, as such, is basically in accord with Liberalism.

No rational person will maintain it to be abstractedly just, that a small minority of mankind should be born to the enjoyment of all the external advantages which life can give, without earning them by any merit or acquiring them by any exertion of their own, while the immense majority are condemned from their birth, to a life of never-ending, never-intermitting toil, requited by a bare, and in general a precarious, subsistence.[17]

Unfortunately, it must be admitted that this condition is expedient, for if it were otherwise no one would have any motivation to labor beyond the attainment of subsistence, for fear that he or his heirs would be deprived of the surplus accumulated. It is certainly just, according to Mill, that people should have control of property which they have accumulated by labor or inheritance. It is therefore necessary to take "the path of least injustice" and "recognize individual property and individual right of inheritance." [18] Even the Socialists, he points out, differ as to whether the produce of combined labor ought to be distributed equally or in proportion to effort.[19] Moreover, as a practical matter, the Socialist ideal of cooperation could not provide the same incentive as selfishness. For the present it is impossible to entertain the notion of a society governed by public spiritedness rather than private self-interest.[20] The best that can be hoped for is that society will attempt to balance the just demands for equality with the just demands of self-interest and the need for a system of incentives to industry. A notion of equality is essential in any good social scheme:

We hold with Bentham, that equality, though not the sole end, is one of the ends of good social arrangements; and that a system of institutions which does not make the scale turn in favour of equality, whenever this can be done without impairing the security of the property which is the product and reward of personal exertion, is essentially a bad government—a government for the few, to the injury of the many.[21]

This formula—the balance of equality against individual liberty—is one of the hallmarks of late nineteenth century Liberal thought. Those who opposed government intervention identified equality with justice, and justice with laws validating inequality —because these laws applied equally to all. Mill saw through this flimsy bit of semantic obfuscation well in advance of Sir Leslie Stephen's tract[22] later in the century. Everyone maintains, Mill wrote in his *Utilitarianism*, that "equality is the dictate of justice, except where he thinks that expediency requires inequality. The justice of giving equal protection to the rights of all, is maintained by those who support the most outrageous inequality in the rights themselves." [23] Even though he used the formula himself, Mill recognized that it was necessary to provide the notion of equality with a substantive meaning taking due account of individual liberty. Lamartine's exposition of equality struck him favorably. Equality, Lamartine had said, was undoubtedly a legitimate social ideal: "Whatever tends to constitute inequality of instruction (*lumières*), of rank, of condition, of fortune among mankind, is impious." But it must be admitted that grave difficulties pursue the attempt to realize the ideal. It is impossible, Lamartine had declared, to reconcile with equality of goods the inequalities of virtues, of faculties, and of exertions, which distinguish mankind from one another. Between the active and the inert, equality of conditions is an injustice, for the one produces and the other merely consumes. In order that this community of goods may be just, we must suppose in all mankind the same conscience, the same application to labour, the same virtue.

In fact, no such supposition can be sustained. If therefore a society were to insist upon equal rewards and equal industry, it would have to make itself an omnipresent, omniscient judge willing and able to compel every individual "to the same labour and the same virtue." This, however, would be the destruction of liberty; the society of equals would be a "universal slavery." Nor would it be much better if society were to forego compulsory equalization and adopt instead a scheme whereby each individual would receive a share in the social product exactly proportional to his daily labor. Because such a result could presumably not be expected from the ordinary workings of the economic system, it would require state regulation of labor and distribution of goods. In such a case the state would again be put in the position of a judge over the individual. Like Proudhon, Lamartine objects to the assumption of such a function by the state as an abridgement of liberty, except that Proudhon believed the same result could be attained through the mechanism of free exchange. Lamartine dismisses all attempts to impose equality artificially and concludes that

imperfect human wisdom has found it easier, wiser, and more just to say to everyone, 'Be thy own judge; take to thyself thy own recompense by thy riches or thy indigence.' Society has established property, has proclaimed the freedom of labour, and has legalized competition.

This attempt to draw a compromise between the ideal of equality and the ideal of individual liberty by establishing free competition is admittedly not without its difficulties:

. . . property, when established, does not feed those who possess nothing . . . freedom of labour does not give the same means of labour to him who has only his hands, and to him who possesses millions of acres . . . competition is the code of egoism; a war to the death between those who work and those who give work; those who sell and those who buy; those who revel in abundance and those who starve. Injustice on all hands! [24]

Like Lamartine, Mill recognized both the ethical validity of the Liberal notion of competitive equality and the disparity between this ideal and the practice enforced by the conditions of production and distribution actually prevailing. He understood that the Socialist theory of Saint-Simon sought to apply the Liberal belief in reward according to labor, "every individual being required to take a share of labour . . . all being classed according to their capacity, and remunerated according to their work." [25] Nevertheless, he found the authoritarian benevolence proposed by Saint-Simon an abhorrent solution, not as tyrannic as other forms of despotic authority but still unsuitable for a free society. [26] If freedom is to be preserved, the ideal of reward according to labor must be kept as a standard of value and enforced in a way that would not impair individual liberty. Even as he urges support for the working class, of a kind to encourage individual liberty of action and initiative, Mill in effect pleads with the wealthier classes to make a greater effort to demonstrate the justice of unequal distribution. The owners and managers of industry should justify, "by the superior capacity in which they contribute to the work, the higher remuneration which they receive for their share of it." [27] The dilemma of Mill—the dilemma of Liberalism—with respect to the property question was that moral exhortations of this sort could hardly be relied on to produce anything more than marginal mitigations of glaring injustices.

The difficulty Mill experienced in attempting to assimilate the Socialist critique of the distribution of property to his fundamentally Liberal position reappears in the reception he gave the Conservative critique. Mill lauded Tocqueville's *Democracy in America* as "the beginning of a new era in the scientific study of politics." [28] He defended Tocqueville against the charge of bias: "his theories are of an impartiality without example." [29] Yet when he entered into a detailed examination of Tocqueville's arguments Mill found it necessary to confute a number of the most important of them on grounds which point up, directly and indirectly, the distinctions between the Conservative and the Liberal views of equality. Tocqueville had made a mistake, Mill argued, in imputing to the rise of democracy, or equality of conditions, certain of the characteristics of modern society which actually derive from the advance of industrialism. Tocqueville, Mill observed,

has, at least apparently, confounded the effects of Democracy with the effects of Civilization. He has bound up in one abstract idea the whole of the tendencies of modern commercial society, and given them one name—Democracy; thereby letting it be supposed that he ascribes to equality of conditions, several of the effects naturally arising from the mere progress of national prosperity.[30]

Mill points out that wherever equality of conditions exists apart from an advanced stage of industrialization it does not exhibit the characteristics which Tocqueville attributes to the equality of conditions in America. The French Canadians, among whom there is also an equality of conditions, lack the American "go-ahead spirit" and class mobility. In addition, like other nonindustrial peoples, they retain the habit of deference to superiors.[31] This difference of interpretation is more than a technical or scientific difference. For Tocqueville, American restlessness and mobility were rooted in the desire for equality of conditions because the ideal of equality was largely a rationalization of envy. Mill's criticism of Tocqueville's theory implies that mobility is ethically neutral and that the desire for equality ought not to be blamed for civilized corruption. He also rejected Tocqueville's attempt to associate the loss of individuality with the tendency toward equality. If anything, Mill was even more concerned about the loss of individuality than Tocqueville, but he did not accept Tocqueville's contention that the equality of conditions was to blame for it. Once again he argued that the advance of industrial civilization bears the chief responsibility.

It is not because the individuals composing the mass are equal, but because the mass itself has grown to so immense a size, that individuals are powerless in the face of it; and because the mass having, by mechanical improvements, become capable of acting simultaneously, can compel not merely any individual, but any number of individuals, to bend before it.[32]

The modern disrespect for antiquity, and the idolization of

progress and perfectibility, which Tocqueville also attributes to equality, are similarly credited by Mill to the rise of machine technology. Indeed, virtually all the unfortunate aspects of modern life, Mill argues, would still have to be combatted even if an aristocracy continued to rule, because they originate in the rise of commerce and industry.[33]

Mill does not stop at taking exception to Tocqueville's view of equality; he provides, in the form of a brief sketch, an alternate history of the rise of equality which, like his criticism, points up some of the differences between the Liberal and the Conservative approach to the understanding of equality. The history which Mill outlines presents the traditional Liberal view: modernity consists in a transition from feudal domination to the gradual liberation of the individual, a liberation in the process of extension to all mankind. Under feudalism, landholders exercised an almost total sovereignty over the inhabitants of the land. With the collapse of the feudal order these inhabitants won their personal freedom and became equal among themselves, and with the large landholders, before the law. This legal equality "was at first little more than nominal." Now that the poor could acquire property by their labor, however, it was not long before legal equality came to have a real significance. Wealth replaced birth and the ownership of land as the standard of power and prestige. Hereditary honors became "less a power in themselves, than a symbolic ornament of great riches." [34] In politics the democratic tendency was strengthened by the articulation of public opinion and the achievement of liberty of petition and other similar rights. Thus, as far as English history is concerned, Mill sees the advance of equality as an aspect of a general liberation of individuals from feudalism. He certainly does not regard this history as a narration of the revolt of the ignorant and the envious against an aristocracy which had ceased to perform its function in society. Neither does he regard the absolute levelling of all distinctions as the inevitable end result of these great historical changes. The tendency toward equality of conditions in England is "much less than M. de Tocqueville contends for." [35] In fact, it may well be argued that in England the tendency is toward the reverse of equality:

The passion for equality which M. de Tocqueville speaks about as if it were the great moral lever of modern times, is hardly known in this country even by name. On the contrary, all ranks seem to have a passion for inequality. The hopes of every person are directed to rising in the world, not to pulling the world down to him.[36]

Mill admits that there are indeed contradictory influences, such as are expressed in the decline of respect for the upper classes. Among those who feel they simply cannot rise above their low station in life, "a levelling spirit is abroad."[37] But there is no necessary logic, such as Tocqueville conceived, according to which equality must ultimately crush all distinctions. "There is a democracy short of pauper suffrage,"[38] as there is an equality in the distribution of property short of communism. Actually the dominant tendency of modern history, which Tocqueville sees, but to which he does not attach enough importance, is the rise to power of the middle class. The effects which Tocqueville attributes to democracy are often the traits of middle class democracy in an industrial and commercial context. America is so rich an example of Tocqueville's view of democracy just because "America is *all* middle class."[39] Given this condition there is surely little danger that in America levelling tendencies will have much effect:

where all have property, either in enjoyment or in reasonable hope, and an appreciable chance of acquiring a large fortune; and where every man's way of life proceeds on the confident assumption that, by superior exertion, he will obtain a superior reward; the importance of the inviolability of property is not likely to be lost sight of.[40]

The same argument applies to England. Mill was confident the middle class would share its power with the lower class when the lower class was ready to exercise power responsibly: when, in short, a number of the advantages enjoyed by the middle class (sufficient to implant respect for middle class values) were also enjoyed by the lower class. The right to vote does not belong to all citizens indiscriminately, but only to those who are prepared to make use of it properly. Mill, as a spokesman for the enlightened segment of the middle class, is confident that education and prosperity will spread among the populace and that the middle class will crown their improvement with the gift of suffrage once they demonstrate their readiness for it:

in proportion as the working class becomes, what all proclaim the desire that it should be—well paid, well taught, and well conducted; in the same proportion will the opinions of that class tell, according to its numbers, upon the affairs of the country.[41]

The credulous optimism with which Mill confronts the egalitarian sentiments of the middle and working classes alike contrasts sharply with the fears excited in him by the demonic forces of his day—the illiberal, irrational phenomena of mob violence, and the antipathies of religion, party, and race. These forces are unloosed wherever there is a failure to extend education sufficiently and, especially in modern times, whenever conformism in opinion and pressures against individuality are allowed to take root. The chief dangers to democracy, according to Mill, derive not from equality, but from tendencies toward uniformity and ignorance. The monopoly of power by the middle class is a more serious danger than any tendency toward levelling. Mill acknowledges his debt to Tocqueville, "the Montesquieu of our times," for having called attention to the dangers of the centralization of power in modern politics.[42] He agrees with Tocqueville that constitutional safeguards against the monopolization of power are a vital condition for the preservation of liberty. He even suggests that opposition to the middle class ought to be cultivated among the agricultural, the leisured, and the learned classes.[43] At the same time he recognizes, as Tocqueville does not, that the dangers to liberty arise not only from the monopoly of power by a single class or group, but from the dissolution of individuality which occurs when, as in feudalism, class affiliation determines individual attitudes. This is a danger which affects men no matter which class they happen to belong to. "No rank in society is now exempt from the fear of being peculiar . . . Hardly anything now depends upon individuals, but all upon classes, and among classes mainly upon the middle class."[44]

Mill's underlying commitment to Liberalism precluded a total acceptance of the Conservative critique of equality. He believed too deeply in the value of individualism to accept the view that the maintenance of class divisions alone was sufficient to secure liberty in society. He believed too deeply in the value of rationality and in the capacity of all men to attain at least a minimal level of rationality through education to accept the idea that the masses ought to be indoctrinated with myths in order to train them to habits of deference. He joined the Conservatives, however, for the short run. Until education was sufficiently diffused, the masses represented a threat to order, to reason, to culture. In Mill's assent to constitutionalism—in the form of the balance of class power, in his advocacy of a superior voice for the educated in government and of a democratic suffrage which would be restricted to the selection of qualified governors—lay his concession to this critique. It is unnecessary, he wrote,

that the many should themselves be perfectly wise; it is sufficient if they be duly sensible of the value of superior wisdom . . . if they be aware that the majority of political questions turn upon considerations of which they, and all persons not trained for the purpose, must necessarily be very imperfect judges; and that their judgment must in general be exercised rather upon the characters and talents of the persons whom they appoint to decide these questions for them, than upon the questions themselves. They would then select as their representatives those whom the general voice of the instructed pointed out as the *most* instructed; and would retain them so long as no symptom was manifested in their conduct of being under the influence of interests or of feelings at variance with the public welfare.[45]

Mill thought that the philosophic resolution of his difficulties with Liberalism could be found in Utilitarianism. Bentham's doctrines seemed to provide a more scientific, hence more realistic, basis for Liberalism. Instead of the unverifiable doctrine of natural rights, Utilitarianism provided the law of greatest happiness, which was, according to Mill, a scientifically demonstrable principle of social behavior. Happily, this scientific doctrine in no way contradicted the essential values of Liberalism. "Everyone to count for one, and none for more than one," was simply a better way to express the Liberal idea of the equality of free individuals. Between utility and "the pursuit of happiness" there was hardly any difference at all. Indeed, the trouble with Mill's solution was that the difficulties he experienced with Liberalism also plagued him as a Utilitarian. His doctrine of Utility made the fundamental assumption not only that men were self-interested but that they were all capable of improvement. "Better to be a human being dissatisfied than a pig satisfied; better to be Socrates dissatisfied than a fool satisfied. And if the fool, or the pig, are of a different opinion, it is because they only know their own side of the question."[46] As a test of the objectivity of the Utilitarian doctrine this argument is plausible, but it does not make Utilitarianism any more realistic than Liberalism, since it too seems to require a degree of education which Mill had already admitted did not yet exist. Even in the context of his argument for Utilitarianism, Mill implicitly admits as much:

> Now there is absolutely no reason in the *nature of things* why an amount of mental culture sufficient to give an intelligent interest in these objects of contemplation, should not be the inheritance of every one born in a civilised country.[47]

If his Utilitarianism diverges at all from his Liberalism, it is in respect to the concern for social as well as individual welfare. Yet it is by no means clear to Mill precisely how the doctrine of Utility, expressed in terms of "the greatest happiness of the greatest number," will decide the pressing questions of social welfare. Should the distribution of goods be made a function of industry or need? Should taxes be levied in numerically equal amounts, proportionally, or in graduated rates? These questions, Mill argues, cannot be answered by an abstract idea of justice, of which there are too many varieties. They can only be answered satisfactorily by the consideration of social utility.[48] Curiously, however, Mill does not indicate what social utility ordains in either case, and, as a rather self-defeating postscript, he soon observes that conceptions of what is expedient have enshrined the most ignoble inequalities:

> The entire history of social improvement has been a series of transitions, by which one custom or institution after another, from being a supposed primary necessity of social existence, has passed into the rank of a universally stigmatised injustice and tyranny. So it has been with the distinctions of slaves and freemen, nobles and serfs, patricians and plebeians; and so it will be, and in part already is, with the aristocracies of colour, race, and sex.[49]

Mill's examples only serve to indicate that Utilitarianism, like Liberalism, makes certain assumptions about the human capacity for the recognition and acceptance of virtue and about the likelihood of progress and perfectibility. Mill no more resolved the crisis of Liberalism by his adoption of Utilitarianism than he did in his attempt to merge Liberal aspirations with the more realistic appraisals of the existing situation which he found in Socialism and Conservatism. At most, he laid the foundation for practical compromises which Liberals could make with their opponents without altogether losing their identity. It remained for later generations and later theorists, among them T. H. Green in England, to modify Liberalism to such an extent that it could become a viable doctrine for the advocates of the welfare state. Meanwhile, Liberals who preferred their principles in older, unadulterated form could only find comfort from advocates of *laissez faire*, chief among whom was Herbert Spencer.

SPENCER: THE TACTIC OF POSTPONEMENT

On a philosophical rather than an ideological level, there would seem to be no two systems of thought farther apart than Lockean Liberalism and the organicist-evolutionary doctrines of Herbert Spencer. As against the Lockean view of nature as a benevolent provider and ethical guide, Spencerian nature is a ruthlessly efficient officer in charge of perfectibility. Far from offering mankind the possibility of happiness at any point in time at the cost only of diligent labor and faithful adherence to the moral law, Spencer's nature ordains that men should be compelled to compete against each other for survival itself for the sake of some faroff perfect adaptation to environment. Given the Spencerian view, how could nature have suggested a social contract at the foundation of society? As against the theoretical individualism of traditional Liberalism, Spencer asserted that, for most of history, nature considered the species more important than the individual and society an organism rather than an atomistic collection of individuals. These theoretical differences also carried different ethical corollaries. If the dictate of nature is adaptation, then the substantive content of the moral law is not an absolute code of natural rights but a shifting standard designed to promote survival in changing circumstances. In primitive times, according to Spencerian ethics, it could not have been morally wrong to kill another creature who posed an obstacle to one's own survival. Happily, according to the same theory, conditions had so changed that now it had become inappropriate to justify murder as an incident of the effort to survive. Thus, even where there is a congruency between Spencerian doctrine and traditional Liberalism, it takes the form of a meeting between two originally divergent lines of thought.

How then did Spencer come to be recognized as a major spokesman for Liberalism in the nineteenth century? The answer to this question provides a critical clue to that bifurcation of Liberalism in the last century which has expressed itself ever since on a practical level in the debate over the role of the state in the regulation and reform of social conditions. Incidentally, it also accounts for the different attitudes toward equality which these conflicting positions maintain.

Notwithstanding the misanthropic reputation he has acquired as a result of a number of uncongenial shifts in the climate of opinion, the fact is that Spencer recognized as fully as Mill and the other Benthamite reformers the contradiction between the social conditions of industrial England and the ethics of Liberalism. As much as he lauded and sought to defend the great strides toward individual freedom which had been accomplished under the aegis of Liberalism and industrialism, Spencer found deplorable the exclusion of the working class from the benefits of this progress. For the workers, he observed, it was the peculiar paradox of progress that they should have been emancipated from one form of coercion only to suffer another even harder bondage.

The wage-earning factory-hand does, indeed, exemplify entirely free labour, in so far that, making contracts at will and able to break them after short notice, he is free to engage with whomsoever he pleases and where he pleases. But this liberty amounts in practice to little more than the ability to exchange one slavery for another, since, fit only for his particular occupation, he has rarely an opportunity of doing anything more than decide in what mill he will pass the greater part of his dreary days. The coercion of circumstance bears more hardly on him than the coercion of a master does on one in bondage.[50]

Confronted by a proletarian misery which seemed to belie the promise of Liberalism, Mill had begun by attempting to reform conditions within the bounds of Liberal individualism and ended by modifying this individualism in the direction of the welfare state. Unlike Mill, Spencer steadfastly refused to compromise the Liberal ethic. Instead he met the incompatibility between that ethic and the prevailing social conditions by postponing the application of Liberal ethics to a later period in history when presumably the contradiction would be overcome through the process of evolution. To fix the moral code for human existence, Spencer argued, it is wrong to search, as Locke had done, for "the original of society," because the ideal form of social ethics would only be attained at the end of evolutionary development.

The moral law, being the law of the social state, is obliged to ignore the pre-social state. Constituting, as the principles of pure morality do, a code of conduct for the perfectly civilized man, they cannot be made to adapt themselves to the actions of the uncivilized man, even under the most ingenious hypothetical conditions—cannot be made even to recognize these actions so as to pass any definite sentence upon them. Overlooking this fact, thinkers, in their attempts to prove some of the first theorems of ethics, have commonly fallen into the error of referring back to an imaginary state of savage wilderness, instead of referring forward to an ideal civilization, as they should have done; and have, in consequence, entangled themselves in difficulties arising out of the discordance between ethical principles and the assumed premises.[51]

For those Liberals who, for practical and philosophical reasons, would not follow Mill into the modification of Liberal values, Spencer's tactic of postponement provided an agreeable alternative. Locke's and Condorcet's ideal of individual perfectibility could be reread in the light of a fashionable scientific theory and transformed into a doctrine of social evolution. The claims of the underprivileged could now be met not only with the older, increasingly suspect doctrines of Malthus, but with a fresh analogy from nature itself. The Liberal image of society could be held in abeyance, suspended above the travail of evolution, as a utopia due to be installed by a providential nature at some conveniently later date. When this period would finally be reached, the contradictions between Liberal values and social reality would be dissolved. In the meantime, however, whatever promoted the advance toward this finale, even though it might conflict with Liberal values, would have the provisional justification of a requirement for evolution.

Spencer's critics among the Liberals did not appreciate the ingenuity and the utility of this revision, especially since they were not so concerned as the Spencerians to keep Liberal values perfectly intact. A late nineteenth century critic who excoriated Spencer for his facile analogies with biology and his want of humanitarian feeling praised Mill, because at least "his thinking is in a process of transition from the extreme doctrines of individualism and *laissez faire*, in which he was brought up, to a more adequate conception of society." [52] Had Spencer's conception of society been merely inadequate it is unlikely that he would have exerted so widespread an influence upon Liberal thought and opinion in Europe and America for over half a century. Indeed Spencer and those who accepted his arguments would not have admitted that there was a conception of society more adequate than that of Liberal individualism—so long as it was understood that this society would only be realized in the long run. What accounts to a considerable extent for the popularity of Spencer's doctrines is that it enabled Liberals who would not be reconstructed, to avoid the *crise de conscience* which Mill and those who shared his problems could only overcome by modifying Liberalism.

More perceptive critics argued that Spencer had twisted his biological analogies to fit his Liberal preconceptions. In a "postscript" to a chapter of his *Principles of Sociology*, Spencer replies to one such criticism offered by Henri Marion, a French commentator. Marion had asserted that Spencer's theory of social evolution dovetailed with Liberal principles too neatly not to have been deliberately contrived for this purpose. He noted that Spencer had drawn an analogy between the development of individual organisms and society but, having done so, had not followed the logic of his argument to the same conclusion in both cases. Spencer had argued that the more developed its central nervous system the "higher" would an organism rank in the scale of evolution. At the same time he held that a society with a highly developed central regulatory system ranked low in the scale of social evolution. The higher society, Spencer argued, was that in which the nutritive function was more highly developed than the regulatory function, and in which the individual members of the society maintained their existence successfully with a minimum of central regulation. As a naturalist, Marion had observed, Spencer could be expected to regard highly centralized societies as the superior form, but "as an Englishman of the Liberal school" he is prejudiced against such organization: "bientôt le moraliste en lui combat le naturaliste," and Spencer opts for individualism rather than regulation.

Spencer's reply to this criticism points up the manner in which he conceived of Liberalism as the ultimate goal of social evolution. He argues that individuals differ from societies in that the requirements for individual survival demand a constant emphasis upon mechanisms of defense and aggression. Central regulation enhances these faculties and is therefore the mark of those organisms best able to survive. It is otherwise, however, with societies. During the militant stage of history, social survival (like that of the individual organism) depends upon military capacity. In this period, therefore, centrally organized states would be best able to survive challenges to their continued existence. The militant stage of history, however, was in the process of yielding to the industrial stage, in which the requirements for survival would be altogether different. In the industrial stage of history the vitality of societies depends less upon military power than "on those powers which enable them to hold their own in the struggle for industrial competition." Similarly, Spencer observes, there is a difference between the individual and the social organism in regard to internal composition. In the individual organism the components act for the sake of the central nervous system, which monopolizes all feeling in the organism, whereas in society all the units have feelings, expressing the intention of nature that the aggregate should exist for the benefit of the individuals who compose it. Therefore, Spencer concludes, "social organization is to be considered high in proportion as it subserves individual welfare . . . and the industrial type is the higher because it subserves individual welfare better than the militant type" when the challenges to its successful adaptation to environment are not primarily military.[53] The Liberal image of a society in which individuals compete through industry to attain happiness and fulfillment is considered to be the goal toward which history is tending and the state of existence which nature had intended for man. Spencer elaborated the same fundamental theory of social evolution in his adoption of Sir Henry Maine's theory of the transition from status to contract. Status is the type of social organization which corresponds to the militant period, contract the type which corresponds to the industrial period.

To this historical theory Spencer added a conception of the ethical code which would govern the final stage. He used the term "equal freedom" to describe the social relations of the industrial-contractual period, asserting that this was the law of social life, from a biological as well as a moral point of view. The law of equal freedom asserts that the expression of his faculties is the natural and proper aim of every human being, and a necessity of evolution: unless organisms are free to exercise their faculties they will not develop characteristics appropriate to their environment, and slough off other characteristics inhibiting adaptation. So long, however, as men retain their primitive predatory characteristics, it is necessary that individual freedom be limited, because no one can be expected to stop short of sacrificing others for his own ends. The law of equal freedom therefore provides that "every man may claim the fullest liberty to exercise his faculties compatible with the possession of like liberty by every other man."[54]

"Equal freedom" is Spencer's formulation of the Liberal doctrine of competitive equality. He attacks the Benthamite modification of Liberal equality as a subversive introduction of Socialism. The greatest-happiness principle, Spencer exclaims, "explodes into the astounding assertion, that all men have equal rights to happiness—an assertion far more sweeping and revolutionary than any of those which are assailed with so much scorn."[55] Justice and nature demand that men have equal rights not to happiness but to the pursuit of happiness:

if an equal portion of the earth's produce is awarded to every man, irrespective of the amount or quality of the labour he has contributed towards the obtainment of that produce, a breach of equity is committed. Our first principle requires, not that all should have like shares of the things which minister to the gratification of the faculties, but that all should have like freedom to pursue those things . . . It is one thing to give each an opportunity of acquiring the objects he desires, it is another, and quite a different thing, to give the objects themselves, no matter whether due endeavour has or has not been made to obtain them. Nay more, it necessitates an absolute violation of the principle of equal freedom.[56]

Taken by itself, out of the context of Spencer's general revision of Liberalism, this statement would seem to indicate a total acceptance of the Lockean formulation of competitive equality. It seems to justify unequal reward on the ground that the effort expended to obtain the rewards will vary from one competitor to another. But this statement is followed by another which indicates that, unlike Locke, Spencer does not believe that all individuals have more or less the same capacity to be productive. It is not entirely a question of industry, but of differences in innate capacity as well. If, he writes,

out of many starting with like fields of activity, one obtains, *by his greater strength, greater ingenuity, or greater application,* more gratifications and sources of gratification than the rest, and does this without trenching upon the equal freedoms of the rest, the moral law assigns to him an exclusive right to all those extra gratifications and sources of gratification; nor can the rest take them from him without claiming for themselves greater liberty of action than he claims, and thereby violating that law.[57]

Spencer's addition of the claim of superior talent to the traditional Liberal demand on behalf of industry is an indication of his attempt to combine Liberalism and evolutionary necessity. Superiority in capacity will only exist in the interim period before perfect adaptation is attained; it is therefore accorded the same value as industry. Indeed Spencer goes beyond this modification of Liberalism in an effort to make social ethics practical. He argues, as Mill did earlier, that while the equation of merit, expressed in industry, with reward is the principle of abstract justice, it is "no longer practicable" now that the simple agrarian economy has been superseded. In conditions of commerce and industry it is impossible to know whether the ideal is followed or not, except insofar as the working of the law of supply and demand approximates it. Given a complex economy, he asks, how can the proportion between merit and reward be determined? The Lockean test of labor admits of no such application, Spencer objects, because it is impossible to know how much labor gives a man a claim to what is originally common, greater than that of all others. Nor can anyone know how to set the limit which Locke prescribes in order to prevent any individual from acquiring so much that there is not enough left for others.[58] Spencer's revision of the Lockean formula cut to the very roots of the Liberal conception of justice, a conception which drew much of its ethical validity from the assumption that, once artificial privileges and restraints were removed in favor of equal rights, men would all begin their pursuit of happiness from the same starting point.

Spencer was no less critical of another major thesis of the Liberal doctrine of equality, the belief that all men were sufficiently rational to know the moral law. While Locke had recognized differences of rational capacity, he had asserted that all men had a sufficient rational capacity to justify their equal claim to authority in matters affecting the precepts of the law of nature. Spencer argued against Bentham that the principle of greatest happiness, Bentham's Utilitarian substitute for Locke's moral law, would not be agreed upon by all men because everyone had a different standard of happiness.[59] On this point, as well as on the issue of competitive equality, Spencer seems to have diverged significantly from the traditional Liberal view.

In his historical theory Spencer went even further from any idea of equality. The moving force of history was not the group as a whole, but the exceptional individual who broke through all tendencies to conformity. Compulsory cooperation, which is the general feature of feudalism, gives way to voluntary contract only because the superior individuals will not consent to be reduced to the level of their inferior contemporaries:

Though need for mutual protection caused cohesion of relations in clusters, there was at work from the beginning a cause of dissolution ready to show its effects as soon as surrounding conditions allowed. Always the diligent and skillful felt annoyance at being unable to profit by their superiorities. They were vexed on seeing the idle taking equal shares of benefit with themselves.

The disintegration of the medieval guilds occurred, according to Spencer, because superior journeymen left them to establish themselves as independent artisans in the suburbs. These exceptional individuals paved the way for the total decline of feudal economic relations by demonstrating the superior efficiency of free labor.[60]

From an evolutionary point of view, superiority should be more highly valued than inferiority. As it is an axiom of nature that the fittest survive, it is both inevitable and just that those most capable of adaptation reap the greatest rewards, and that those whose incapacity puts them in the way of evolutionary progress receive lower rewards and in some cases are denied existence itself. Spencer admits that society does not satisfy the ideals of a vague humanitarian belief in equality: "The strong divisions of rank and the immense inequalities of means, are at variance with that ideal of human relations on which the sympathetic imagination likes to dwell."[61] But nature takes no account of sentimental illusions— her only concern is that the level of the species be advanced through natural selection, in the social as in the animal and botanical universes. Those who are unworthy of survival, whether because of "incapacity or misconduct,"[62] are eliminated for the sake of this general advance. "It seems hard," Spencer admits, that widows and orphans should be compelled to struggle for sheer survival, or that an accidentally incapacitated laborer should have to compete against men who suffer from no physical handicaps, but otherwise the process of evolution could not be continued.[63] "Is it not cruel," he asks of humanitarians, "to increase the sufferings of the better that the sufferings of the worse may be decreased?"[64] Besides, to ask superiors to yield the benefits of their talents to inferiors is "psychologically absurd." For this to occur without compulsion, "the intensity of fellow-feeling" must be "such as to cause life-long self-sacrifice."[65]

Important as these anti-egalitarian beliefs are for Spencer's theory of evolution, they do not imply an ultimate rejection of equality. Equality, like other Liberal values, must wait until the limit of evolution is reached. By then natural selection will have developed a race of men all of whom will be equipped with the characteristics necessary for survival. In this sense—for Spencer the all-important sense—they will then be equal. Since the conditions for survival will be industrial, it is implied that men will then compete as equals in industrial capacity. Reward and merit will automatically become adjusted and it will no longer be necessary that some members of society be sacrificed, since, theoretically at least, no one will possess characteristics unsuited for adaptation. Moreover, the development of industrial characteristics would gradually expel the predatory survivals from earlier periods and men would live together in harmony.

In the meantime, however, it was essential that nothing be done to interfere with evolution. Although Spencer's evolutionary theory seemed to assure the eventual attainment of Liberal individualism, he was apprehensive lest the difficulties of the transition should induce a regression to compulsory hierarchical organization. He saw both Socialism and the Benthamite modification of Liberalism as philosophies of a "New Toryism" which, if successful, would reverse the evolutionary process and restore the obsolete system of central regulation and its corollary, the annihilation of individuality. Socialism, he predicted, would necessarily entail "established grades and enforced subordination of each grade to the grades above." It would also require a military organization of society in which the officers would constitute a vast bureaucracy charged with apportioning labor and reward and with regulating virtually every aspect of social life.[66] Far from being improved, the condition of the workers would deteriorate under Socialism because they would be deprived of all freedom to choose and change their occupations. Already, Spencer noted, the submissiveness of trade union members to their leaders gave evidence that Socialism would entail the worst tyranny the world has ever known.[67] To the assurance of the democratic Socialists that the bureaucracy would be subjected to rigorous democratic control, Spencer replied that any control would prove utterly ineffectual because a centralized authority with such extensive resources would be bound to extend its power and because the spirit of individualism in the people would tend to be extinguished. The bureaucracy would become a new ruling class and the people would be reduced to the level of abject inferiors, as under feudalism. If anything, Socialist tyranny was likely to be worse than feudal tyranny, thanks to improved means of compulsion.[68]

Spencer's alternative to Socialism, as the ultimate goal of social evolution, was not the ruthless individualism which he believed necessary in the interim period between the militant stage and the completion of the industrial era. He predicted that as the challenge which evoked aggressiveness suffered a gradual diminution there would be a softening of individualism by the natural faculty of sympathy. He found this tendency already exemplified in love relations:

Every one must have observed the carefulness with which those who are on terms of affectionate intimacy, shun anything in the form of supremacy on either side, or endeavour to banish from remembrance, by their behaviour to each other, whatever of supremacy there may exist.[69]

Until evolution reaches its limit, the ends of self-maintenance and race-maintenance can only be met "by destruction of other beings, of different kind or of like kind."[70] In social groups evolution remains incomplete while there is still antagonism between groups and between members of the same group. "Hence the limit of evolution can be reached by conduct only in permanently peaceful societies." In conditions of peace "perfect adjustment" will be obtained—an adjustment in which life can be sustained "by each without hindering others from effecting like perfect adjustments."[71] Adjustment is not complete, however, until it assumes the positive form of cooperation and mutual help, after the stage of mutual toleration has been reached. Industrialism will provide the necessary context for this development "in proportion as the activities, becoming less and less militant and more and more industrial, are such as do not necessitate mutual injury or hindrance, but consist with, and are furthered by, co-operation and mutual aid."[72] Beyond the mere avoidance of direct and indirect injuries to others, the limit of evolution will be characterized by "spontaneous efforts to further the welfare of others."[73]

In the actual organization of industry the passage from passive to active association, from egoistic to altruistic individualism, will take the form of the advance from wage-work to a cooperative system. This advance would extend the law of equal freedom to the working class to a degree it did not yet enjoy under the prevailing factory system. Spencer admits that "so long as the worker remains a wage-earner, the marks of status do not wholly disappear." Workers who are paid a wage are generally not treated as distinct individuals but as a class of producers without regard to their special talents or productivity. Piece-work payment is, in principle, a recognition of individuality; but under the existing organization of production it is unlikely that principle and practice will be united. The production of the piece-worker is taken by employers as the basis for raising the regular norm of production; the workers come to realize this and therefore join together to restrict individual initiative. The best corrective for this circle of abuses would be the cooperative organization of production, which would therefore represent a higher form of industry.

Under such a mode of co-operation . . . the system of contract becomes unqualified. Each member agrees with the body of members to perform certain work for a certain sum, and is free from dictation and authoritative censure. The entire organization is based on contract, and each transaction is based on contract.

Only under such a system can contractual justice be attained. In this stage of development "the general law of species-life, and the law applied in our conception of justice [a law Spencer regarded as otherwise impracticable]—the law that reward shall be proportionate to merit," will be fulfilled.[74] Cooperation, however, is not merely an arrangement which can be introduced at any stage of the development. It must await changes both in individual character and in environmental conditions before it will be appropriate.

While Spencer's apparent differences with the Lockean tradition may thus be resolved theoretically by taking proper account of his attempt to postpone Liberalism, it is nonetheless true that Spencer himself did not always maintain the distinction between the transitional period and the ultimate period. In part this is probably due to rhetorical considerations. To persuade a Liberal audience that it was necessary to forego Liberalism in the short run in order to assure its ultimate triumph would have been more difficult than to argue, as Spencer did, on Liberal grounds where it seemed possible and on grounds of evolutionary necessity in other cases. As a result his discussions of equality seem sometimes to be contradictory. But perhaps the most serious difficulty with Spencer's egalitarianism is that, since the attainment of Liberal equality is a matter for the future, the only immediately relevant conclusions which can be drawn from his doctrines are antiegalitarian. To sustain such an ambiguity required a much greater confidence in the progressive character of history than a good many Liberals found warranted by subsequent events, and, equally important, required an ability to keep ultimate goals in mind while practicing contradictory immediate expedients. By Spencer's own understanding of human nature, this was surely too much to expect.

Neither Spencer nor Mill succeeded in resolving the crisis within Liberalism. At most they clarified the alternatives and made it possible to act pragmatically either to reconcile old ideals to a changing reality or to seek to alter reality in accordance with those ideals. This pragmatism was to prolong the life of the Liberal conception of equality, but the atrophy of the philosophic function that inevitably accompanied it meant that Liberal egalitarians would find themselves gravely handicapped. Soon they would have to confront the unforeseen perplexities of mature industrial society guided only by the philosophers of its early and middle ages.

The Conservative Paradox

T<small>HE</small> <small>EARLY</small> critics of the French Revolution had no intention of coming to terms with this or with any other manifestation of the levelling temper. Edmund Burke, Joseph de Maistre, Louis de Bonald, and Adam Müller, to take the leading figures, were Conservatives in the sense that they wished to see the Revolution undone and the old order restored. Their social theories were conceived in direct opposition to all that had inspired the revolutionaries. Against natural right they put historical precedent and tradition. Against the chaos of revolutionary overthrow they put established order with only the most gradual change. Against abstract reason they put sentiment and prejudice, against atomistic individualism organic pluralism—and against equality hierarchy.

After this first wave of die-hard resistance, other critics took a less defiant attitude. Virtually all the later Conservatives began from the assumption that the old order could not be restored. As Conservatives they retained a commitment to the principles of the old order, but as practical philosophers they had to consider how these principles might be re-established in the new context of egalitarian society. Alexis de Tocqueville reiterated the Conservative critique of democracy, but he went on to suggest a modification of what were, from a Conservative point of view, the worst dangers of democracy. In its Tocque-

villean version the Conservative concept of equality thus became the basis of a more temperate, more conciliatory, and—
from the point of view of Liberals and Socialists—a more in-
sidious opposition than had been offered by the first spokesmen
of reaction.

Some of those who shared Tocqueville's dislike of democracy
would not accept the political compromise he proposed. They
sought instead to transcend the political dilemma altogether by
addressing themselves to more fundamental questions of morality and the place of man in the universe. They denounced the
rise of mass society as a challenge to higher values and as an
utterly false response to the question of human purpose, but they
could see no satisfactory alternative either in a restoration of
aristocracy or in a modification of democracy. Instead they
called for a new, nonpolitical individualism—a new man to stand
against the tide of mass men. Kierkegaard saw this man as a
man of faith, not in the conventional sense of piety, but in the
sense of a passionate struggle to transcend all finite experience.
Only by confronting with fear and trembling the grounds of
all being, he urged, could the self realize the fullness of its own
existence. Max Stirner saw the new man as a wholly self-sufficient individual, refusing to recognize any external obligations
and answering the threats of the collectivity with the demands
of his own absolute self. Nietzsche saw the new man, the *Übermensch*, as a creator of values—as a man who would transform
the ethically and aesthetically neutral force of his nature into
something noble and unique.

It was only a short step from the Conservative critique of democracy to the theories of a new elitism, fashioned either out
of the charismatic attraction of the heroic individual or out of
the organizational necessities of mass society. It was a longer
and perhaps a more significant step to the social theory of Freud,
which, in a number of ways, sums up and synthesizes all the
nineteenth century tangents to the Conservative concept of
equality. Like Tocqueville, Freud recognized that the demand
for equality could not be ignored, even though it represented
only a covert wish to make frustration universal. Like Kierkegaard, Stirner, and Nietzsche, he also recognized and championed

the effort to create a superior man dedicated to the higher aims of life. As a social philosopher he brought both of these concerns together. Until all men might become capable of sustaining these higher aims, the illusion of equality would remain a social necessity; but, in order that this society be directed to higher values, it was essential that government be entrusted to an aristocracy of the enlightened. In this prescription, at once classical and contemporary, in which equality is denounced as an ideal of reform but pressed into service as a myth of order, Freud expressed in modern form the peculiar paradox of the Conservative reaction to levelling.

TOCQUEVILLE: THE DANGERS OF DEMOCRACY

No one in the nineteenth century was more deeply convinced of the importance of the idea of equality than the aristocrat Alexis de Tocqueville. In all his political studies it was the pivot, repeatedly acknowledged, about which he traced his understanding of the tendencies of modern history. Equality, he believed, was the keynote of the age in which he lived, the central dogma of "a new social and political order," [1] the capstone of a revolutionary attempt to "establish a social science, a philosophy, I might almost say a religion, fit to be learned and followed by all mankind." [2] The convulsive waves of revolution that continued to sweep over the remnants of the "old regimes" of Europe during his own lifetime confirmed this conviction. But he did not rest his belief in the importance of equality upon the revolutions themselves. The visible work of revolution, he believed, was predated and made possible by deeper and more persistent tendencies in social organization and opinion. The magnitude of these events, and the unity which seemed to embrace them all, led Tocqueville to a single focus of inquiry: equality of conditions, he confessed, was "the central point at which all my observations constantly terminated." [3]

It ought not to surprise a generation schooled in the sociology of knowledge to find that an aristocrat should have been an assiduous student of equality. What *is* surprising is that he should have been able to approach the subject with a relatively receptive serenity. Even this apparent anomaly can be accounted for, to some extent, by his position in history. Had he come to maturity during the highest tides of the French Revolution, Tocqueville might conceivably have shared the unqualified revulsion of Burke and Maistre, who looked upon the egalitarian revolution as an intolerable affront to divine order. But Tocqueville was of a later, more chastened generation of aristocrats. To be sure, his father had narrowly escaped the guillotine at the height of the Terror, and he himself was sufficiently impressed by the accounts of Robespierre and Napoleon to picture Caesarism as the permanent shadow of the age of equality.[4] At the same time, he recognized that no matter how subtle the machinations of the Talleyrands and the Metternichs, and however "legitimate" the several claims of Bourbon, Bonapartist, and Orleanist pretenders—among the last named, the heirs of "Philippe Égalité"—it was hopeless to think that the old order could be permanently restored. Burke, he observed, had erred profoundly in thinking that the French Revolution might have modeled itself upon the Glorious Revolution. The English wanted liberty, the French equality.[5] The deepest aim of the French revolutionaries was the destruction of the traditional legitimacy which, according to Burke, the English revolutionaries sought only to reaffirm.[6] Nor was this new kind of revolution confined to Europe. Tocqueville went to see for himself how the same phenomenon had occurred without resistance in the comparatively ideal laboratory of the New World. The evidence plainly indicates that in Tocqueville, as in other aristocrats who joined less detached bourgeois proponents of order in the camp of Guizot, blind rage had given way both to sober reflection and to resignation. Faced with the alternative of living as permanent exiles within their native country, they chose to think and work on behalf of their interests within the context of democratic society.

Tocqueville's angle of vision is important to recognize because it imposed a definite construction upon what he saw. The democracy Tocqueville observed was democracy seen through the eyes of an aristocrat. The egalitarianism he took to be the motive force of history was represented in his work as it appeared to a Conservative. In his interpretations of the historical rise of democracy, in his prognosis of its further development, in his diagnosis of the threat it posed to civilization, in his prescriptions of curative action, it is apparent that Tocqueville is a friend to democracy only for the sake of saving it from itself.

History assumed a cardinal importance in his understanding of egalitarianism. For Tocqueville, history was a succession of organic periods, each giving different stress to the constant elements of human nature. He took as his unit of study the Western nations, and although he frequently called attention to the political, ethnic, religious, and regional differences among them, he was convinced that fundamentally they constituted one society. As he saw it, this society was in a process of evolution in which each of the component nations pursued the same path at different rates of speed. In the *Old Regime* he sought to explain why the revolution had come first to France, but at the same time he observed that the underlying causes would in time affect the other nations. In *Democracy in America*, even as he was minutely attentive to the differences between France and America, he wrote that "in spite of the ocean that intervenes, I cannot consent to separate America from Europe." The Americans were "that portion of the English people who are commissioned to explore the forests of the New World." [7]

In America he saw the future of the entire Western society. From all those in which the democratic revolution had occurred, "I have selected the nation, from among those which have undergone it, in which its development has been the most peaceful and the most complete, *in order to discern its natural consequences.*" [8] This notion of the "natural" development of an historical period indicates the overriding emphasis Tocqueville ascribed to the guiding principles of each historical period. America was the best place in which to study the outlines of the future not because the absence of a feudal prehistory was to make for a radical difference between America and Europe, but rather because it meant that equality would there have already taken the course it would take in Europe after the temporary, incidental dislocations of revolution had subsided. [9] For Tocqueville, the whole of Western society was in a period of transition from feudalism to democracy and the forms the future would take, like the forms previous epochs had taken, would be at least similar in all countries.

But Tocqueville's theory of history did not stop simply at identifying this transition; it was also an attempt to account for it. Why was the triumph of equality so inevitable? Why had the old order been so completely overthrown? Tocqueville's most comprehensive answer, only partly hidden by the detachment with which he assembled a chain of concrete events, such as the centralization of power, the breakup of manorial holdings, the rise of a moneyed aristocracy, the destruction of the rigid barrier between classes by the introduction of legal equality, was essentially that the events of the transition were due to a combination of the will of God and the fault of man. The recognition of "that irresistible revolution which has advanced for centuries in spite of every obstacle" promoted in him "a kind of religious awe." For however pernicious its effects, no historical movement could have demonstrated such power of persistence unless it were divinely sponsored.

It is not necessary that God himself should speak in order that we may discover the unquestionable signs of his will. It is enough to ascertain what is the habitual course of nature and the constant tendency of events. I know, without special revelation, that the planets move in orbits traced by the Creator's hand.

Thus the "gradual and progressive development of social equality" conferred upon this tendency "the sacred character of a divine decree."[10] How else could all the events of history have so conspired to advance equality?

. . . all men have aided it by their exertions, both those who have intentionally labored in its cause and those who have served it unwittingly; those who have fought for it and even those who have declared themselves its opponents have all been driven along in the same direction, have all labored to one end; some unknowingly and some despite themselves, all have been blind instruments in the hands of God.[11]

Tocqueville's theory of the divine direction of history was, like the events it described, a theory in transition. He joined the moderns in viewing the providential guidance of history not as a work of intermittent intervention, but as a long evolutionary process in which all men were vessels of the *telos*, willingly or not. But in other crucial elements he is closer to the older tradition of history as theodicy, running from Augustine through Bossuet to Maistre and Bonald, for whom the course of history is by no means necessarily progressive. Tocqueville associated the idea of the indefinite perfectibility of man with the democratic age,[12] but he did not adopt it in his own theory of history. He saw the rise of democracy not merely as a transvaluation of values but as a challenge to all values. Maistre and Bonald had denied both that equality was inevitable and also that it was divinely sanctioned. Tocqueville reversed both of these judgments, but even so he could not extend a genuine welcome to the historical forces he granted were legitimate. For democracy, he remarked, he had a "goût de tête," [13] an intellectual recognition, but no passion of the soul. Rather than exhorting his contemporaries to further the clearly indicated will of God, he counseled them to *"make the best* of the *social lot* awarded to them by Providence." For "to attempt to check democracy would be . . . to resist the will of God." [14] That it was difficult for Tocqueville to accept his own judgment of the divine intention is evident from such negative descriptions of the proper course for the religious believer to follow. *"Perhaps,"* he reflected with patent uneasiness, "after all, the will of God is to distribute a mediocre happiness among the totality of mankind, not to concentrate a large amount of felicity upon a small number or to bring certain ones to perfection." [15] To the reactionaries who preceded him the purpose of history was a good deal more inspiring, and the assent to history, when it was divinely directed history, could be offered in the spirit of a crusade. In Tocqueville all that is left of the older aristocratic attempt to historicize the divinity is an inability to reject a phenomenon with such deep roots and irrepressible power as a monstrous historical sport, and, coupled with that forced recognition, the pose of dignified submission.

But in Tocqueville's case this submission was not entirely gratuitous. For in his theory of history—and this is a second point at which he approaches the older tradition—there is also an assumption that in directing history God works according to principles of justice, meting out punishment and reward. Without saying explicitly, as Maistre did, that equality is a divine punishment, he put much the same thought in another form by associating cause and responsibility in his analysis of history.

History, Tocqueville suggested, is a compound of general causes and immediate accidents and incidents, the general causes being the influence of ideas and changes in the social structure. Early egalitarian ideas had been without effect, because "for doctrines of this kind to lead to revolutions certain changes must already have taken place in the living conditions, customs and mores of a nation and prepared men's minds for the reception of new ideas." [16] Now that historical conditions were favorable, the egalitarian cause was bound to succeed. In the fifteenth century the feudal system was still too strong; now it was weak beyond all possibility of survival. The revolution, as Tocqueville took great pains to point out, was only the culmination of a process which originated in the decay of feudalism. The heart of his causal analysis—and at the same time of his moral judgment—rests in his understanding of the way this weakening took place.

The decay of feudalism was not primarily the result of a combination of historically neutral forces, beyond will and values. Nor was the feudal ruling class overthrown because external forces led the nobility to so oppress the lower classes that in desperation they rose up to overthrow their masters. On the contrary, according to Tocqueville, it was the foolish generosity of the aristocracy in acceding to some of the demands of the lower classes that intensified their other grievances and gave them a new recognition of the possibility of improvement. "The very destruction of some of the institutions of the Middle Ages made those which survived seem all the more detestable." [17] Moreover,

it was precisely in those parts of France where there had been the most improvement that popular discontent ran highest. This may seem illogical—but history is full of such paradoxes. For it is not always when things are going from bad to worse that revolutions break out. On the contrary, it oftener happens that when a people which has put up with an oppressive rule over a long period without protest suddenly finds the government relaxing its pressure, it takes up arms against it.[18]

In describing this mechanism of democratic revolution as a "paradox," Tocqueville sought to dissimulate in irony what struck him on a deeper plane as a tragedy compounded of ignorance and vice. The ignorance and avarice of the masses was part of it— but who could have expected better from them? Far worse was the failure of the guardian elite, the feudal aristocracy. No matter how he qualified his conclusions, Tocqueville could not escape the judgment of the Revolution as a tragedy brought upon itself by the aristocracy, not so much out of excessive generosity as out of ignorance, plain vice, and indifference to its own code of ethics.[19] Two new roads to power, one of money, the other of knowledge, contributed heavily to the destruction of the feudal order; but both were opened by the aristocracy itself. "In the eleventh century, nobility was beyond all price; in the thirteenth, it might be purchased. Nobility was first conferred by gift in 1270, and *equality was thus introduced into the government by the aristocracy itself.*"[20] As to the influence of civilization and knowledge, which produced a literary "arsenal open to all, where the poor and the weak daily resorted for arms,"[21] Tocqueville observed pointedly that the French revolutionaries "took over from the old regime not only most of its customs, conventions and modes of thought, but even those very ideas which prompted our revolutionaries to destroy it."[22]

The clearest evidences of aristocratic responsibility are monarchical self-ruin in great enterprises, and the nobility's waste of resources in private wars, while the middle classes enriched themselves in commerce. The nobility extended power to the lower classes in order to limit the King; the King did the same in order to gain greater power over the nobility.

In France the kings have always been the most active and the most constant of levellers. When they were strong and ambitious they spared no pains to raise the people to the level of the nobles; when they were temperate and feeble, they allowed the people to rise above themselves. Some assisted democracy by their talents, others by their vices. Louis XI and Louis XIV reduced all ranks beneath the throne to the same degree of subjection; and finally Louis XV descended, himself and all his court, into the dust.[23]

Was it the revolutionaries, Tocqueville asked, who established centralized national government and its structural corollary, equality before the law, at once a total subversion of feudal order and an invitation to easy rebellion? His answer, abundantly documented in the *Old Regime*, was that it was the ambitious monarchs, typified by Louis XIV, who removed power from local authorities guided by the landed aristocracy and undermined the quasi-independent judicial authority of the *parlements*. Behind far-reaching events such as these, and behind the breakup of the landed estates, the establishment of an independent peasantry, and the creation of a nobility of the purse lay all the vices which afflicted the feudal aristocracy—ambition, pride, a taste for luxury and for martial glory, and mutual jealousy. The monarchy, by sapping the foundations of aristocracy, prepared its own path to the guillotine. The aristocracy, by abdicating its function as guardian of feudal liberty and shepherd of its subjects, dissipated what was left of its moral and physical authority in the cultivation of debilitating luxury and fratricidal wars.

Reflecting upon these causes of egalitarian revolution, Tocqueville could not exactly blame the lower classes for rebelling. The aristocratic standard of social justice, the sacred equation of privilege and responsibility, had been violated by the aristocrats themselves. The more the functions of keeping order, administering justice, superintending the execution of the laws, and guarding the common welfare were no longer performed by the nobility, "the more uncalled-for did their privileges appear—until at last their mere existence seemed a meaningless anachronism."[24]

It was in this sense that Tocqueville, like Maistre, saw equality as a divine punishment. And it was with an equally religious feeling that he regarded the expulsion from the feudal paradise as an irrevocable expression of the divine will. But the aristocracy had suffered and learned its lesson.

The same families that were most profligate fifty years ago are nowadays the most exemplary, and democracy seems only to have strengthened the morality of the aristocratic classes. The French Revolution, by dividing the fortunes of the nobility, by forcing them to attend assiduously to their affairs and to their families, by making them live under the same roof with their children, and, in short, by giving a more rational and serious turn to their minds, has imparted to them, almost without their being aware of it, a reverence for religious belief, a love of order, of tranquil pleasures, of domestic endearments, and of comfort.[25]

Would the democracy need to undergo the same experience? Apparently moved by a spirit of repentance, Tocqueville sought to cast aside his innate pride in the higher aspirations of a society ruled by the nobility—to suppress rancor and repugnance. Only in this way could he become a tutor to the democracy, a self-impressed Athenian in the academy of the New Rome.[26] In attempting to restrain the future from betraying its own ideals and succumbing to its own temptations, the aristocracy might hope to pay its debt to mankind and play its last great historical role as a benefactor of civilization. For Tocqueville was convinced that if democratic society should repeat the failure of feudal society, the consequences to humanity would be even worse.

The dangers of democracy were uniquely difficult because, according to Tocqueville, they lay in the fulfillment of its aspirations rather than in the corruption of them. The principle of equality, and the character traits and social structure justified in its name, all represented a threat to the existence of civilization and culture. Tocqueville's understanding of civilization was rooted in the traditional notion of a hierarchy of virtues, talents, status, and authority. Because he believed in the organic character of periods of history, he feared that the levelling of social conditions would inevitably entail the rejection of the values associated with hierarchical society. For this reason, his resigned acceptance of democracy is deeply qualified by his apprehensions. Virtually every aspect of democracy appeared to him to be charged with dangers to civilization so great that the full realization of equality would be catastrophic.

Tocqueville gave vent to these fundamental misgivings even in his description of the principles and conditions of democratic life. Unlike the democratic theorists themselves, he did not begin from the premise that equality was an irreducible principle, whether of justice or of divine creation. On the contrary, he made every effort to reduce the desire for equality to some category below the level of intrinsic values. Tocqueville was deeply convinced that the desire for equality was not entirely "healthy." He tried to separate the experience of violent hatred in the revolutionary period from democracy itself, but he was not very successful. In his own mind he could not make the separation. Democracy was conceived out of envy and in Tocqueville's view it was bound to be forever tainted with the marks of its birth. From the standpoint of aristocratic ethics the revolution was justified; but, for the mobs which carried it out, the principal motivation was naked envy. If actual violence passed with the successful completion of the revolution, the psychology of resentment remained. In the halcyon days of feudalism, if we are to believe Tocqueville, there was never much occasion for invidious feelings. Before the aristocracy degenerated into a caste, before guilds became corrupt and peasants owned their own land, and before centralized and absolute monarchy unraveled the clusters of isolated, well-knit communities, hostility was usually muted by a familial solidarity, solemnized by its seeming permanence.[27] But the subversion of the feudal order produced actual, sensed barriers of hostility among the various classes. The privileges and the distinctions accorded to the few, now divorced from responsibility and abstracted from the matrix of custom and affection, seemed wholly illegitimate to those who suffered what Tocqueville described as "spiritual estrangement."[28] In attacking the holders of privilege, however, the populace sought not to protest an imbalance but to despoil the favored few, to gain for themselves the marks of privilege they professed to find intrinsically unjust. It was this attitude which Tocqueville placed at the center of the desire for equality. Envy of the privileged, he asserted, was the "democratic disease."[29]

It is not difficult to recognize in Tocqueville's portrait of democratic society the equation of equality with envy. In democratic America, Tocqueville observed, "everyone is in motion, some in quest of power, others of gain."[30] Where there were neither limits to desire nor assurance of security, no man could be content with his lot. In previous times the acceptance of established ways of life led to an indifference toward worldly things and assisted the mind to remain attentive to the image of a kingdom above and beyond that of this world. But the preoccupation with worldly advantages which the breakdown of feudalism had inspired produced in the democracy a perpetual and dogged competition for advantage. Each man now looked with avid eye to the enjoyments of his neighbors and sought to equal and surpass in wealth all those around him. Because of the natural disparity in talents, most were doomed to fail of their goal, but because of their dogmatic refusal to recognize the existence of these natural inequalities and because of their belief in infinite perfectibility they would be "forever seeking, forever falling to rise again."[31] Thus the social mobility which Tocqueville found so characteristic of America and of democracy in general was not a demonstration of vigor but a pathological symptom. The same sickness was responsible for the principled individualism of the democrat, which Tocqueville contrasted with the spontaneous, instinctive egoism of aristocratic times.[32] The utilitarian mentality which directed the efforts of this new man was for Tocqueville a fitting, if loathsome, expression of the same disease. And the social structure of democracy, in which the bonds of affection, lodged in "ties of family, of caste, of class and of craft,"[33] are all dissolved, was the perfect format for the fullest exploitation and nurture by every man of his own cancer.

The social structure and the psychology of equality worked together to produce a set of sub-attitudes. The constant experience of change led to a contempt for tradition and fixed forms, and at the same time reinforced the belief in infinite perfectibility. Isolation and selfishness made men indifferent to public questions, and the belief in the equal intellectual capacity of all men twisted what was otherwise a rugged individualist into a slavish worshipper of public opinion. In government democratic man insisted upon representation, but in his parliament, even though he yearned for it secretly,[34] he could not achieve discipline. For while there was yet "freedom," not only would he refuse to defer to genuine superiors but he would rout out from politics all men of quality.[35]

Taken together, these changes of attitude and social organization which Tocqueville traced to the impact of the idea of equality indicated a radical downward shift in social aspiration. The values which accompanied the levelling of hierarchy were, almost by definition, lower ones expressed in the materialism, the contempt for leisure and meditation, the selfishness and the envy he found characteristic of democracy. In literature and the arts he saw a trend from the ideal to the real which struck him as but another aspect of the general development. The democratic drama, he said, was "more striking, more vulgar, and more true."[36] The democratic poet, he observed, in what is at least superficially a remarkable anticipation of Whitman, would no longer seek to describe outstanding men but, catering to the taste of the populace, would provide them with a "survey of themselves."[37] Even in material production itself the denigration of taste had already become evident. No longer did craftsmen labor to produce painstaking work for a small appreciative market. Instead they were given over to satisfying the expanded wants of a virtually anonymous clientele which demanded only utility, not specimens of art.[38] In manners, honor and dignity were words which simply had outlived an appropriate style of life.[39]

Politically the most important general consequence of the rise of democracy, according to Tocqueville, was the high degree to which the passion for equality displaced the concern for liberty. Tocqueville credits some of the early revolutionaries with an attachment to both liberty and equality,[40] but in this he does them no especial courtesy. For it should not be supposed that Tocqueville's conception of liberty is that of the Liberal enlightenment. On the contrary, he conceived of liberty, much as Montesquieu did, largely in terms of restraint upon a monopolistic exercise of power. Thus there was liberty where clusters of aristocratic power could be brought to bear against decisions of a central monarch which were conceived to be "arbitrary," that is, unpopular or against common usage. Tocqueville's position may best be described as that of an aristocratic constitutionalist concerned with limiting the exercise of arbitrary power by distributing it among various groups high in the social hierarchy. This is evident in his discussion of liberty in the *Old Regime*, where he describes the role of the nobility, local governments, the church, and the independent judiciary, in resisting authority, as the very substance of freedom.[41]

His implicit refusal to accept the democratic definition of

liberty as expressed in modern natural right doctrines indicates that Tocqueville was not so firmly committed to historicism as a method and a moral touchstone that he believed all values to be relative. He had enough respect for the authority of history to submit to the general conditions it imposed. But he was not content simply to regard the new values which he saw in democracy as of the same intrinsic rank as the values which he held as an aristocrat. The fact that democracy engendered materialism was bad enough. Worse still was the danger that this materialism might be made a virtue. If democratic society did not exalt the romantic quest of aristocratic sensualism, it did inculcate a petty and ritualistic pursuit of the possible, capable of inspiring only a race of shopkeepers.

The reproach I address to the principle of equality is not that it leads men away in the pursuit of forbidden enjoyments, but that it absorbs them wholly in quest of those which are allowed. By these means a kind of virtuous materialism may ultimately be established in the world, which would not corrupt, but enervate, the soul and noiselessly unbend its springs of action.[42]

The danger he saw in egalitarian dogma was far less the threat to peaceful order that earlier aristocrats had emphasized than a general paralysis of the spirit. Variety and genuine individualism were, he felt, vanishing from life under the impact of democracy. Stimulated by indifference and spiritual isolation, as well as by a preoccupation with the pursuit of material well being, democratic man's latent instincts for discipline and subordination might precipitate a frantic quest for security at all costs. In the presence of a highly centralized and powerful state this quest for security might easily be answered by a tyrannical democratic Caesarism which would dwarf in oppressiveness all the tyrannies that preceded it. Equality, Tocqueville observed, was born in the worst days of the Roman empire, not because the populace wished to be emancipated but because it was accustomed to considering itself a society of equals—under the absolute sway of an emperor.[43] Similarly, those who in the heyday of the French Revolution had stood most strongly for equality and liberty were the very ones who abandoned their ideals and turned "their backs on freedom, to acquiesce in an equality of servitude under the master of all

Europe," Napoleon Bonaparte.[44] As democracy was born in envy, so did it seem to Tocqueville, its particular tragedy, its "paradox," was to end in the grip of a spiritless hunger for security which would find its just desert in a new Caesarism.

The danger, however, was not inevitable. Tocqueville indeed held that democracy was much too powerful a movement to be stopped, but, because its progress was "not yet so rapid that it cannot be guided,"[45] the dangers could be averted.

Tocqueville's various prescriptions for the maladies of democracy fall into four categories: (1) the promotion of "political liberty"; (2) the recognition and support of natural inequalities; (3) the promotion of religion; and (4) the organization of certain important facets of government and society according to the principle of functional hierarchy. Like his assessment of the dangers in democracy, the correctives Tocqueville proposed in order to provide this "guidance" were derived from an aristocratic notion of what was desirable. Wherever possible he sought to introduce aristocratic elements into democracy by manipulating democratic institutions and tendencies for aristocratic ends.

Under Tocqueville's constitutionalist definition, political liberty included voluntary association, local self-government, federalism, and the separation of powers in the central government. All these institutions, of course, were in existence in America, which led Tocqueville to assert that they were adaptable, if indeed not "naturally" intrinsic, to democracy. He thought them beneficial because as he saw them they functioned as substitutes for the limitation on monarchical power provided by feudal social organization. The democracy had "destroyed those individual powers which were able, singlehanded, to cope with tyranny."[46] In this vacuum of opposition, other forms of organization, including voluntary associations, might "take the place of the individual authority of the nobles, and the community would be protected from tyranny and license."[47] Voluntary association, as in the formation of parties and pressure groups, served to create a climate of discussion in which issues could be clarified and the power of the majority tempered by persuasion. Unlike the democratic theorists themselves, who were so concerned with dismantling a corporate society that they paid little attention to the positive role of groups, Tocqueville noted not only that interest groups could exist in democratic America, in and out of the representative framework, but that they found two important sources of stimulation from democracy. The tendency of people to regard their own interests naturally led them to make common cause with others who shared a particular interest; and the basic ideological harmony of Americans, which made differences of opinion "mere differences in hue," encouraged the formation of loosely knit and peaceable associations.[48] Tocqueville hoped that the existence of these groups would modify the extreme individualism of pure democracy. But he did not face the question of how, in the absence of American harmony, groups could ever be expected to play the same role. In this instance, Tocqueville's theory that democracy would unfold naturally in America served to obscure an important difference in historical conditions and to provide a propagandistic justification for the adoption of similar institutions in Europe. Had he been as uncompromisingly scientific as he claimed, Tocqueville would have been forced to admit that what might have served in America as a "natural" check on democracy could only have served the same purpose in Europe if imposed artificially.

This manipulative attitude also influenced his discussion of local government. Whatever belief Tocqueville had in the intrinsic value of local self-government, the reason he encouraged it was that he felt it would aid the division of functions among betters and inferiors. The democracy could be thrown the bone of local self-government and thus be led to feel it was governing itself. So long as the functions of such government were restricted to minor services, the democracy would be rendered less harmful.[49]

Tocqueville was equally "subversive" of democracy, as he conceived it, in his treatment of the role of private property. Repeatedly he warned that the egalitarian movement would not stop before the right of private property. "Can it be believed that the democracy which has overthrown the feudal system and vanquished kings will retreat before tradesmen and capitalists?"[50] And again, declaratively,

The French Revolution, which abolished all privileges and destroyed all exclusive rights, has allowed one to remain, that of property. Let not the proprietors deceive themselves, nor think that the rights of property form an insurmountable barrier because they have not as yet been surmounted; for our times are unlike any others . . . today, when the rights of property are nothing more than the last remnants of an overthrown aristocratic world; when they alone are left intact, isolated privileges amid the universal levelling of society; when they are no longer protected behind a number of still more controversible and odious rights, the case is altered . . . property will form the great field of battle.[51]

At the same time he was reassured to find that one of the great strengths of American democracy was its basis in private property, particularly in the system of small holdings. The wide distribution of property tended to make for a greater sense of responsibility. In addition it provided a way for natural inequalities to express themselves and to create the conditions for a kind of hierarchy, based upon differences in wealth, which was more congenial to the materialistic ethics of democracy than the older aristocratic forms of hierarchy.[52] Communism was the final term of equality by logical extension from that principle itself, but a democracy in which property rights were important could be arrested at a pre-communist stage because property rights created a protective social structure and responded to a social psychology, both of which were congenial to democracy. Thus again Tocqueville's assertion that the American experience indicated the natural direction of egalitarianism served him as a convenient way to make yet another suggestion designed to introduce aristocratic principles. The ease with which he was willing to make use of the very materialism he deplored in correcting the faults of democracy suggests that Tocqueville was himself a victim of the same instrumentalism which he said characterized the thinking of democratic man.

Tocqueville's advocacy of religion as a kind of antidote for democracy is inspired by a similar readiness to accept expedients. He remarks the religious origin of the idea of equality. He speaks of the revolution as a kind of reformation, he refers to equality as a dogma of belief, and he sees it as divinely supported. He goes to great lengths in order to dissociate the attack upon the clergy in the revolution from antireligiosity. He observes that democratic men are even more drawn to religion than others because of their susceptibility to nonrational and mythic beliefs. Why so much effort to join religion and democracy? Precisely because only religious belief could ultimately undo the worst effects of equality. Faith, because it would lift attention from earthly preoccupation to the contemplation of things beyond, could prevent the exaltation of sterile materialism. Tocqueville did not suggest that religion be superimposed upon or set against the materialism of democracy, but rather that materialism itself be turned into an instrument of religious education. Governments, he suggested, must "restore to men that love of the future with which religion and the state of society no longer inspire them." They must

teach the community day by day that wealth, fame, and power are the rewards of labor, that great success stands at the utmost range of long desires, and that there is nothing lasting but what is obtained by toil.

When men have accustomed themselves to foresee from afar what is likely to befall them in the world and to feed upon hopes, they can hardly confine their minds within the precise limits of life, and they are ready to break the boundary and cast their looks beyond. I do not doubt that, by training the members of a community to think of their future condition in this world, they would be gradually and unconsciously brought nearer to religious convictions. Thus the means that allow men, up to a certain point, to go without religion are perhaps, after all, the only means we still possess for bringing mankind back, by a long and roundabout path, to a state of faith.[53]

It is clear from these remarks that while Tocqueville did not mean to confuse materialism and religion, he saw in materialism a possible way to faith because it might be used to turn the mind toward the future and to relate good works with rewards. It is difficult to avoid seeing in this position not only a strongly utilitarian conception of religion, but also an acceptance of materialism. It is surely remarkable that such a value-conscious aristocrat should have sought to foster the religion of success in the belief that true religion was close behind.

Tocqueville's prescriptions for the illnesses of democracy, like his diagnosis, are designed from a Conservative, aristocratic point of view. Like Plato in the *Republic*, Tocqueville saw history as a process of degeneration, marked by the steady growth of appetite, and due to culminate in universal materialism and envy. To check this development, it would be necessary to modify and thwart the natural tendencies of egalitarianism by making use of egalitarian attitudes and institutions to block their worst consequences. The fact that these attitudes do not reflect the self-understanding of democracy should not disqualify them from a claim to consideration, but any such consideration must reckon with the Conservative character of Tocqueville's thought if his analysis is to be properly evaluated. The importance of this point of view to Tocqueville's work in general and his analysis of equality in particular cannot be overemphasized. It is true that his general acuteness and his awareness of his own value premises are admirably well developed. In some respects it is impossible to say of him that he was "limited" by the perspective of his time or his birth. When he paid careful attention, for example, to the change in inheritance customs from primogeniture to multiple partition,[54] he was simply remarking, as a singularly probing social scientist, one of the manifestly important aspects of the decline of feudalism. Nevertheless, it would be a mistake to impute to Tocqueville the intentions of "value-neutral" historiography. In his work there is a continual interplay between observation and evaluation: cause and responsibility are often two sides of the same coin, and actors, institutions, and customs are assigned their relative roles in the strategy of history precisely with respect to the values they promote or deny. Tocqueville paid scarcely any attention to a number of historical tendencies which loom rather large in retrospect. One serious instance of how a particular inattention affected his assessment of historical tendencies is his prediction of civil war in the United States. He was "right," of course, in thinking there would be one, except that he thought the war would be waged between Negroes and whites.[55] Had he taken into account factors other than the principle of equality, such as nationalism and sectionalism, which also promoted antagonism, he might have made a more balanced prediction. Nor did his recognition of the tensions which had developed between agrarian and urban interests lead him to examine the more complex and more important problem of the general impact of capitalism and industrialization upon society, or the compounding of these and other developments in nineteenth century imperialism. And, although he was the admired correspondent of the young Count Gobineau, he did not foresee the historical significance which the racist doctrines of Gobineau and others were to assume. It is not simply that such factors were outside his scope of interest, but rather that to some extent at least they were simply not illuminated by the light in which Tocqueville regarded history.

KIERKEGAARD, STIRNER, AND NIETZSCHE: THE ONE AND THE MANY

Although Tocqueville could only contemplate the fulfillment of democratic tendencies with apprehension, others who understood these tendencies in much the same way came to think that they might contain a blessing in disguise. Kierkegaard, Stirner, and Nietzsche all condemned egalitarianism as the bearer of mediocrity, materialism, and conformity, but they also saw the possibility that a wholesale levelling might clear the ground for the emergence of a new individualism, higher than any petty egoism that went by the same name, and far more attractive to men of insight than the appeals of humanitarian democracy.

Kierkegaard made only one or two pronouncements on social equality, but in these he left no doubt of his position. The present age, he wrote, was one in which the passion for equality had succeeded in overturning all historical precedent. The dialectic of the past, as he put it, had consisted of a relation of leaders to followers in which the mass existed for the sake of the great individual. The dialectic of the present made the leader the representative of the mass and thereby subordinated the great individual to the collectivity.[56]

The new power of the masses, Kierkegaard asserted, had already brought a severe degeneration in the quality of social life. The "public," an abstraction composed of unreal individuals, was held up as the only source of values. The press poked at every scandal to appease the insatiable curiosity of its phantom master.[57] Politicians would soon also bend entirely to the popular will. Even the most mediocre "establishment" was preferable to the authority of public opinion, but politics could not be insulated against the general trend. The "rational State" was coming to an end, Kierkegaard prophesied, and the style of politics was bound to change: "The art of statesmanship will become a game. Every-thing will turn upon getting the multitude pollinated, and after that getting them to vote on his side, with noise, with torches and with weapons, indifferent, absolutely indifferent, as to whether they understand anything or no." [58]

Yet, precisely because of these changes for the worst, Kierke-gaard could hope that the perennial appeal of the religious way of life might become all the greater. If all values were buried in a senseless pursuit of pleasure, might the result not be a degree of boredom in itself educational? Levelling, after all, was only the final phase of a long and ill-conceived effort to solve in worldly ways problems which could only really be approached religiously. The world is inherently the realm of difference and inequalities, of prodigious varieties of more and less. The vain attempts of social reformers to change this reality could only be ridiculed. What difference did it make to try this or that panacea when nothing could alter stubborn reality? One reform is tried out and fails and another appears only to fail in turn. Now

comes the new ministry which does less for the beer-sellers, more for the candle-makers, and then you take more from landowners and bring the proletariat more to the fore, equalize priests and deacons, and above all make a humpback watchman and a bowlegged black-smith's apprentice into straight and equal men.[59]

Faced with the repeated failure of all schemes of social reform, might people not at last consider the prospect of eternity as the only radical alternative to the limitations of worldly life? The levelling spirit would seek to destroy all independence of mind, but the individual might see in this threat an ultimate danger and might respond to it by turning to God. "The sharp scythe of the leveler makes it possible for every one individually to leap over the blade—and behold, it is God who waits." [60] In the past the confrontation of man and God has been channeled through many intermediaries. When those intermediaries are gone, the oppor-tunity for faith will be all the greater. "God will himself come directly into relation with the single individuals, not through ab-stractions, neither through representative persons, but God will himself, so to speak, undertake to educate the countless indi-viduals of the generation." [61]

It was even possible that the religious and the secular alternatives might come to confront each other on the plane of equality itself, once the coming generations grew to understand the meaning of the levelling they had experienced:

. . . there would be present the two greatest possible contrasts, striving with one another about the interpretation of this phenomenon. On the one hand *communism*, which would say, This is the correct worldly way, there must not be the slightest difference between man and man; riches, art, learning, rule, etc., etc., are of the evil one, all men ought to be equal like laborers in a factory, like cattle in a barnyard, partake of the same dimensions, etc., etc. On the other hand *pietism*, which would say, This is the right Christian way, that one makes no difference between man and man, we ought to be brothers and sisters, have all in common: riches, art, learning, etc., etc., are of the evil one: all men should be equal as it once was in little Christenfeld [an example of Christian communism] all dressed alike, all pray at fixed times, marry by casting lots, go to bed at the stroke of the clock, partake of the same food, out of one dish, and at the same time, etc., etc.[62]

For Kierkegaard the subtle difference between these two versions of equality was all-important. The Christian, in being a Christian, is already so indifferent to worldly distinctions that he takes no notice of inequalities that do in fact distinguish one individual from another. Nor would he wish to make men alike in worldly ways. The Christian is not troubled by worldly inequality or by the opposition of power, talent, or numbers. He does not need to struggle for an opportunity to succeed or prove himself as good as someone else. "In a worldly sense one must wait in the tension of uncertainty to see what follows after suffering, whether victory follows. In a Christian sense there is nothing to wait for, victory was long ago placed in one's hands by faith." [63] The contrast was clear to Kierkegaard; it might now become clear to others.

If levelling played a potentially benevolent role for Kierkegaard, it played an indispensable role in the development of the kind of individualism that Max Stirner advocated. Stirner followed Hegel in conceiving the process of history as the gradual unfolding of perfect freedom. Christianity he believed, had announced freedom in spiritual terms, and the Reformation and the French Revolution had brought it closer to complete realization.

But the democratic revolutions had resulted in a powerful society which stood as the last barrier to individual emancipation.

Stirner identified three phases in the development of the egalitarianism of the French Revolution. The liberalism of the bourgeoisie asserted that men had equal rights as citizens but that property should be the reward of the deserving. Socialism arose as a second phase of liberalism to demand an end to economic egoism and the "slavery of labor."[64] But social liberalism was in its turn as incomplete as political liberalism. Socialists conceived of man as a worker and property as the key to his fulfillment. In addition it brought regimentation: "Before the supreme *ruler*, the sole *commander*, we had all become equal, equal persons, *i.e.* nullities."[65] A third, humane liberalism therefore arose whose advocates sought to replace the conception of man as a citizen and a worker with the more universal conception of man as a creature with a destiny and with needs and faculties transcending his political and economic role.

Even this humane liberalism would not provide a final emancipation. It was only the penultimate stage in the realization of freedom and it raised fresh barriers to be overcome. Just because humane liberalism conceived of man in abstract terms—of man in general rather than men in particular—it provided the basis for a universal moral orthodoxy which was bound to be a coercive instrument against the individual. Humane liberalism was therefore only "the last metamorphosis of the Christian religion," putting universal man in place of universal spirit. It would be no less oppressive than Christianity had been because it provided the secular state with a standard for moral conduct which could be used to stifle nonconformity.[66]

Against all these forms of liberalism Stirner posed what he regarded as the last necessary step in the fulfillment of history: the apotheosis of the self. Liberals had tried to establish universal right in universal nature. Socialism had removed one fetter to impose another: "Communism rightly revolts against the pressure that I experience from individual proprietors; but still more horrible is the might that it puts in the hands of the collectivity."[67] Stirner did not shrink from the consequences of his rejections: "it is right for *me*," he proclaimed, "therefore it is right."[68] If necessary, let

rights to property be settled by the war of all against all; if necessary, let others defend themselves against the demands of the self.
History seeks for man, and that man is "the individual, the finite,
the unique one." [69]

Like Kierkegaard and Stirner, Nietzsche attacked levelling
tendencies—"this brutalising of man into a pygmy with equal
rights and claims" [70]—yet at the same time considered them a
necessary step in the development of a higher man. But egalitarian reform had by his time become so associated with the cause
of humanitarianism that Nietzsche feared his own teachings would
be confused with those of the reformers. "Some preach my
doctrine of life," Zarathustra declares, "and are at the same time
preachers of equality and tarantulas . . . They wish to hurt those
who now have power." Higher men should not be deceived:

> I do not want to be mixed up and confused with these preachers
> of equality. For, to *me*, justice speaks thus: 'Men are not equal.'
> Nor shall they become equal! What would my love of the overman
> be if I spoke otherwise? [71]

Did Zarathustra mean to take the side of the aristocrats against
the commoners? "Our 'good society'?" he answers, "It is indeed
better to live among hermits and goatherds than among our
gilded, false, painted mob—even if they call themselves 'good
society,' even if they call themselves 'nobility.' " [72] Nietzsche was
still more scornful of those who peddled so-called aristocratic
values in the form of what he called the "mendacious race
swindle." [73] The reactionaries were no better than the levellers.
It was a case of "mob above and mob below." [74]

When Nietzsche attacked the belief in equality, it was not to
defend social aristocracy but to make it possible to create a new
hierarchy of values.[75] Egalitarianism, he believed, had originated
in a departure from the natural order and had brought into being
a morality contrary to nature. Before it would be possible to
transcend a merely natural morality, it would be necessary to
expose equality as a departure from nature and to train out of
human character and intellect the dishonesty and cunning that
had made the illusion of equality seem a value.

In nature, he theorized, values must have been dictated by the
strong barbarian groups to subjugated weaker groups, perhaps

debilitated by culture. In the course of time, those enslaved to the barbarian races, inflamed by declassé aristocrats and power-seekers, must have risen in revolt against their masters. The ideology of this slave revolt is exactly the reverse of the ideology of the strong. When the new morality is triumphant, the "trans-valuation of values" has occurred. In place of the inborn right of the superior to rule, the masses raise the sovereignty of the people. In place of glory and honor they put pity and love.

The earliest systematic expression of the slave morality occurs in Judaism and Christianity. When Christianity triumphed over paganism, the new morality established its hold over the whole of Western civilization. From then on, the superiority of the lowly went unchallenged: "the wretched are alone the good; the poor, the weak, the lowly, are alone the good; the suffering, the needy, the sick, the loathsome . . . are to be saved, and not the powerful and rich." Pagan pleasures become Christian vices; pride yields to prudence as a test of will; boldness is replaced by cunning; and Sabbatarian narcosis puts an end to heroic contest.[76]

But the triumph of Christianity is a victory for the slave morality only in the sphere of ultimate ends. When the masses are no longer satisfied by promises of far-off reward (and far-off revenge), they turn upon their masters, including even the priests who had announced the slave morality in the first place. The French Revolution opens the last great effort of the slaves to make their triumph in values a triumph in fact, by despoiling the possessors of privilege and wealth and degrading all culture to their own level. Democracy, Liberalism, Socialism, Anarchism—all are only variations of the levelling spirit signifying that the masses will not be content with triumphs in the sphere of ethics. The revolutionary movements are only advanced expressions of Christianity, except that the newer versions of the "pity morality" exalt immediate happiness rather than eternal bliss.[77]

When the slave morality takes political form, the challenge to the natural values becomes more apparent than ever. The slave morality, as expressed in the various doctrines of equality, exalts precisely what is worst in man—his weakness in the face of frustration and envy. Fittingly, Utilitarianism in philosophy is the counterpart of egalitarianism in politics. The idea that man is a pleasure-seeker, and the ideal of the good of the greatest number, capture perfectly the urge to materialism and mediocrity which moves the masses to revolt. The explanation of justice and punishment on grounds of utility similarly serves as a convenient mask for the aggressiveness and vengefulness that lie only just below the surface of the egalitarian mentality.[78]

The very fact that the egalitarian ideal seemed so near to complete fulfillment provided Nietzsche, as it had Kierkegaard and Stirner, with a certain degree of hope for the future. If the disguise of the slave morality could be penetrated, the last remaining illusion would be dispelled. Corrosive criticism and honesty even in self-appraisal could prepare the way for the appearance of an "overman." The overman was not to be a reinstatement of some primitive barbarian character but an entirely new type of man who would have been restored only to innocence. The overman would employ the same forces of nature that had given rise to aristocrats and egalitarians, in order to transcend this level of choice entirely. With the help of honesty and innocence, he would seek instead to create his own new values.

The overman could not be produced by social or political reform. Nietzsche rejected all political and social approaches to resolving the problem of values just as did Kierkegaard and Stirner. Nietzsche sought to attack them at their source when he denounced the Hobbesian glorification of the state and security as the worship of the "new idol." No sooner had the old God been vanquished, said Zarathustra, than the Leviathan was established in his place. But the state was no mortal god; it was only a mortal monster. "State is the name of the coldest of all cold monsters. Coldly it tells lies too; and this lie crawls out of its mouth. 'I, the state, am the people: on earth there is nothing greater than I: the ordering finger of God am I'—thus roars the monster." The state claims to serve life by providing security, but the life it exalts is only a slow dying. For real life, life that is an effort to transcend mere existence, the state is only an obstacle.[79] Might a solitary individual find politics an outlet for creativity? Nietzsche does not say, but his attitude toward Napoleon—"that synthesis of Overman and Monster" [80]—indicates that at least one great empire-builder did not meet the test.

Indeed, Nietzsche did not define precisely what he hoped the overman would be, except to characterize him as a man who would accept nature but seek always to impose his unique stamp on his own endowments. Plainly he did not think just any expression of the will to power the sign of an overman. He realized that the overcoming of moral inhibitions would make it possible not for one but for two new men to appear—the overman and the "last man."[81] He knew the dangers of unchaining the evil instincts or "wild dogs" in man.[82] He seemed to suggest that the proper response to mass society lay in the direction of individual creativity, but he did not come to grips with the question of whether this individual creativity might coexist with mass society. It remained for Freud to consider this problem and to propose just such a coexistence.

FREUD: EQUALITY AS MYTH

The Conservative character of Freud's understanding of equality contrasts sharply with his humanistic effort to assist mankind to emancipate itself from the hold of irrationality and of internal and external forces acting beyond the control of man himself. This contrast, however, is essential to any adequate understanding of Freud and to an appreciation of the latest and perhaps most relevant turning in the Conservative concept of equality.

Like the less ambivalent prophets of emancipation who preceded him, Freud regarded the *intellectual* history of humanity as a progressive advance from animism to religion and finally to science.[83] Psychoanalysis, as the science of individual and social psychology, represented the last great step. Copernicus and Darwin had shattered animism and religion in the understanding of the natural universe; psychoanalysis would deal the final blow to the immature human ego.[84] The revelations of this new doctrine, at once a science, a therapy, and a philosophy of life, would make men aware of their limitations and of the sources of their involuntary delusions, evasions, and feelings of guilt and anxiety. Once enlightened, they would be enabled to live realistically, free of the burdens of guilt and ignorance, free from unwilling subservience to instinctive drives. They would be compelled to reconcile themselves to the necessary sacrifice of instinctual gratification for the sake of maintaining life and civilization, but these sacrifices, as acts of conscious will, would not entail the psychic injury of repression.

This emancipation was open to individuals, although not to all individuals in the same degree,[85] but it was not open to society. Although Freud held that "from the very first, Individual Psychology is at the same time Social Psychology as well," [86] he distinguished between the prospects open to individuals and those open to society. Upon superior individuals psychoanalysis could confer the direct and supreme benefit of consciousness and freedom; to the inferior masses, it could offer only the indirect and lesser benefit of government by their superiors in reason. Domination, according to Freud, is inevitable in all social relations. "One instance of the innate and ineradicable inequality of men is their tendency to fall into two classes of leaders and followers." The followers "stand in need of an authority which will make decisions for them and to which they will for the most part offer an unqualified submission." The utopian expectation, as Freud saw it, is not that all men should become free and rational, but that an elite should arise which would govern society in accordance with the "dictatorship of reason." [87]

It is just as impossible to do without government of the masses by a minority as it is to dispense with coercion in the work of civilization, for the masses are lazy and unintelligent, they have no love for instinctual renunciation, they are not to be convinced of its inevitability by argument . . . It is only by the influence of individuals who can set an example, whom the masses recognize as their leaders, that they can be induced to submit to the labours and renunciations on which the existence of culture depends. All is well if these leaders are people of superior insight into what constitute the necessities of life, people who have attained the height of mastering their own instinctual wishes.[88]

Superior individuals might heal the wounds of past traumas, repressions, and defensive reaction-formations, but society could never surmount the awful circumstances in which it originated. These circumstances, expressed in the myth of the slaying of the primal father, are the fountain of all law and authority and, at the same time, of social coercion and unfreedom.[89] No constitutional or moral modifications could successfully or permanently alter the basic form of society. All revolutions, no matter what their substantive aims, merely re-enacted the primal crime and were fated always to be followed by a restoration of coercive authority.[90]

For Freud as for Hobbes, there are only two real alternatives—civilization, with domination and repression, or the war of all against all.[91] The very survival of society is predicated both upon repression and upon the existence of certain emotional relations, apart from common interest, which contradict individual freedom and self-consciousness. If all men could be expected to attain the rational prophylaxis of psychoanalysis, then possibly an entirely different form of society might develop. Men like themselves, Freud wrote to Einstein, were pacifists by nature,[92] but he held out no hope that society as a whole could attain a similarly lofty outlook. Even in the best of circumstances, where leadership was in the hands of a (psychoanalytically) mature and wise elite, social relations would remain fundamentally irrational and repressive.

Underlying Freud's distinction between the prospects for society as a whole and for individuals is his belief that men are not equal with respect to their capacities for understanding. They are unequal in other respects as well. Even the two sexes, despite the denials of the feminists, exhibit fundamentally different psychological characteristics which make it unscientific to regard men and women as "completely equal in position and worth."[93] Different basic libidinal types account for differences of personality and character.[94] Inequality in rational capacity is the primary ground of inequality in social relations. Even where authority does not in fact correspond to superiority in wisdom, obedience is predicated on the illusion of superiority. The family, as the nuclear model of society, provides the first and fundamental form of all social inequality. In society one man will convince another, not by rational persuasion, but by "setting an example" or by assuming the role toward the other which in the family is taken by the father.[95] As the domination of the children by the father rests on irrational obedience, so does the authority of the political leader over the followers. For Freud, in effect, the masses are society's children. Although the father, or father-surrogate, may not in fact be gifted with superior reason, he is thought to be so gifted. He is obeyed because of his supposed omniscience and because, in fact, he is able, by irrational persuasion, to guide opinion and conduct.

From a scientific point of view, it follows that the notion of human equality, with respect both to natural capacities and to social relations, cannot be anything but an illusion. Illusions, however, are never without foundation in reality. The illusion of equality expresses an idealized notion of what is actually the case, but this idealization performs an extremely important function. Society, like the family, rests on the illusion that all the lesser members share equally in the love of the father. In the church and in the army, the institutions which Freud takes as his models for all organized social groups, "the same illusion holds good of there being a head—in the Catholic Church Christ, in an army, its Commander-in-Chief—who loves all the individuals in the group with an equal love." [96] In the church "believers call themselves brothers in Christ, that is, brothers through the love which Christ has for them." The same is true for the army: "The Commander-in-Chief is a father who loves all his soldiers equally, and for that reason they are comrades among themselves." [97]

This apparently simple formulation, however, is the result of a complicated set of changes in attitudes which, according to Freud, necessarily occurs in social history and in family relations. Ideally each individual would like to be the leader, to take the place of the father and so enjoy the pre-eminence and privileges. He "learns" that this involves too great a risk and therefore seeks a psychological gratification of the same impulse which need not involve such disastrous consequences. If only he can attain the love of the leader, he and the leader will be as one, and the pre-eminence of the leader will become, in a psychological sense, his also. Alas, even this is somewhat beyond his reach, for there are competitors for the love of the leader. From envy of the superior he turns to envy of his co-competitors. When he and the others realize that no one of them can hope to possess the love of the leader exclusively, the demand for equality arises.

Unless the demand is fulfilled, their mutual rivalry threatens perpetual fratricide. This threat is only overcome by the fabrication of the illusion that the leader loves all of them equally.

Because of this supposed common possession of the love of the leader, each of the followers identifies himself with the leader and with his fellows. Equality is thus an illusion, but an illusion grounded in a psychologically real relation. It functions to preserve an arrangement which, apart from its psychological representation, is in reality a relation of domination. The continued existence of society requires both actual domination and the illusion of equality. Without either of them, mutual envy among the followers themselves and their collective envy of the privileges of the powerful would erupt into violent antagonism. Society would then be too weak internally to withstand the slightest external threat. Indeed it might collapse even without an external threat, because the ties of rational self-interest are too weak to sustain order without the support of emotional ties. Thus even as Freud, in the name of science, exposes equality as an illusion, he regards this illusion as an indispensable constituent of social order. Even though it celebrates a spurious value which is in reality only an idealistic rationalization of brute envy, the belief in equality has psychological validity.

In several different contexts Freud expounds this viewpoint in an attempt to account for the historic development of the idea of equality and to join this development to specifically psychoanalytic theory.

In his letter to Einstein on the causes of war, Freud suggests that the idea of equality developed out of the struggle for power in which social life originated. At first, he speculated, conflicts of interest and opinion must all have been settled by violence. "Domination by whoever had the greater might" was probably "the original state of things." In principle this condition lasted through the invention of tools, except that technological advance made intellect a force to be considered in the struggle for power.[98] At some point, the weak probably banded together to challenge the few who were superior in strength and intellect, and when they succeeded communal law and right must have been first established. Law, which had represented the strength of the few superiors, now stood for the might of the community. This community, however, could only have remained viable while it was composed of equally strong individuals. In fact conditions are never so appropriate. "The community comprises elements of unequal strength—men and women, parents and children—and soon, as a result of war and conquest, it also comes to include victors and vanquished, who turn into masters and slaves." Law "becomes an expression of the unequal degrees of power" in the community.[99] Democracy is overthrown and the community reverts to its previous oligarchic form.

While oligarchy is closer to the prescriptions of nature, as a guardian of social stability it is weak because it rests on sheer strength and is therefore liable to be overthrown whenever the weak can be persuaded to band together. Society therefore takes a major step toward social stability when the notion of equality is made an adjunct to domination. Psychological equality answers the demand of the weak for real equality, which would otherwise be unanswerable and threatening. The illusion of equality serves to pacify the rebellious, and the result is a state of society both appropriate and enduring.

In *Totem and Taboo* Freud sets forth a similar historical theory in which his argument is couched in more specifically psychoanalytic terms. The "hypothesis" of the primal crime joins "static" psychoanalytic theory to the historic account of the rise of psychological equality. Government first arises out of the superiority in strength of the primal father. Motivated primarily by sexual envy, the sons band together to kill the father. This common motivation at once brings the brothers together, and yet makes it impossible for their union to last beyond the act of parricide.

Sexual need does not unite men; it separates them. Though the brothers had joined forces in order to overcome the father, each was the other's rival among the women. Each one wanted to have them all to himself like the father, and the new organization would have perished. For there was no longer any one stronger than all the rest who could have successfully assumed the role of the father.[100]

The prohibition of incest inhibited the fratricidal tendencies of the democratic union, but it did not remove either the underlying

desire or the fact of its frustration.[101] Much time must have
elapsed before bitterness abated and the brothers established in
the place of the father "an ideal . . . having as a content the fullness of power and the freedom from restriction of the conquered
primal father, as well as the willingness to subject themselves to
him." Original democratic equality "could no longer be retained."
This ideal is that of an omnipotent God to whom all men are
equally and utterly subordinate.[102] The real conditions of inequality which had been overthrown are partly restored through the
institution of separate families in which the brothers, as *pater-
familiae*, enjoy the prerogatives of the primal father on a smaller
scale. But the longing after absolute power, and the unconscious
recognition that it cannot be attained, express themselves in the
worship of the tribal god.[103]

Freud's discussion of the rise of equality out of the primal
crime is renewed in *Group Psychology and the Analysis of the
Ego*, where it is explicitly linked to the psychology of modern social groups and to the psychoanalytic theory of identification.
After recounting the argument of his earlier work, Freud goes on
to suggest that the re-establishment of domination on the limited
scale of the family was only the beginning of the full re-establishment of the original inequality. It was inevitable that one man
should again assume the role of the social father and restore the
original single-family structure, because otherwise the anarchic
tendencies of egalitarianism would destroy society altogether.
The fact is that the desire for equality is "simply an idealistic
remodelling of the state of affairs in the primal horde, where all
of the sons knew that they were equally persecuted by the primal
father, and feared him equally." [104] In forming the totemic community of brothers, all with equal rights and all bounded by the
totem prohibitions, they succeeded only in repressing temporarily
the desire which each felt to replace the father. The creation of
the family was a means of extending this possibility to all of
them on a small scale, but this meager concession could not contain their desires for absolute power. As democracy had given
way to a society of separate and antagonistic families, the family
society had in its turn yielded to a restoration of absolute domination by one father figure. Finally "the group appears to us as a

revival of the primal horde," in early history as in modern times.[105] *"Many equals, who can identify themselves with one another, and a single person superior to them all*—that is the situation we find realized in groups which are capable of subsisting."*[106]

The stable society combining real domination and psychological equality is made possible by the growth of "aim-inhibited" sexual drives. The whole of life, according to Freud, is a perpetual combat between two forces—*Eros,* seeking to preserve organic matter and to create ever larger organic units, and *Thanatos,* seeking the disintegration and death of all organic unity. *Eros* in the form of the sexual drive brings about the union of the sexes and the procreation of life; in its aim-inhibited form it creates "libidinal ties" which unite men in society.[107]

With this social function of *Eros* in mind, Freud suggested to Einstein that the way to modify aggressiveness was to bring love into play against it. By "love" Freud here meant the libidinal ties of aim-inhibited sexuality through which social unity is achieved. In every group there is a dual form of asexual love: all the members identify with a leader or father surrogate, and they identify with each other through this common relation to the leader. Of the Catholic Church Freud writes: "there is no doubt that the tie which unites each individual with Christ is also the cause of the tie which unites them with one another." [108] So long as men live without such ties there is antagonism, and domination is resented and felt as domination. Once the ties are created, illwill disappears.

The whole of this intolerance vanishes, temporarily or permanently, as the result of the formation of a group, and in a group . . . individuals behave as though they were uniform, tolerate other people's peculiarities, put themselves on an equal level with them, and have no feeling of aversion towards them. Such a limitation of narcissism can . . . only be produced by one factor, a libidinal tie with other people.[109]

To explain how this libidinal tie, or identification, rests on "the nature of the tie with the leader," Freud uses the psychoanalytic theory of the relation of the ego to the ego ideal. The ego "introjects" the ego ideal into itself. A primary group is therefore one in which a number of individuals substitute the same object for their ego ideal, identify themselves with this ego ideal, and thereby identify with one another.[110] A primary group is not ordinarily entered into merely out of admiration of the leader or out of common interest, as in the case of a group which elects a leader because he represents a point of view to which most of the group subscribes. The demand for equality arises in early childhood and finds expression in libidinal ties. In a nursery, children come to regard each other as companions only after they are brought by harsh experience to the recognition that no one of them can hope to receive the love of the nurse exclusively. Identification of the children with one another develops "as a reaction to the initial envy with which the older child receives the younger one."

The elder child would certainly like to put its successor jealously aside, to keep it away from the parents, to rob it of all its privileges; but in face of the fact that this child . . . is loved by the parents in just the same way, and in consequence of the impossibility of maintaining its hostile attitude without damaging itself, it is forced into identifying itself with the other children. So there grows up in the troop of children a communal or group feeling, which is then further developed at school. The first demand made by this reaction-formation is for justice, for equal treatment for all . . . If one cannot be the favourite himself, at all events nobody else shall be the favourite.[111]

The demand for equality is not to be taken at face value, but rather as an outgrowth of frustrated egoism, as an expression of grudging selfishness making a virtue out of failure. From the nursery to the factory, all demands for equality represent a process that starts with individual failures to find gratification and ends in unconscious efforts to enforce similar deprivations upon others. The cry for social justice is always inspired by the wish to impose an equality of frustration:

No one must want to put himself forward, every one must be the same and have the same. Social justice means that we deny ourselves many things so that others may have to do without them as well . . . This demand for equality is at the root of social conscience and the sense of duty.[112]

As critical theory, the psychoanalytic notion of equality claims to unmask Liberal and Socialist values as idealistic reconstruc-

tions of egoistic, covetous sentiments. Liberalism disguises the
desire of the mass for an authority which it could not normally
possess and for rights to possess and enjoy which, in reality,
would make deprivation and prohibition universal. The Liberal
argument that men ought to have equal rights because they are
equally capable of rational understanding is rejected as without
scientific justification. Against the Socialists, Freud argues that to
achieve abundance for all would not be to end inequality. The
Bolsheviks "hope to be able to cause human aggressiveness to disappear by guaranteeing the satisfaction of all material needs and
by establishing equality in other respects among all the members
of the community. That, in my opinion, is an illusion."[113] Communism repeats the messianic promises of Judaism and medieval
Christianity with no more chance of fulfilling them. Like the
religions, Communism seeks "to compensate its believers for the
sufferings and deprivations of their present life." [114] The root
causes of deprivation, however, will remain long after material
goods are made available to all; and the necessarily inegalitarian
structure of authority will not be affected by changes in the
relations of production.

In effect, Freud recognized that the demand for equality must
in some way be met if there is to be stability and unity in society.
Society needs both a structure of authority, which cannot be
egalitarian, and ties of identification; Freudian doctrine makes it
possible to have both by promoting psychological equality as a
complement to actual inequality. Freud did believe, as a recent
commentator has suggested, that the only effective way to combat aggressiveness was to enlarge the sphere in which love could
find expression; but he did not believe that to increase the role
of love, in the form of aim-inhibited sexual relations, the only
appropriate social form of love, would decrease the degree of
domination in society.[115] Indeed, as he understood it, the function of social love was to serve as an ally of domination. In his
discussion of *Eros,* Freud was reminded of the Platonic *Symposium* where Aristophanes describes love as an original whole-
ness lost in the creation of separate individuals, and the quest for
love as the effort to restore the wholeness that has been lost.[116]
Freudian *Eros* has the similar goal of reuniting the separate ele-

ments of organic life in society,[117] but this reunification presupposes an order of domination and makes the achievement of love in society an illusion. For Freud, as for the other Conservative theorists of equality, the assumption of human depravity, out of which equality arises, is also the basis for the conclusion that domination is necessary for social stability. Since equality is not considered an ideal, but only a derivative of the passions, it is bound to be subordinated to the requirement of order.

Freud's solution, couched as it was in the most modern of all systems of social science, thus returned the Conservative conception of equality to its Platonic origin. The royal lie would reassure the masses of their ideal equality with the superior classes, but power would be wielded only by a philosophically trained elite.

For all its similarities to the most ancient of Conservative prescriptions, Freud's conclusion has a disquieting relevance to contemporary conditions. To dismiss the notion of a mass society, managed and manipulated by benevolent elites, as a figment of the Conservative imagination would be to ignore too much of modern experience. At the same time, it is sobering to consider how many elements of Freud's theory are familiar from earlier Conservative theories composed in very different circumstances, and how much it is itself vitiated by its ambivalent attempt to undercut egalitarianism as science while accepting it as a necessary support of any social order.

CHAPTER EIGHT

The Socialist Dilemma

B EFORE MARX initiated an intellectual restoration, the discussion of equality in the Socialist thought of the earlier decades of the nineteenth century bore only superficial resemblance to previous Socialist egalitarianism. Socialist literature either reproduced Liberal notions of equality or adopted the reactionary belief in the necessity for hierarchy. With the exception of Cabet, whose complete utopianism sets him apart from the others, the social philosophers considered by Marx and Engels to be the precursors of scientific Socialism do not espouse a clearly Socialist conception of equality. Communism of possessions, to take a central point, is rejected by Fourier and Saint-Simon, as well as by Proudhon. The notion of a physical equality of need, which had been introduced by Mably and Babeuf as a kind of Socialist counterpart of the Liberal notion of an equality in mental and physical capacity, is also either rejected or ignored.

Marx and Engels were quick to perceive that as far as equality is concerned none of these theorists took a truly Socialist position. Proudhon is exposed by Marx, and Dühring by Engels, as Liberals in proletarian disguise. Had they been contemporaries, it is not unlikely that Saint-Simon and Fourier would have been similarly criticized for their partially Liberal, partially Conservative attitude towards equality. As it was, Marx and Engels were more interested in incorporating certain of the ideas of these "utopian Socialists" into their own "scientific" theory—in particular the dialectical historicism of Saint-Simon, and the theories of class distinctions and class antagonisms put forth by both Saint-Simon and Fourier, each in his own fashion.

In this process of rejection and assimilation Marxism acquired a theory of equality which in many respects is very similar to the earlier religious versions of Socialist egalitarianism, but which adds a notion of technological-economic determinism completely without precedent in pre-nineteenth century Socialist thought. This theory was set forth as the scientific Socialist substitute for the Liberal egalitarianism which was espoused alike by Marx's Liberal and Socialist contemporaries. From the point of view of the history of egalitarian thought, the Marxian formulation is especially interesting because it is the first Socialist conception of equality to be developed in explicit opposition to a Liberal concept. The differences between the two doctrines therefore become quite apparent. Perhaps the most comprehensive difference is that for Marx the achievement of equality was to render all forms of domination and individual antagonism completely obsolete, whereas, for the Liberals, equality could never be more than a context for authority and an expression of individual competition. In the Marxian scheme of history, Socialist equality would push far beyond the transitory phase of Liberal equality of rights into an era in which egoistic individualism would be replaced by an identification not only of interests but of human character. The groundwork for this transformation of moral values lay in the attainment of material abundance. The emancipation of mankind from the drudgery of specialized labor, and the achievement of economic abundance, would end the division of labor, with its separation of men into classes of status, wealth, vocation, and power. A new society would arise in which men would be free of concern for material goods, and so versatile that they could perform any number of occupations. In these conditions government would have only administrative functions, since, according to Marx, the sole reason for the existence of the coercive state is antagonism among individuals and classes. Economic progress would therefore provide the necessary conditions for the expression of the truly human qualities: scientific consciousness through the knowledge of the laws of social development; universal creativity in the exercise by every individual of his manifold talents and interests; and, in the place of egoism, egalitarian love.

Liberals, considerably less millenarian in their goals, were rather attached to the values Marx condemned. They did not conceive of the elimination of antagonism, and with it of government, as a real possibility. Moreover, the fundamental individualism of Liberalism stands against the effort to overcome all egoism, all separate individuality. Self-interest and self-fulfillment in privacy are for Liberals both assumptions of fact concerning human nature and values as expressions of human uniqueness. Liberal theorists tended to assume that all differences in status, wealth, and authority, except for those due to unfair privileges or handicaps, should be respected because they reflect differences of effort. The difficulty of reconciling this point of view with the actual conditions of modern industrial economy was well exposed by Marx, but he failed to appreciate the set of values it embodied because he considered it a merely transitory reflection of a stage of production rather than a description of what is essential to man as man. At the same time, the Marxian critique of Liberalism had the intellectually salutary effect of making it clear that, next to Socialism, Liberal egalitarianism is a sober, compromising attempt to adjust certain absolute "natural" values to the conditions of a fallen state where reason must be safeguarded against passion and self-interest continually enlightened.

Although Marx himself emphasized those aspects of his theory which deal with the conditions for the achievement of Socialist equality, no understanding of Marxian Socialism is complete without a consideration of the more traditional elements which he combined with his theory of technological and economic determinism. Between Müntzer and Winstanley on the one hand and Marx on the other, there are remarkable affinities which tend nowadays to be overshadowed by what is peculiarly Marxian. An important link in the understanding of this continuity is the work of the young Hegel. Because this phase of Hegel's work stresses religious themes, it exhibits what is common both to the religious Socialists of an earlier period and to Marx, in more explicit terms than the latter day Socialists might wish to acknowledge. In terms of goals and values there is scarcely any difference between the Hegel of "The Spirit of Christianity and its Fate" [1] and the Marx of "Private Property and Communism," [2] with the almost semantic qualification that what Marx calls man's true essence, Hegel describes as a divine spirit. Like Marx after him, the young Hegel propounded a theory of historical progress due to culminate in an age of love. Hegel's vision of the future was a "reunion of the separated" which would put an end to domination and alienation. History was the process in which man as material object and man in his spiritual essence had been separated but would finally come together again. Hegel too regarded Liberalism, expressed for him in Kantian ethics and Kantian logic, as an episode in this historical evolution. Like Marx, the young Hegel believed that love would only be fully realized if property could be removed as an obstacle to a total identification in love. But Hegel did not so emphasize the property question that it became the overriding consideration, after which all other obstacles would disintegrate. Hegel saw acutely that the fundamental issue was not property but individuality. He recognized that property was one of the concrete forms of individuality (even if it were to be held in common), but he also insisted that love, to be complete, would have to extend its sway not only over property but over all individualism—in politics, in organized religion, and in the human mind and character. There is more than a hint of a similar recognition in the early work of Marx. For Hegel, however, the recognition of the obstacles to love cast a pall of disillusionment over his otherwise progressist theory of history. Because he did not turn away from these obstacles, Hegel had a better glimpse of the darker side of Socialist egalitarianism than Marx himself. Hegel realized that the total triumph of (Socialist) equality might well require the annihilation of individuality. He saw also that although communism in property was a condition of this achievement it would not of itself bring it about. It was necessary that a spiritual transformation accompany what Marx called the change in the relations of production before true communism would be achieved. To attempt to inhibit egoism by coercion and to develop fellow-feeling by a manipulation of the external environment would have seemed to Hegel, and to some extent to Marx as well, as a foredoomed effort to achieve the ends of love by the agency of domination.

THE YOUNG HEGEL: EQUALITY AS LOVE

Equality was a principle with the early Christians; the slave was the brother of his owner; humility, the principle of not elevating one's self above anyone else, the sense of one's own unworthiness, was the first law of a Christian; men were to be valued not by honors or dignity, not by talents or other brilliant qualities, but by the strength of their faith. This theory, to be sure, has been retained in all its comprehensiveness, but with the clever addition that it is in the eyes of Heaven that all men are equal in this sense. For this reason it receives no further notice in this earthly life.[3]

Hegel's first discussion of equality merely expressed, in a moving way, his dissatisfaction over the compromising of the original Christian ideal. It was only as he sought to overcome such contradictions between the ideal and the real through the device of the dialectic that he made his unique contribution to the development of Socialist egalitarianism. Marx accepted the dialectical method of Hegel as a general instrument of analysis, but for Marx it did not carry the symbolic character with which Hegel had originally invested it. Marx was metaphysician enough to accept the description of property as a "Greek fate," [4] reconciled in the final synthetic "moment" of the dialectical triad. Beyond this, Marx attached no extramethodological significance to the dialectic. For Hegel, however, especially in the early period of his work, the dialectic was at once a mode of understanding and a statement of the essential process of human relations. As Paul Tillich has remarked, "It can be said without exaggeration that Hegel's dialectical scheme is an abstraction from his concrete intuition into the nature of love as separation and reunion." [5] In his fragment on "Love" (1798), Hegel makes this association in a discussion of sexual love. The relation of the lovers is a process of "unity, separated opposites, reunion." The lovers come together in sexual union, and "separate again, but in the child their union has become unseparated." [6] The same association is expressed in terms of asexual love in "The Spirit of Christianity and its Fate" (1799), which, like the fragment on

"Love," is included in Hegel's *Theologische Jugendschriften*. Here Hegel examines ethical and religious history under the aspect of the striving for union in love. Although he regarded Christianity as a transitional phase in this history, Hegel credited Jesus with pointing the way toward the fulfillment of love by declaring himself "against personality, against the view that his essence possessed an individuality opposed to that of those who had attained the culmination of fellowship with him." [7] In the era of fulfillment, separate individuality would be replaced by an identification in love. A man "who lived entirely in beholding another would be this other entirely, would be merely possessed of the possibility of becoming different from him." [8] Hegel regards this identification as the ultimately desirable relation not only between man and man but also between man and God. "The hill and the eye which sees it are object and subject, but between man and God, between spirit and spirit, there is no such cleft of objectivity and subjectivity. [O]ne is to the other an other only in that one recognizes the other; both are one." [9]

In these early statements, written in the years when Hegel was in the throes of a Romantic ambivalence between enthusiastic optimism and bleak despair, and before he undertook the more comprehensive task of providing an integrated account of all cultural history, Hegel produced both an important link between nineteenth century Socialist thought and its precursors in the left wing of the Reformation, and a penetrating examination of the obstacles to Socialist equality. Hegel's vision of an age of love when domination would be succeeded by equality, in the form of a common recognition of the identity of the human essence, follows the pattern of the millenarian Socialist thought expressed earlier by Müntzer and Winstanley. The mystic notion of direct revelation and the identification of man with God which accompany the Socialist doctrines in the Reformation are again expressed in Hegel. The notion of a progressive incarnation of Spirit in history joins and translates religious and secular millenarian doctrines into the language of modern secular Socialism.

Both Marx and Hegel conceived of history as the process in which the alienation of man from himself is to be overcome. For both of them alienation involves both separation and domination as general principles. For Marx it is the labor process which creates this separation (between men and between man and the product of his labor), through the division of labor, and which also creates domination, in the class relations which develop out of the division of labor and in the general determination of social relations by the products of labor. For Hegel, on the other hand, separation and domination result from a failure to appreciate fully the relevance of "Spirit" to the existential conditions of life, a failure which is expressed in conceptions of the ideal as something distinct from man and opposed to him. For Hegel, property, whether private or common, poses an obstacle to the overcoming of alienation which is much less amenable to correction than the philosophic sources. To possess property is to be tied to "dead" objectivity, which cannot, like other relations of life, be made spiritual and vital. Marx comes closest to this view of property when he argues in "Private Property and Communism" that to make property common is not necessarily to overcome egoism, because forms of possession do not of themselves create changes in attitude and understanding.

Hegel was optimistic with respect to the realization of love on a spiritual, philosophical level, but he recognized that if love did not transform the relations of spirituality to the objective world, unification would always remain precarious and incomplete. Because he could not see how this transformation might occur, Hegel ended both his early essays on a note of despair. A union of two people in love where ties to property exist, Hegel wrote in the fragment on "Love," "seems to be possible only if it comes under the dominion of both," for "the one who sees the other in possession of a property must sense in the other the separate individuality which has willed this possession." To make the use of the property common is no solution, because the question of the right of possession would remain as an unresolved taint of individuality. "But," Hegel concludes the fragment, "if the possessor gives the other the same right of possession as he has himself, community of goods is still only the right of one or other of the two to the thing." [10] This is to say that property is always an inanimate object which cannot exist in relation to human beings in any way other than a legal, juridical way. This legal relation presupposes the separation of individuals, and their government by rules which, unlike love, have an existence apart from man himself and create relations of right, which are relations of separation and domination opposed to relations of identification in love.

The difference between Hegel and Marx with respect to the question of property reflects a basic difference of approach. Whereas Marx opposed communism to Liberalism and capitalism, Hegel opposed an era of love to a juridical order which he equated with an order of alienation. These conceptions are similar in that they conceive of an opposition between separate individuality and identification in love; between the notion of man as his activity (Marx: as a producer; Hegel: "as his deeds") and as his true self; between government as a guardian and agent of individual rights, and spontaneous self-government. They differ in that Hegel recognized perhaps more adequately than Marx that to create a society of love would require an overcoming of all individuality, with respect to feelings, to philosophic understanding, and to material possessions, each of which posed peculiar problems.[11]

To elucidate these similarities and differences, and to indicate in more detail the continuity of the early Hegelian philosophy with that of the religious Socialists, it is essential to enter into an exegesis of "The Spirit of Christianity and its Fate," the richest and most nearly complete of the *Early Theological Writings*.

The argument of the essay lends itself remarkably well to the Trinitarian image of historical development[12] introduced by the thirteenth century Franciscan mystic, Joachim of Flora. Schematically this can be represented as follows:

Father (*Juridical*)	*Son* (*Faith*)	*Holy Spirit* (*Love*)
Conceptual	Vital but incomplete	Integrally vital
Logic	Analogy	Dialectic
Dependence	Dependence	Mutual recognition (equality)
Externality (man as his deed)	Internality (man as his intention)	Conscious will
God as alien	God as one man	God as all men

The juridical order, which appears historically in Judaism and in Kantian ethics, is the first stage of dialectical movement. It is an order characterized by the coercion of law, standing in opposition to the individual as a universal to a particular, and registering the fundamentally antagonistic character of social relations.[13] In the chapter on the moral teachings of Jesus, which is even more crucial to the understanding of this phase than the sections explicitly devoted to the subject, because it discusses the juridical order critically, Hegel writes: "Retribution and its equivalence with crime is the sacred principle of all justice, the principle on which any political order must rest."[14] In the juridical order, authority derives from a source external to the individual, issues in commands, and is instrumented by violence. The law is a universal opposed to the particular in that it regards man only in the light of his actions; in the eyes of the law a criminal is not a person but his transgression. A human judge may mediate between the law and the criminal, but this does not affect the essential order, because man, judge and criminal alike, remains a dependent. Indeed, in this order even God is a dependent, for he is merely the administrator of the law[15] as man is its slave. The unity of this order is therefore a conceptual one, in the sense that it is a regulation of antagonism rather than an integration in love.

The whole artificial structure of right and justice, including private property, must be transcended: this is the message of Jesus to his followers.[16] Only in this way can freedom (self-determination) be attained, for in the realm of the juridical order man is not himself but his actions. Insofar as he is considered moral it is because he performs actions he is commanded to perform, not those he freely determines to do. Man exists in freedom only when "his character and deeds become the man himself,"[17] when he makes for himself the distinction of virtue and vice.[18] The gaining of this freedom is not the ultimate end, which is love, but it is a necessary precondition.

Christ's opposition to the juridical order is the second, antithetic moment of the dialectic. He alone succeeds in transcending the juridical order because he recognizes that to do so one must negate the juridical order entirely. Transcendence cannot be accomplished through crime because the transgressor either suffers punishment (a disruption of life) or feels guilt (bad conscience). In either case he begins to long for the innocence and the whole-ness he has lost, and in his longing he at least indicates the step which must be taken: "opposition is the possibility of reconcilia-tion."[19] But if a man confines his activity within the limits of the juridical order, he cannot succeed. Whether he risks his life in defense of his right or submits passively to deprivation, he remains under the domination of the law. In the first case the engagement is fought on behalf of right; in the second, right is not renounced but only forfeited through want of the will to defend it. Jesus, as the "beautiful soul," united both courses and thereby overcame this bondage. The virtue of courage, which asserts self-control, remains in the ethic of Jesus, while opposition (to an adversary, for right) is forsaken; the virtue of passivity, which is to renounce right, remains, but the grief over the loss of right disappears.[20]

Hegel celebrates the achievement of Jesus as a progressive step towards love, but he regards it as an insufficient and tragic step. The beautiful soul renounces property and all other ties to the juridical order (including "father, mother, and everything") and thereby transcends it[21] in two specific ways: he is no longer bound to "objects," and he determines his own actions. In order to maintain this absolute independence, however, the beautiful soul has to annihilate himself, has to give up his life (thus, Jesus crucified).[22] But in principle the beautiful soul has succeeded in achieving freedom without injury to love. Because he renounces whatever is his by right, he does not offend against love, he has no desire for revenge, and he can be reconciled with his fellow men.[23] In renouncing retribution he renounces the juridical order and becomes autonomous: his disdain of those relations to the juridical order is his own will, his free choice.[24] In discovering his hu-manity, the beautiful soul overcomes alienation from himself. He recognizes that "the sinner is more than a sin existent, a trespass possessed of personality; he is a man, trespass and fate are in him. He can return to himself again, and if he does so, then trespass and fate are under him . . . in love life has found life once more."[25]

Hegel distinguishes between Jesus (the beautiful soul) and the Christian community which he founded. The Christian com-munity passes from the juridical order of Judaism into the realm of faith. Faith offers the possibility of mutual recognition between God and man: "a knowledge of spirit through spirit," of like by like, rather than "feeling one's own reality as inferior to his in might and strength, and being his servant."[26] But faith is only the possibility, not the consummation. Knox, the translator of Hegel's *Theologische Jugendschriften*, points out that Hegel renders the Scriptural phrase, "While you have light yourselves, believe in the light," as "*Until* you have light,"[27] indicating clearly his view that faith is not the ultimate phase of Spirit. With the death of Jesus the tentative approach of the Christian community to love comes to an end. While Jesus was alive the Christian community experienced the vitality of the love-feast existentially, not merely as an intellectual conception.

> The connection between the blood poured out and the friends of Jesus is not that it was shed for them as something objective to them for their well-being, for their use. The connection . . . is the tie between them and the wine which they all drink out of the same cup and which is for all and the same for all. All drink together; a like emotion is in them all; all are permeated by the like spirit of love. If they are made alike simply as recipients of an advantage, a benefit, accruing from a sacrifice of body and an outpouring of blood, then they would only be united in a like concept. But because they eat the bread and drink the wine, because his body and his blood pass over into them, Jesus is in them all, and his essence, as love, has divinely permeated them.[28]

In the absence of Jesus, the love-feast becomes merely a dispensation of grace rather than an immediate experience of love. As a religious ceremony the love-feast involves a "confusion between object and subject rather than a unification . . . Something divine, just because it is divine, cannot present itself in the shape of food and drink."[29] The gap between faith and the sensation of objects cannot be bridged: "To faith it is the spirit which is present; to seeing and tasting, the bread and wine." Love as living spirit dies with the person of Jesus. "When the (statue of) Apollo is ground to dust, devotion remains, but it cannot turn and worship the dust. The dust can remind us of the devotion, but it cannot draw devotion to itself."[30] Similarly, upon the destruction of the incarnation of love, a

regret arises, and this is the sensing of this separation, this contradiction, like the sadness accompanying the idea of living forces and the
incompatibility between them and the corpse. After the supper the
disciples began to be sorrowful because of the impending loss of their
master, but after a genuinely religious action the whole soul is at peace.
And, after enjoying the supper, Christians today feel a reverent wonder
either without serenity or else with a melancholy serenity, because
feeling's intensity was separate from the intellect and both were one-
sided, because worship was incomplete, since the divine was promised
and it melted away in the mouth.[31]

At the same time, faith opens the way to dialectical consciousness. Hegel equates judgment, the activity of the juridical order,
with logic: "judgment (in law) is a judgment (in logic), an
assertion of likeness or unlikeness, the recognition of a conceptual
unity or an irreconcilable opposition."[32] Faith is superior to logic,
for logic cannot "grasp absolutely different substances [human
and divine nature] which at the same time are an absolute unity."
Because the Jews were dominated by logic, they could not receive
the message of Jesus. They elevated the intellect, which Hegel describes as "absolute division, destruction of life," to "the pinnacle
of spirit."[33] The same criticism would apply to Kantian practical
reason, for as the dialectic is the epistemological mode of love,
ordinary logic is the form of thought appropriate to the juridical
order. The stage of faith, as a closer approach to the stage of love,
reveals for the first time both the vital experience of love in the
life of Jesus and the principle of dialectical consciousness in the
form of faith.

In opposition to Kant, Hegel holds that the virtue ethic embodied in the reign of love is not a principle which can be stated
as a general rule with application in specific duties. That would
make love a determinate, conceptual "unity" of virtues, rather
than a "living" one. Virtues under the aspect of love are distinguished from virtues in the realm of right and law in that the
latter are designed to provide rules of conduct in specific situations. As a result there is a multiplicity of such virtues, and inevitable conflict among them, when the area of activity comprehends several situations, each with its own appropriate rule of
conduct. In such a conflict, sin, in the sense of a denial of one or
the other virtue, must result from the attempt to act in accordance

with the law. If love is the source and substance of the virtues, no conflict can occur, for, according to Hegel, love by its nature "restricts *itself* in accordance with the whole of the given situation."[34]

One may plausibly extrapolate from this the conclusion that in the reign of love there would not be any necessity for external arbitration (government) to decide which of the virtues is to be sacrificed. In different circumstances love will take different shapes, but it is forever the same and it cannot be imprisoned within a felicific calculus. Unlike law, love can never have the force of a "universal opposed to a particular," because while law mediates between the two terms in opposition, love exists in their unification. Moreover, love does not bring unification in concept but in Spirit. There is no gap between universal and particular because "to love God is to feel one's self in the 'all' of life, with no restrictions in the infinite."[35]

But this identification with the totality in divine love is not yet possible in the phase of faith. The value of the incarnation is that it evoked faith, revealing the divinity in man. Faith is only possible "if in the believer himself there is a divine element." Man is thus revealed to us (though not necessarily to himself) as the bearer of divinity, of Spirit, of freedom. Man in faith does not become illuminated as a dark body receiving a foreign light: "his own inflammability takes fire." In his most forthright passage, Hegel unveils the radical character of his dialectical understanding and his dissatisfaction with existing religion:

> *The middle state between darkness (remoteness from the divine, imprisonment in the mundane) and a wholly divine life of one's own, a trust in one's self, is faith in the divine.*[36]

Thus Christianity, the religion of faith, is not the end of the process toward the actualization of Spirit, but only a step nearer it, a middle state. This passage indicates more clearly than any other in the essay the outlines of the young Hegel's post-Christian dream. Jesus was the first divine man. His followers were not divine in themselves but were only related to divinity in the dependence of faith in Jesus. John the Baptist "only bore witness of the light," whereas Jesus was "the light individualized in a man." As long as Jesus was alive among them, his followers remained believers only; with his death the possibility arose for the Holy Spirit to animate their whole being as it had the being of Jesus.[37] The dialectical statement of the development toward autonomous love is revealed as the Trinity in history.

The culmination of faith, the return to the Godhead whence man is born, closes the circle of man's development. Everything lives in the Godhead, every living thing is its child, but the child carries the unity, the connection, the concord with the entire harmony, undisturbed though undeveloped, in itself. It begins with faith in gods outside itself, with fear, until through its actions it has (isolated and) separated itself more and more; but then it returns through associations to the original unity which now is developed, self-produced, and sensed as a unity. The child now knows God, i.e., the spirit of God is present in the child, issues from its restrictions, annuls the modification, and restores the whole. God, the Son, the Holy Spirit! [38]

With the Jews there is recognized the notion of God, but the notion is conscious only as fear of an alien power. Jesus as the son of God is man made aware of the original unity of man and God, the prelude to an age when the unity will be not only sensed but actualized in the divinity of everyman, the age of Spirit, of love. The restrictions to be annulled are the oppositions which are the basis of the juridical order.[39]

The Christian community did not achieve the goal announced in the incarnation of Jesus because it existed as a community in virtue of the common relation of all the members, not in an all-inclusive love but in the (incomplete) religion of Christianity, in love as faith. Love was thus fixed in a determinate activity, the activity of religious practice. This restriction of love, this attachment of love to a determinate mode of activity, was its undoing. Man's social existence is not circumscribed by his relation to God and by the pleasures of life (including property) which the Christian community kept in common. Beyond these and "beyond the single activity of spreading the faith . . . there still lies a prodigious field of objectivity which claims activity of many kinds." [40] Christian love, which is confined to the realm of faith, does not extend to those other activities. The conflicts which arise for the Christian engaged in these other activities can only be met

by an "inactive and undeveloped love," a love which flees from
most of the determinate modes of living.[41] The elevation of love
to a preoccupation with religion is thus "contra-natural," even
as it is in one sense the highest expression of love. Love as faith
leads on the one hand to the fanaticism of the proselytizer, on the
other to the fanaticism of the ascetic.

The rejection of the political state is an instance of the incom-
pleteness of love as faith. "With this [passive] relation to the
state one great element in a living union is cut away." [42] Political
reality—the state and Jewish legalism—was an abomination, so
Jesus renounced it. But the result was that he could find freedom
only in the void. "The earthly life of Jesus was separation from
the world and flight from it into heaven; restoration, in the ideal
world, of the life which was becoming dissipated into the void."
The fate of the Christian community consists in its having followed the example of its founder in separating itself from the
world. Love in the Christian community "could not and was not
supposed to be a union of individualities; it was a union in God
and in God only." For

faith can only unify a group if the group sets an actual world over
against itself and sunders itself from it. Hence the opposition [to the
rest of the world] became a fixed and essential part of the principle
of the group, while the group's love . . . retained the form of . . . faith
in God, without becoming alive, without exhibiting itself in the specific
forms of life.[43]

Whatever connection the Christian community attained to the
divine Spirit was effected in Jesus. "His individuality united for
them in a living being the indeterminate and the determinate
elements in the [entire] harmony." [44] With his death, Christian
love was denuded of its relation to life. The image of the resurrected Christ becomes objective for the group only in the sense
that it becomes the "presentation of the love uniting the group," [45]
an exclusive love which is clearly inadequate. The Christian God
comes to hover between heaven and earth, between the infinite
and the determinate. God comes to be apprehended intellectually,
and hence in a divided aspect as both human and divine but not
as a unity. Ultimately the Christian community reverts to what
is essentially the condition of Judaism. The love it set up as an

ideal becomes divorced from life and is therefore something alien and abstract which comes to dominate the group. There ceases to be recognized any equality between man and God. Christianity becomes a "community of dependence, the community of having a common founder, and in this intermixture of historical fact with its life, the group recognized its real bond and that assurance of unification which could not be sensed in a love that was unliving."[46] The dilemma of Christianity, as Hegel sees it, is twofold: insofar as it regards ties with the world as profane, its love is incomplete; and insofar as its philosophical consciousness is undeveloped, it is caught in a tension between God and the human Christ. Hegel sees the dilemma represented in the difference between the Roman Catholic and Protestant churches. The Catholic Church only regards the activities of life as sanctified because they express man's servitude and impotence, and the Protestant church sets up an absolute gulf between the divine and the human. It is the fate of Christianity, according to Hegel, that within its own framework these contradictions can never be resolved. "It is its fate that church and state, worship and life, piety and virtue, spiritual and worldly action, can never dissolve into one."[47]

To go beyond Christianity to the complete fulfillment of love is therefore to advance toward an integration of Spirit with the activities of life and toward the dialectical understanding of the relation between man and God. The egalitarianism which Hegel describes as mutual recognition, or the knowledge of Spirit by Spirit, is the expression of love in social relations and in philosophic understanding. It demands the overcoming of individualism by the recognition on the part of every member of society that he and his fellows share the same divine Spirit. Self-dependence is only a "moment" in the advance to absolute love. In the *Phenomenology* this self-dependence takes the form of the statement, "The Self is Absolute Being," which is the prelude to the "unhappy consciousness."[48] There can be no adequate mutual recognition without dialectical understanding, for otherwise it would be impossible to conceive of the synthetic unification which love demands. Philosophic recognition is impossible so long as natural relations and objects are taken to represent reality. To speak of man as the son of God the Father is to oppose a barrier to dialectical understanding, because it indicates that God and man are still strangers to each other.[49] To put this relation in terms of objects such as bread or wine is to erect a similar barrier, because the understanding can grasp the meaning of these objects only by analogy. Analogy, however, is not to be confused with dialectical synthesis. In the parable "the different things, the things compared, are set forth as severed, as separate, and all that is asked is a comparison, the thought of the likeness of dissimilars." In the love-feast as an experience, on the other hand, in the connection of bread and persons, "difference disappears, and with it, the possibility of comparison. Things heterogeneous are here most intimately connected." [50] Hegel indicates a preference for the Gospel of John because the notion of the Logos becoming flesh is a dialectical statement of the relation between man and God.[51] The key to Hegel's repeated assertion that "love is less than religion" is his understanding of religion, in its complete form, as a unification of reflection and love,[52] or mutual recognition as a social and philosophic event. Christianity is inadequate as religion, both because in it love is not fully developed and because its religious consciousness is not fully dialectical. For the most part, the relation between man and God is still represented as domination, either as the natural relation of Father to sons or in the relation of giver to receivers. In the *Phenomenology* Hegel describes the natural relations and other elements of the Christian consciousness as "pictorial" or "representational" rather than dialectical.[53] Domination and pictorial thought are bound together; in order for mutual recognition to arise, they must both be overcome.

In this early work Hegel did not yet conceive of Spirit in history as a dialectical juggernaut. Even as he looked toward the fullness of development, he recognized that there were obstacles in the path of Spirit which could not easily be reconciled. Unlike Marx he was not tempted to regard the transformation of character and understanding which would be required for the realization of love as a mere reflex of changes in relations to property. Property, like all spheres of objectivity, including politics, and all manifestations of individuality in thought and in action, could not easily be invested with Spirit or contained within the love relation. Even as Hegel, with the enthusiasm of youth, urged the attempt to go beyond Christianity, his apprehensions fore-shadowed the resignation of his later work. Equality in the matrix of dialectical understanding was the goal of history, but perhaps, Hegel seems to have concluded, the fate of its contradictions would be too powerful to be overcome.

THE NON-MARXIAN SOCIALISTS

With respect to equality, the religious Socialism of Hegel was more indicative of the future path of Marxian thought than the work of the secular utopians and social theorists who were generally acknowledged as kindred spirits by Marx and Engels. Both Saint-Simon and Fourier, whom Marx and Engels counted among their most important forebears, rejected all but one aspect of equality, and that a feature of Liberal equality. They explicitly denied the validity of the eighteenth century conception of natural equality, in its Liberal and Socialist forms, and they also decried communism in property. They were collectivists only in the sense that they advocated a fully planned organization of production and an organically integrated society. Their Socialism, if it may indeed properly be given the name, rests on an attempt to integrate the several classes which derive from the natural inequalities in human nature. Proudhon was anything but a collectivist. He opposed all but transitory, *ad hoc* association, preferring what he called an "equilibrium" which would result from the "mutualism" and "reciprocity" of voluntary contractual relations among individuals, each of whom would express his own faculties and aspirations through labor and exchange. Saint-Simon, Fourier, and Proudhon sought to unite capitalists and proletarians, as the laboring, productive segment of society, and to eliminate idleness and its privileges. They did not propose, however, that the products of collectively organized labor be divided equally. In this respect they were Liberals, advocating a competitive equality among individuals, and a return proportionate to labor, resources, and talent. In the case of Liberalism, however, the doctrine of competitive equality rests on a belief in natural equality. In the case of the Socialists, it rests on the assumption of natural inequality. The result is that their justification of unequal reward is not sustained by the usual Liberal ethical argument.

In addition to this quasi-Liberal position, there is in Fourier and Saint-Simon much that is derived from the Conservatives. The emphasis on the passions that is so pronounced in Fourier, and the belief in hierarchical organization that is essential both to Saint-Simon and Fourier as an adjunct of their organicist, functionalist, and pluralist conceptions, are elements which bring them closer to Maistre than to Marx. If their work is, nevertheless, most important to the history of Socialism, it is largely for the reason that Marx adopted a number of their ideas. Their conception of classes arising out of natural inequality and out of the distinction between producers and idlers influenced Marx. The relations of production which they made the focus of reform played the same role for Marx, although he ignored those aspects of the earlier Socialist theories that stressed the autonomous role of the passions, the nature of individuality, and the indispensability of the division of labor. Finally, their common concern to end the exploitation of man by man was of course restated by Marx in the context of communism.

Both Saint-Simon and Fourier brought into question the belief in natural equality which had been important for eighteenth century French Socialism—Saint-Simon by adopting the typology of the physiologist, Bichat, who had enumerated three basic types: "the brain, motor and sensory." In Saint-Simon's scheme the "industrials" were the motor type, the savants the brain type, and the artists the sensory type. Each of the three types constituted a separate class, and the classes would be arranged hierarchically. Saint-Simon's ideal society is thus a hierarchy of classes based upon the assumed natural differences among men. Education and social organization were to be designed to take maximum advantage of these differences, in contrast to the Liberal theory of education which would provide the same instruction to all in disregard of any such fundamental natural differences.[54] The result would be a society composed of highly specialized functional groups. Saint-Simon did not conceive of this society as a mere continuation of feudalism. It was his intention to substitute the criteria of natural inclination and talent for the feudal standards of wealth, birth, and status. Superiority in talent would, he assumed, be readily recognized, thus eliminating the possibility of rivalries for power, such as occurred under feudalism.[55] The hierarchical system would not be a system of domination, but an organization in which every individual would participate as an active self-determining agent. In this society "each person enjoys a measure of importance and benefits proportionate to his capacity and to his investment. This constitutes the highest degree of equality possible and desirable." [56] The equality of communism is rejected because it would violate the natural inequality of human nature and the principle that reward should be attached to merit. The poorer classes would be bound to benefit from such a scheme, because it would remove distribution from the realm of chance and it would prevent the privileges of birth and inheritance from determining a man's share of the social product. At the same time, private property would not be tampered with except where it promoted "the impious privilege of laziness." [57]

Like Saint-Simon, Fourier rejected both the idea of natural equality and the social equality of communism. Men were governed by a number of passions, each of which was dominant in a particular man and corresponded to a special vocational inclination. The harmonious society would group men according to their passional identities. They would be assigned to labor which they could be expected to enjoy. Each man would receive dividends out of the produce of the community according to the capital, labor, and talent that he contributed.[58] The ideal society, Fourier wrote, is as incompatible with equality of fortunes as it is with the false notion of the identity of characters. The organization of production and social relations ought to correspond to the variety of passions in society. The phalanx is therefore designed according to an "échelle progressive" in which men are grouped according to their particular passions,[59] so that society is, in effect, a harmony of extreme contrasts. In such a community, equality would be "political poison." [60] Laziness will be overcome only if labor is made more attractive, through the application of the theory of the passions, and if men are given an incentive to produce. To accommodate differences in wealth there should be four or five dinner tables. The diners ought not to be too rigidly separated. It should be possible for the poorer members to dine at the first table fifty times annually in order to learn "the polite customs of the superiors." [61]

Thus, insofar as Saint-Simon and Fourier accept equality at all, it is the Liberal equality which sanctions a competition among individuals (without the artificial barriers of privilege) and a system of rewards proportionate to individual labor and initiative, except that Fourier would permit those who joined the phalanx to profit from any accumulated resources they might bring with them. Otherwise the theories of human nature and social organization proposed by Fourier and Saint-Simon are sharply antiegalitarian.

The egalitarianism of Proudhon is even closer to the Liberal pattern, inasmuch as it is not accompanied by a demand for hierarchy. To the "official" Liberals of his day, with their post-revolutionary concern for order and stability, Proudhon could only appear to be a dangerous anarchist. Proudhon surely was anarchistic, but his is an anarchism with a close affinity to Liberal principles, especially to the Liberal conception of equality.

According to Proudhon, history had been marked by three great revolutions and was to be marked by still another. The first was the announcement of equality before God, made in the Gospels; next came the revolution in philosophy (Bruno, Descartes, and Luther, among others), which established equality on grounds of reason; then, the revolution of the eighteenth century which made all men equal before the law. The final revolution, the task of the contemporary generation, would bring to an end the exploitation of man by man.[62]

This final revolution, however, is not to issue in communism, as in the case of Babeuf's transition to "égalité réelle," but in a system of perfect competition. Proudhon attacked both the utopian communism of Cabet and the state-directed Socialism of Louis Blanc.[63] According to him, as to the Liberals, equality ought not to replace liberty but to complement it. Even as he argued for the improvement of the proletarian lot, Proudhon recognized that the masses did not appreciate the value of individual and group liberties. They wanted only centralization of authority so as to assure equality. In order to avoid tyranny, however, it was necessary to "marry" the bourgeoisie and the proletariat so that liberty would be united to equality.[64] Equality of wages, or the Socialism propounded by Blanc, would inevitably entail tyranny. In order to prevent such tyranny, equality must be understood as the equal freedom of each individual to pursue his self-interest without interference from another man or from a majority. Louis Blanc had stated the goal of Socialist equality: from each according to his capacity, to each according to his need. Proudhon's objection to this doctrine is that it puts the state in the position of deciding what is the capacity and the need of each individual. In such a circumstance, Proudhon declares, he would straightway leave the society. Only if the individual is free to negotiate, with the state as with other individuals, what he is to contribute and what he is to receive, can there be an equality which is also libertarian. The state has no right to invade the privacy of the individual, and work is one of the most private of his activities.[65] "Work is, with love, the most secret function, the most sacred of man; it fortifies itself with solitude, it is decomposed by prostitution." [66]

Against tyrannical Socialist equality Proudhon opposes an "equilibrium" of individual producers working separately and exchanging freely among themselves, without capitalist or state intermediaries. Under such a system, the value of commodities would be determined solely by the labor required to produce them. Equal quantities of labor embodied in one product would exchange for the same quantities of labor embodied in another product. If a man wished to acquire more goods he would simply work longer, but since all labor would be rated in equal individual units, no man would be compelled to labor for another man's profit. Reward would be accorded each man on the basis of his exertion. Thus, Proudhon declares, "Labor and exchange" are the "*alpha*" and "*omega*" of the revolution.[67] Under free exchange a unit of labor would become equal in value to that of any other unit. This would substitute commutative justice, or the "reign of contract," for the distributive justice Proudhon identifies with feudal, military, and statist regimes.[68]

The equalization of the value of labor was for Proudhon a step toward eventual equality in property. The mistake of the statists was to impose equality a priori. Equality is a priori only a condition of human dignity. From a priori equality, whether of the communist type or of the "personal" type of Rousseau, can only come *"immobilisme"* and a sharing of misery. Equality should be a hope, an anticipation, but not the beginning principle. Otherwise men become fixed in their station, much as in a caste society, progress is impossible, and individual spontaneity is overridden by the state.[69] The division of labor, if it is adopted as a central guiding principle, makes it possible to achieve whatever is needed in the way of social cohesion without at the same time sacrificing progress. Only through industrial progress could the interest of labor be promoted, providing there was complete freedom to produce and exchange.

Proudhon indicates clearly that he does not think men are equal in their capacities or are likely to be equal in the effort they put forth, and he assumes that reward should be commensurate with both. Without economic equilibrium—which is not an a priori equality, but an inequality arrived at under circumstances in which all the participants, as free contractors, are equal at their entrance—"the most ignorant, the most incapable of humans would have the right to be as well treated as the wisest and most valiant."[70] This would give the worthless man an indemnification for his weakness and ignorance. Equality of goods will come about only when men all deserve to share identically. Until then there should be inequality of possessions. Proudhon's social theory is in principle very much in accord with the Liberal understanding of equality, insofar as he advocates an equality of free individuals competing amongst one another for status and wealth. In rights there must be complete equality, but in the distribution of goods justice demands equilibrium—the distribution of wealth according to individual labor and free contractual exchange.

THE MARXIAN CRITIQUE OF LIBERAL EQUALITY

It was a source of constant annoyance to Marx and Engels to find Socialism advocated in the name of "equality." In the first place, they argued, the belief in equality is only an ideological expression, not a scientific principle. In the second place, the content of this ideology is not Socialist equality but Liberal bourgeois equality. German Socialism, Marx wrote to a correspondent, ignores the materialistic basis of history for "modern mythology with its goddesses of Justice, Freedom, Equality, and Fraternity."[71] Engels echoed this irritation in a criticism, addressed to August Bebel, of the wording of a party program: " 'Doing away with all social and political inequality' is . . . a very questionable phrase in place of 'the abolition of all class differences.' " This "notion of socialist society as the realm of equality," he explained,

is a superficial French idea resting upon the old 'liberty, equality, fraternity'—an idea which was justified as a *stage of development* in its own time and place but which like all the superficial ideas of the earlier socialist schools, should now be overcome, for they only produce confusion in people's heads and more precise forms of description have been found.[72]

The trouble with the term equality, however, is not only that it is vague and inexact, but also that, insofar as it is equated with Socialism, what is in reality a scientific theory of social history is presented as mere ideology. According to scientific Socialism, the idea of equality is an ideological reflection of material relations. Scientific Socialists cannot countenance the claim of any such idea to historically absolute validity. They reject, Engels writes,

every attempt to impose on us any moral dogma whatsoever as an eternal, ultimate and forever immutable moral law. . . We maintain on the contrary that all former moral theories are the product, in the last analysis, of the economic stage which society had reached at that particular epoch.[73]

Only unscientific idealist Socialists such as the philosopher Eugen Dühring can make equality out to be an eternally valid moral principle from which Socialism is derived. Dühring asserts that the touchstone of all social theory is the notion that "two human wills are as such *entirely equal to each other.*" This is taken to be the norm of justice to which all social laws and arrangements ought to conform. Engels challenges Dühring by measuring his theory against actual social relations. Two people may be "unequal" in sex. From this difference of male and female there arises the domination of the wife by the husband in the family, which is the microcosm of all social relations.[74] Insofar as social relations are considered—and Dühring's theory requires a relation between two people—equality does not in fact govern the relation. Only if the two people were, so to speak, abstracted from social relations and from their particular individual qualities would it be possible to speak of equality between them.

In order to establish the fundamental axiom that two people and their wills are also absolutely equal to each other and that neither lords it over the other, we cannot use any couple of people at random. They must be two persons who are so thoroughly detached from all reality, from all national, economic, political and religious relations . . . from all sex and personal differences, that nothing is left of either person beyond the mere idea: person—and then in fact they are 'entirely equal.'[75]

In any conceivable real situation, inequality is bound to assert itself. The wills of two men otherwise isolated from society by a shipwreck may be equal in the abstract, but their personal characteristics will form relations of inequality between them. One will be lazy, the other energetic; one intelligent, the other stupid. The likelihood is, Engels argues, that the one with the superior characteristics will tend to impose his will on the other, perhaps by persuasion or by the unconscious growth of an habitual relation of domination.

Even Dühring, Engels points out, qualifies his doctrine of abstract moral equality by admitting that dependency and domination are justified under certain conditions.[76] Some dependency is to be allowed on the ground that the dependent lacks the quality of self-determination—a qualification which Engels argues can logically serve and has in fact served as a bogus justification for imperialism, and not merely for the relation of parents to children which Dühring cites. Two persons, Dühring further suggests, may be "morally unequal," which also justifies domination. To this Engels replies that inasmuch as there is a touch of the beast in all of us, the entire race having evolved from the lower form of animal life, this distinction cannot apply.[77] Dühring further compromises his theory by admitting mental inequality. Who is to decide, Engels asks, when a man or group of men is so mentally inferior as to justify their subordination? Only an elite, in which case there is again no equality. Worse yet, this qualification promotes the paradoxical and pernicious conclusion that some men may be dominated and forcibly coerced against their will in the name of equality. Engels concludes that Dühring's theory, whenever it is compelled to address itself to real relations must collapse in its own contradictions. For "every difference in the quality of the two wills and in that of the intelligence associated with them—justifies an inequality of treatment which may go as far as subjection." [78]

Dühring's theory of equality is, according to Engels, representative of all contemporary egalitarianism, whether espoused by bourgeoisie or proletarians. The modern conception of equality is a deduction from the assumed "common characteristics of humanity, from that equality of men as men," of "a claim to equal political or social status." [79] The trouble with this conception, as with all bourgeois doctrines, is that it expresses ideals which are supposedly general and universal, but which in fact serve only to delude the proletariat and to mask the class interest of the bourgeoisie. The American Constitution confirms Negro slavery in the same breath with which it announces the universal rights of man. The slogan of the French Revolution is limited, in its application, to an equality before the law—a law which is determined according to the interests of the privileged classes and operates to maintain those privileges and an equality of rights, chief of which is the right to private property.[80] As theory, the bourgeois conception of equality suffers from a failure to recognize that all values are relative to historical conditions and cannot be derived from some abstract notion of human nature; as ideology, it is merely the expression of class interest.

Marx and Engels granted the validity of the bourgeois conception of equality in the context of capitalism. They criticized it on the ground that it was "anything but an eternal truth," [81] and they criticized Socialists for adopting a bourgeois conception. Engels' attack against Dühring is an attempt to expose the unscientific and bourgeois character of non-Marxian Socialist egalitarianism. Marx's attack against Proudhon makes the same point, with more specific reference to the attempt to make the ideal of equality the basis for economic organization. Proudhon argued that equality would be a necessary consequence of a natural organization of production and exchange on the ground that, as Marx summarized his argument, "given an equal quantity of labor, the product of one will exchange for the product of another. All men are wage-workers and equal wages pay for an equal time of labor. Perfect equality presides over the exchange." [82] This equality, of course, would not necessarily mean that all producers would possess the same amount of goods, but only that each producer would have an opportunity equal to that of any other producer to satisfy his wants through his labor.

Marx pointed out that this theory derived from Ricardo and had been best expressed by John Bray, an English Socialist. Bray's formulation indicates even more clearly than Proudhon's (which is beclouded by an unexplained belief that natural conditions would ultimately produce an equality of possession) the Liberal, individualistic conception of equality from which it springs. The starting point of Bray's argument is the belief that every man has the right to whatever his honest labor produces. In order to assure that this equality of right is effective, it is not sufficient merely to make men equal before the law or to remove a rich tyrant. The cause of all inequality, all relations of master and slave, owner and wage worker, is the inequity of capitalist relations of production, in which the producers receive only a small share of the value they produce. Remove the capitalist intermediary and inequality will cease, because no one will receive unearned income. Existing inequalities, Bray argued, were not due to "the assumed inequality of bodily and mental powers" which the apologists for capitalism cited, but to the divergence of actual economic organization from the Liberal principle that every man is entitled to the fruits of his labor.[83]

Mark recognized that, despite their adoption by critics of capitalism, these theories of labor value were Liberal and not Socialist in respect to their ethical underpinnings. Thus Marx could write of Bray's egalitarian ideal that it is in fact "nothing but the reflection of the existing world." [84] Ricardo's doctrine, because it was more scientific and therefore less concerned with the ethics of distribution, is at once praised by Marx for its rigor and damned as a "pitilessly" bourgeois doctrine.[85] Similarly, the theory of Proudhon, according to Marx, would not emancipate labor, but only give additional justification to its enslavement.[86] Proudhon, Marx concluded, using the most pejorative epithet in his polemic arsenal, was, "from head to foot, the philosopher and the economist of the petty bourgeoisie." [87]

The weakness of these theories, Marx believed, was scientific as well as ethical. In the capitalist industrial system all producers do not engage in production upon equal terms, each of them having nothing but his labor to contribute. "To say that this exchange of products . . . has, for its consequence, the equal remuneration of all the producers, is to suppose that equality of participation has existed anterior to the exchange."[88] In fact, the value received in the exchange of any product is distributed not only to labor, but to those who own the factors of production. The share of the laborer, moreover, is determined not by the value of the commodities he produces, but by the minimal requirements for his subsistence. Liberals justified the remuneration of capital as a factor of production on the ground that capital represented the accumulated labor time of the capitalist. Marx argued that capital was an accumulation of value produced by labor in excess of what it received in wages. If the value of labor in one commodity were exchanged for the value of labor in another commodity, there could be no accumulation, and not only capitalism but all higher forms of industrialization would be impossible. At the same time, the advance of productive techniques and international exchange from small-scale individual or workshop production to "socialized" production rendered the belief in the remuneration of every man according to his individual labor an obsolete, inappropriate doctrine. Production was the result of social labor in the aggregate, not of individual labor and enterprise, as it once had been.

In his *Critique of the Gotha Programme* Marx indicates that the distribution of goods according to individual contributions of labor time can be considered Socialist policy only for the period of transition between capitalism and communism. This transitional period is bound to be "still stamped with the birthmarks of the old society from whose womb it emerges." Its principle of distribution will therefore be the bourgeois standard of individual labor:

Accordingly the individual producer receives back from society [after deductions for administrative costs and reinvestment] . . . exactly what he gives to it. What he has given to it is his individual amount of labour. . . . He receives a certificate from society that he has furnished such and such an amount of labour (after deducting his labour for the common fund), and with this certificate he draws from the social stock of the means of consumption as much as the same amount of labour costs. The same amount of labour which he has given to society in one form, he receives back in another.[89]

"Hence," Marx writes, "*equal right* is still in principle—*bourgeois right,* although principle and practice are no longer in conflict."[90] Socialism, in its transitional phase, realizes the ethical principle of Liberalism. Marx not only recognizes the Liberal nature of this principle of distribution, but, having recognized it and having advocated it for the period immediately following the overthrow of capitalism, he submits it to a Socialist critique.

This critique is important for the understanding of Marxian theory as much as for the understanding of the Marxian conception of equality. It indicates perhaps more clearly than any other single issue that the assumption that the mode of production determines the relations of producers and their value systems is seriously compromised even within Marxism. In part this inconsistency is recognized and accounted for by Marx and Engels by the further assumption that with the overthrow of capitalism the determinism of the mode of production yields to human self-determination, or as Marx put it, there is a leap from necessity to freedom. When Marx asserts that "the nature of individuals depends on the material conditions determining their production,"[91] he apparently means this law to apply only to the pre-communist stages of history. "Universal dependence," Marx predicted, "this natural form of the world historical cooperation of individuals, will be transformed by this communist revolution into the control and conscious mastery of these powers which . . . have till now overawed and governed men as powers completely alien to them."[92] Yet at the same time Marx criticizes other German Socialists for drawing conclusions about equality from a notion of man's essential nature *apart from his historical nature as an effect of the process of production.* The consciousness of equality, he argued, is as much a product of history as the social relations which describe the "nature" of man at given periods of time.[93] When Marx came to discuss the Socialist conception of equality as it would exist in communist society, he seems to have ignored the criticism he addressed to his colleagues.

What Marx envisions for the final stage of history is clear in outline. The Liberal principle incorporated in the transitional stage of Socialism is to be rejected because it sees man only as a worker. Under communism, man will no longer be regarded simply as a producer but as a person with needs and desires; these needs and desires, rather than his contribution of labor, will be the basis for the distribution of goods. Liberal equality, Marx argues, is actually the transformation of natural inequalities into a principle of justice. About the time that John Stuart Mill made the same observation, Marx pointed out that a formal principle of equality may serve as a recognition of inequalities. The Liberal equality of right provides such recognition because those to whom it accords equal rights are not equal in their natural endowments.

. . . one man is superior to another physically or mentally and so supplies more labour in the same time, or can labour for a longer time; and labour, to serve as a measure, must be defined by its duration or intensity, otherwise it ceases to be a standard of measurement. This *equal right* is an unequal right for unequal labour. It recognizes no class differences, because everyone is only a worker like everyone else; but it tacitly recognizes unequal individual endowment and thus productive capacity as natural privileges. *It is therefore a right of inequality in its content, like every right.* Right by its very nature can only consist in the application of an equal standard; but unequal individuals (and they would not be different individuals if they were not unequal) are only measurable by an equal standard . . . *e.g.*, in the present case are regarded *only as workers*, and nothing more seen in them, everything else being ignored. Further, one worker is married, another not; one has more children than another and so on and so forth. Thus with an equal output, and hence an equal share in the social consumption fund, one will in fact receive more than another, one will be richer than another, and so on. To avoid all these defects, right, instead of being equal, would have to be unequal.[94]

Only when Liberal equality of individual rights is superseded by a higher form of equality will the goal of history be realized.

Bourgeois equality will "be fully left behind" and society will "inscribe on its banners: from each according to his ability, to each according to his needs!" This change in values must be prepared by the advance of the forces of production to a point where abundance is possible. It is vain and unscientific to imagine that it can be produced simply by propaganda. To speak of "equal right" and "equitable distribution" is to trade in "obsolete rubbishy phrases" and to pervert "the realistic outlook." The distribution of goods is always "a consequence of the distribution of the conditions of production themselves," which is in turn dependent upon the mode of production. Once the means of production are owned cooperatively, it will follow, as "*a consequence*," that distribution will be organized first according to individual contributions of labor, and finally according to need without regard to labor.[95]

The Marxian critique of Liberal equality thus rejects the belief in equal natural capacities and the claim that individual effort ought to be rewarded upon a competitive basis. These views are said to correspond to, and derive from, the capitalist period of history. As capitalism recedes, they will be retained only in the initial phase of the construction of Socialism and will finally be sloughed off entirely. On the question of how Socialist equality is to be established, there is a crucial ambiguity in the Marxian position. On the one hand, it is asserted that the change in values will follow as "a consequence" from the advance of production; on the other hand, it is argued that when capitalism is overthrown and when the initial stages of Socialism are past, technological determinism will come to an end. Instead, man's essential, "natural" qualities and values will finally assert themselves and make technology a servant rather than a master. On the one hand, the achievement of Socialist equality is regarded as a logical result of the working of the forces of history; on the other hand, it is an achievement which must wait upon the final self-abrogation of the laws of history and which assumes that there is indeed an essential or natural condition of man quite apart from the historical versions of human nature. To examine this paradox more closely it is necessary to pass, as Marx might himself have said, from his critical to his positive theory of equality.

MARXIAN SOCIALIST EQUALITY

The critique of Liberal equality is accompanied in Marxian doctrine by what amounts to a restatement of the Socialist conception of equality as it was expressed by Müntzer and Winstanley, with the important addition of an ambiguous technological determinism. Marx himself only implied the existence of an essential natural man who would reappear, or appear for the first time at the final stage of history. Engels, in adopting the anthropological work of Lewis H. Morgan, provided Marxism with the classic Socialist formula: communist equality exists in the original state of the race, but is abandoned in a lamentable "fall" from innocence; it is followed by successive periods of inequality, continually increasing in severity until finally equality is re-established and all social inequality is annihilated. As scientific as Marx and Engels may have considered their doctrines, and not altogether without justification, it is striking that this historical formula should present itself both in the primarily theological thought of Müntzer and Winstanley, and in the avowedly antireligious, antitheological thought of Marxism. Even though theirs is essentially a progressist theory of history, Marx and Engels apparently felt irresistibly attracted to the notion of paradise regained. Engels seized upon the work of Morgan not only because of its emphasis upon the determinative effect of the process of production, but also because it suggested that communism was the original (and idyllic) state of humanity. In the age of gentile communism, "all are equal and free." There is no slavery, no oppression; primitive men who have not strayed far from this original state are noted for their "personal dignity, uprightness, strength of character." [96] The original state could not be maintained, both because of the inexorable advance of technology and because of human passions. The result is a fall from the purity of the original state:

The power of this primitive community had to be broken, and it was broken. But it was broken by influences which from the very start appear as a degradation, a fall from the simple moral greatness of the old gentile society. The lowest interests—base greed, brutal appetites, sordid avarice, selfish robbery of the common wealth—inaugurate the new, civilized, class society. [97]

The Socialist future of society is regarded as the re-establishment, under advanced conditions of production, of the values at the origin of history. Engels italicizes the conclusion of Morgan that the future society will be "a revival, in a higher form, of the liberty, equality, and fraternity of the ancient *gentes*." [98]

Between this original state and the future state, history is a story of ever increasing, ever more manifold inequality, and, at the same time, of the gradual rise of egalitarian ideology. In tracing this history, Marx and Engels intend to indicate the "scientific content" of the idea of equality, to distinguish the Socialist understanding of equality from its bourgeois and idealist-Socialist predecessors and contemporaries. This understanding rests on the assumption that values do not play an autonomous role in history, but are the reflection of different stages in the organization of production. Equality only becomes a significant ideological battle cry when the forces of production require it. The Greeks, Engels writes, because of the immaturity of the forces of production, knew virtually nothing of equality and considered inequality to be the universal principle of order. The Romans, even though they made the important step of establishing legal and political equality, still maintained the basic distinction between freemen and slaves. Christianity "knew only *one* point in which all men were equal: that all were equally born in original sin." This corresponded to the character of Christianity as "the religion of the slaves and the oppressed." The "traces of common ownership" found in the practices of early Christian groups are dismissed by Engels as a reaction of sectarian solidarity against oppression, rather than attempts to practice Christian values. [99] In any case, Christianity put an end to its egalitarian tendencies in short order as distinctions were allowed to arise between priests and laymen. In the Middle Ages, the highly developed inequality of feudalism issued in an antithesis in the form of "the class which was destined in the future course of its evolution to be the standard-bearer of the modern demand for equality: the bourgeoisie." [100] The economic underpinnings of egalitarian ideology are nowhere more apparent than in the case of the bourgeoisie:

Trade on a large scale, that is to say . . . world trade, requires free owners of commodities who are unrestricted in their movements and have equal rights as traders to exchange their commodities on the basis of laws that are equal for them all. . . The transition from handicraft to manufacture presupposes the existence of a number of free workers—free on the one hand from the fetters of the guild and on the other from the means whereby they could themselves utilize their labour power: workers who can contract with their employers for the hire of their labour power, and as parties to the contract have rights equal with his.

But the "clearest expression" of bourgeois egalitarianism, albeit unconscious, is contained in the value theory of bourgeois economics. Against feudal economic and extra-economic forms of inequality the bourgeoisie sets an equality of men as free producers of value. Once it achieved its own limited class goals, the bourgeoisie sought to limit the application of the doctrine of equality. But the annihilation of privileges claimed by the bourgeoisie for commerce and industry was bound to be extended into other areas. Why should equality not also be the standard for the agricultural peasantry?

Inevitably, with the advance of industrialization, the bourgeois demand for equality came to be "accompanied by the proletarian demand for equality." In the past the proletarian demand was couched in terms of the revival of primitive Christianity. In the conditions of industrialism it takes the more realistic form of a demand that the bourgeoisie make good on its promises and establish real equality—not merely an equality of rights and an equality before the law, but an equality in social status and economic benefits. In principle, however, the proletarian advocacy of equality, when it is not simply a reaction against oppression but a positive expression of ethical principle, rests on the same grounds as bourgeois equality.

In one important respect, however, proletarian equality differs from bourgeois doctrine. The proletarians demand not only the abolition of class privileges, but the abolition of classes.[101] In this demand they come to the verge of scientific Socialist egalitarianism. For the key to the understanding of the problem of equality is not some ethical idea, but the actual historical relation of classes. Bourgeois equality, for all its pretensions, presupposes the dominance of the capitalist class over the proletariat. In fact, however, the existence of classes is the source of all inequality. To speak of equality among the classes, as Proudhon does, is ridiculous. As a history of the division of society into classes continually struggling for dominance, all pre-Socialist history is a history of inequality. In the last analysis this division into classes is the result of the division of labor: classes make their appearance in history as soon as there is division of labor. Division of labor is not, as the bourgeois economists claim, a form in which social harmony results from natural individualism, but an expression of antagonism. When the division of labor between town and country arises, enmity develops between the groups inhabiting the two areas. The same antagonism is felt by journeymen and masters within the guilds. When the division of labor advances to the point where masters and journeymen perform different operations, they become split into antagonistic groups. Another such split occurs when the suppliers of capital and the suppliers of labor are ranged into two separate groups. Under capitalist economic organization, power accrues to the owners of the means of production. This class, the bourgeoisie, becomes the dominant class in modern society.[102]

Inequality makes its first historical appearance in the family, when, as a result of the division of labor, "wife and child are the slaves of the husband." In the opposition of families to each other, the antagonism spreads: from this opposition there results an "unequal distribution . . . of labour and its products, hence property."[103] Finally the division of labor produces class antagonism, and, as a further result, the state arises as a mediator of class conflict. However, even when the state is not merely a creature of the dominant class, it cannot eradicate class antagonisms because these antagonisms derive from the process of production. Only when the process of production advances to a higher stage of development can class antagonism cease, because the division of labor will have been overcome and classes will have been abolished by the productive process.

In this way, and only in this way, will equality replace inequality. The logic of this economic determinism points up the significance of Marx's famous remark about the future society to the effect that men would then hunt in the morning, fish in the afternoon, rear cattle in the evening, and criticize after dinner.[104] In context, as has often been remarked, this deserves to be taken as more than a casual and humorous suggestion, for it states a principle essential to Marxian theory—the overcoming of the division of labor which was the root cause of all inequality. If this were to prove impossible, Marxian Socialism would be contradicted at a most essential point. Marx was confident that the division of labor would be reduced to an obsolete expression of the lower stages of development, as the means of production became so highly automatic and so highly productive that abundance would be possible with a small investment of labor. At this stage, it would no longer be necessary to compel men, for the sake of their own and the social subsistence, to engage in a single occupation. Marx does not specify the exact form of economic and social organization which will supersede the division of labor, on the ground that to do so would be unscientific. Engels criticizes a discussion of the distribution of goods in the future society upon the same ground and in a way which indicates the importance of economic determinism for Marxian theory even in the final stage of development: "But strangely enough it has never struck anyone that, after all, the method of division essentially depends on *how much* there is to divide, and that this must surely change with the progress of production and social organization, so that the method of division may also change." As a social scientist, "all one can reasonably do . . . is (1) to try and discover the method of division to be used *at the beginning,* and (2) to try and find the *general tendency* in which further development will proceed."[105]

In *The Origin of the Family* Engels also develops the argument that equality and inequality are results of the organization of production. In "gens communism" the woman is a co-producer, there is no private property, and as a result there is no inequality. The rise of the monogamous family, with its distinctions of status as between husband, wife, and children, and of wealth among the various families, is linked to "the victory of private property over primitive, natural communal property."[106] The division of labor reduces the woman to the status of "head servant" rather than co-producer. The husband, Engels writes, is like the bourgeoisie, the wife like the proletariat.[107] Monogamy develops because property is made private and attached to families dominated by the male members of society. The first "class" antagonism is therefore the relation of husband and wife; the second, the opposition of families within the society.[108] Under capitalism the domination of the wife by the husband is maintained, but a new element enters into the relationship which augurs a change. The substitution of contract for status has the effect of requiring the consent of the woman to marriage. Under capitalism this free consent is a sham because choice is limited and determined by property relations. The same is true for the "free" contract of the laborer with his employer: legally the parties to the contract are assumed to be equal; in fact they are unequal because the relations of power behind the legal façade are disproportionate.[109] In both cases, however, the equality of legal rights is a step toward actual emancipation. Full realization depends upon the conditions of production. When women are again made co-producers by the advance of industry, and private property is abolished, dependence will also disappear. The monogamous family will either vanish or reappear purged of inequality and exploitation, as a relation of real love.[110]

Implicit in these arguments is the assumption that social relations, and hence equality, derive from the process of production. When the division of labor is made obsolete, inequality will disappear with it. The Socialist conception of equality is therefore no ideological deduction of rights from common characteristics, but a theory which asserts that equality will characterize human relations at a certain period in the evolution of production. Since the process of production carries, as it were, the seed of human social purpose in history, the outcome is to be accounted the highest form of moral relations. Until now, Marx wrote, we have not grasped the relation of industry to man's moral essence. Instead, "we have looked for the actuality of human essential capacities and activity of the human *species* only in the universal existence of man in religion, or history in its abstractly universal essence."[111] This outlook is appropriate only while man still labors under the curse of human self-alienation. This burden begins to be lifted when men recognize that industry is "the exoteric unfolding of human *essential capacities*."[112] Industry is not merely a condition, or one of a set of conditions, in which the human essence may express itself; it is the primary form of that expression itself.

Yet, as we have already indicated, alongside this rigorous technological determinism, embodying the belief that values are immanent not only in history generally, but specifically in the organization of production, there is the other Marxian view which asserts that with the achievement of Socialism this determinism will come to an end. Indeed, Marx goes well beyond this qualification when he asserts in "Private Property and Communism" that technological determinism, even if it reaches into property relations, will not be sufficient to create a Socialist society. In his attack upon "vulgar communism" Marx accepts many of the criticisms made against communism. He admits that communism, in the sense of a levelling of differences in wealth and property, without anything further, will merely universalize greed and materialism (in the pejorative, ethical sense of the word). This form of communism only makes private property universal and, with private property, all the moral vices which characterize it at earlier periods of history. It "overestimates the role and domination of *material* property to such a degree that it wishes to abolish *everything* which cannot be possessed by everybody as *private property*."[113] The replacement of marriage by the community of women, as practiced in vulgar communism, is, Marx urges, the "secret clue" to the character of this form of communism. The woman is not emancipated from her existence as a chattel, but, what is perhaps even worse, she is made the chattel of every man in society.

In the same way that the woman is to abandon marriage for general prostitution, so the whole world of wealth, that is, the material essence of man, goes from the relation of exclusive marriage with the private property owner [to] the relation of universal prostitution with the community. . . Since it completely negates the *personality* of man, this type of communism is only the logical expression of private property, which is just this negation.[114]

Thus what is important for the realization of true communism is not simply the equalization of property but the overcoming of the inhumanity which is the historical by-product of property.

Universal *envy*, constituted as power, is only the secret guise in which *greed* asserts itself and is to be satisfied. The thought of every property owner, as such, is directed—*at least* against the *wealthier* one—as envy and a desire to reduce all to a common level, constituting even the essence of competition. The vulgar communist is only the consummation of this envy and this craving to level down, establishing a certain common denominator . . . [This] is only a retrogression to the *unnatural* simplicity of a *poor* and needy man, who not only has not gone beyond the limits of private property, but has not even attained its level.[115]

This transformation must involve a change not only in the distribution of property but in the attitude toward property. In the past, property has been a kind of Greek fate, hovering over man and controlling him, and the equal distribution of property does not immediately change anything. The key to emancipation lies in the growth of identification among men. It is only possible when "the senses and spirit of other men have become my own appropriation." Then and only then will private property be transcended by the "total freeing of all the human senses and attributes," and an "emancipation" which implies victory in the struggle for the expression of what is really "human" in man.[116] In the true, ultimate stage of communism man will no longer be a creature of his material needs. Men will replace technology as the governors of the social universe and will devote themselves to the realization of human creative capacities; but the precondition of this activity is the triumph over egoism in which men will realize their identity. True communism, Marx believed, would amount to "the return of man to himself as *social, i.e.,* human man, complete, conscious and matured within." It would represent "the *true* solution of the strife between men and nature, and between man and man."[117]

Clearly, Marx recognized with Hegel that the redistribution of property would not of itself bring true communism, in the sense of an overcoming of egoism and antagonism, unless accompanied by a spiritual transformation in human character. Unlike Hegel, he did not allow this recognition to cloud his vision of future fulfillment. But he too glimpsed the dilemma of Socialist egalitarianism that forced itself upon Hegel. Once emancipated, would the essence of humanity prove to be a universal altruism, or would

an unyielding shell of separate individuality remain to frustrate perfect communism? Would it be possible to reproduce this personal
altruism in social institutions without raising a still more oppressive communal authority in the place of a ruling class, without
substituting for the coercion of circumstances a visible and invisible compulsion to conform? No less than Liberal and
Conservative theorists of equality, the Socialists could not escape
their own doubts and difficulties as they struggled to formulate
the governing principles of a reality not yet in being.

CHAPTER NINE

Equality and the Decline of Political Philosophy

⁓⁓⁓⁓⁓

IFFERENCES AMONG philosophers are important only if we concede the importance of philosophy itself. Nowadays it is sometimes said that political philosophy is obsolete—no longer necessary, no longer useful, no longer possible. With rare exceptions, the books written on the subject do not expound new political philosophies but instead examine those that have already been expounded. It would certainly seem that, insofar as we retain an interest in the philosophic tradition, it is as historians and critics rather than as fresh contributors to an endless dialogue renewed in each succeeding generation. Why then should we concern ourselves with the philosophic ambiguities of the problem of equality?

To answer this question we must define what we mean by political philosophy, and then consider what philosophy can tell us about equality. Political philosophy attempts to describe and evaluate systematically the nature and function of government. The normative character of the enterprise makes political philosophy different from political science, and the systematic element lifts it above ordinary political controversy, however rigorous. Political philosophers, we may say, try to reach a level of abstraction on which the issues of the day may be examined in the light of perennial or at least more general principles. The record of political philosophy displays sufficient thematic unity to enable us to speak of it as a tradition of inquiry conducted at two levels: on one, the issue is human nature; on the other, it is the proper ordering of society. As surrounding circumstances change, these themes are restated in different terms. The Greek philosophers probed the analogy between the constitution of the *polis* and that of the soul. In the ages of faith, theologians justified the relation of spiritual to temporal by analogy with the relation of the soul to the body. The contract theorists argued for freedom or for authority as their stress fell on the relative roles of reason and passion in human nature.

It was when all these terms of argument, and in particular those put forward in theories of the state of nature and the social contract, were criticized and dismissed as arbitrary, fictitious, and oblique ways of examining things that political philosophy took a final fateful turning in the direction of empirical science. As it came to be accepted that only empirical research—into the causal relationships of changing patterns of thought and practice, into the regularities of personal and group behavior—could possibly pronounce upon human nature and social order, political philosophy was eclipsed by social science.

Whether the eclipse has provided more or less illumination is debatable. It is now generally admitted that what was intended to be a radical advance from philosophic presumption to scientific certainty has often issued merely in the replacement of one rhetoric with another. Formerly philosophic contentions, miraculously salvaged from the ashcans of history, regularly emerged from their assigned oblivion in chic "scientific" dress. History was the story (depending on the storyteller) of liberty, of the coming slavery, of economic stagnation or cornucopic abundance. Sociological "iron laws" declared the necessity of tradition, authority, and aristocracy and then declared that sociology itself was determined by social perspective and *Zeitgeist*. Psychology unmasked old illusions only to reveal the need for new ones, which were promptly supplied in the form of standards for psychic health and social adjustment.

Not all social scientists have jumped to conclusions so freely;

nor has the effort to create a science of society run its course by any means. It would therefore be wrong and premature to see in all social science merely a naive scientism. It remains true, nevertheless, that no scientific laws have yet been offered which cast comprehensive light on human nature and social order, in terms demonstrably free of value judgment and yet determinate. It may be that science will never be capable of transcending the relativity of values in human experience, because of limitations in the techniques available to social science, because of the volatile, malleable character of social phenomena, and perhaps because there is something in the nature of man in society that makes diversity and indeterminacy ultimate characteristics. No complaint is more frequently heard among social scientists than that which says in effect: "There are too many variables."

But if social science has not been as successful in its positive achievements as it is sometimes made out to be, it has certainly chalked up a critical success against political philosophy. Those with more than an antiquarian interest in the older tradition have had to content themselves with studying the history of this tradition in the hope that something, somehow, would come of it. Some have worked on abstruse questions of political philosophy, others among down-to-earth political ideologies and climates of opinion. The results have not always displayed impeccable academic objectivity. Historical study has in fact sometimes been a surrogate for open philosophizing. No less than social science, the history of political thought has enabled those who study it to resurrect long interred arguments as agents of present controversy. The history of ideas readily becomes an account of degeneration or a progressive revelation culminating in some contemporary set of ideals or dangers.

In an effort to cleanse the scientific enterprise of its philosophic entanglements and to use the study of the history of political thought to destroy the phantoms of the philosophers, at least one fresh alternative has been proposed by adherents of modern analytic philosophy. These theorists tend to argue that controversies among philosophers either amount to misunderstandings or could be resolved by constant reference to concrete facts. They contend, in other words, that political philosophy inflates conflicts, which might otherwise be soluble through prudent compromise, into grand illusions making domestic and international tensions far more acute than they need be. Implicit in this contention is the tacit assumption that apart from ambiguities of language there are no fundamental conflicts over ends, but only disagreements over means best left to practical and scientific study.

As a critical tool analytic philosophy is certainly useful, but the preoccupation with critical tasks is inherently inadequate. Is the demonstration of Rousseau's exaggerations and contradictions nearly as important as the consideration of his insights? Does the shift from ends to means dissolve value conflicts or only relocate them? Insofar as the success of prudent compromise depends upon the achievements of social science, which are as yet so limited, will we not find ourselves with no guidance at all if at this point we abandon philosophy altogether?

The conclusion seems inescapable that whether or not we believe in the ultimate ability of social science to clear up all difficulties in the realm of value, and whether or not we accept the contentions of analytic philosophy, we remain in need—if only in that possibly eternal interim before science makes its final revelations and prudence settles all conflicts—of something very much like political philosophy. Yet it must be admitted that political philosophy can only be reinstated on limited terms. A philosopher who might have the presumption to argue that a particular notion of right and obligation is sanctioned by nature, whereas others are not, would very likely find his position dismissed as arbitrary (or worse, as quaint). Only if political philosophy can come to terms with the relativity of values short of a surrender to nihilism, only if the plasticity of nature can be accepted short of a surrender to naturalism, only as the insights of science are assimilated and ambiguities of language avoided, can the tradition be restored. Such a restored political philosophy might not play the commanding roles it has heretofore been accorded, but it would perform a function in society for which there is always a great need. That function would not be to lay down any laws but to help clarify questions of public purpose and to consider contemporary problems in the light of ultimate values.

How might such a restored political philosophy deal with the issue of equality? The first step would be to recognize the persistence of several concepts of equality, exhibiting several fundamentally different sets of attitudes toward human nature and social order. In describing human nature, the Liberal stresses the capacity for reason and the will to autonomy; the Socialist stresses common humanity, identical needs, and the inclination to productive labor; the Conservative stresses the power of the antisocial passions. For society, the Liberal advocates individualism, the Socialist collectivism; the Conservative poses the choice of anarchy or absolutism wherever graded hierarchy is ruled out. A restored philosophy would have to begin from the recognition that all three definitions of equality must somehow be taken into account.

Conceivably, further reflection might trace the philosophic differences to the more elemental level of temperament. For Socialist, Liberal, and Conservative, could we not write Optimist, Meliorist, and Pessimist? The Socialist calls for a grand reconciliation of all separation and conflict; the Liberal accepts a degree of conflict and even makes a virtue of it, within limits; the Conservative sees so much conflict that he feels a dire need of order. Temperament will not account for all of the substantive differences among the doctrines of equality, but along with historical circumstances it must surely play an important role in any explanation of the persistent attraction these doctrines have exerted.

If we assume that, whatever the ultimate reasons for the persistence of these concepts of equality, they must be accepted as a condition of discussion, we reach the question of their relevance to modern conditions. We must bear in mind, of course, that the decline of political philosophy was not accompanied by the demise of equality as a political issue. Even when the philosophic springs went dry, ideology remained as a reservoir from which the philosophic analysis of equality could be taken and applied to many of the most critical and inflamed issues of modern history, including popular government and the extension of the suffrage; private property, taxation, and welfare legislation; slavery and female emancipation; religious tests and racial discrimination; and the nature and availability of education.

In the industrially advanced nations of the West, most of these once burning issues survive only as dying embers, and the camps of the antagonists are all but deserted. Instead there is virtually universal if tacit agreement that the gap between rich and poor, powerful and powerless, fortunate and unfortunate, ought in some degree and in certain particulars to be narrowed and made more passable. A combination of prosperity and practical compromise has even softened the tone of the residual arguments over what degree and which particulars. Insofar as racial discrimination remains a subject of heated controversy, the debate is hardly conducted (nor was it ever) in philosophic terms. There are, to be sure, those mock philosophers who claim that equal rights contradict individual liberty, as though there could be a genuine liberty that was not reciprocal, a freedom for one individual to deny to others the rights he demands for himself. Otherwise, what intellectual argument there is on this subject tends to invoke the authority of natural and social science. Each side claims its biologists and anthropologists, its sociologists and its separate sets of statistical data. Such a debate is scarcely evidence of the survival of egalitarianism as a philosophic issue. Quite the contrary, it is only additional proof of the utter decline in relevance suffered by a tradition of inquiry that once stood as the highest moral court of appeal for social controversy.

All the nihilistic revolts of the nineteenth and twentieth centuries, including imperialism and reactive nationalism as well as racism, are far less by-products of the philosophic tradition than symptoms of its ebbing vitality. The troublesome and even monstrous consequences of these revolts should not be taken as an indictment of political philosophy, but as a warning against the casual abandonment or the cynical distortion of the entire tradition. As the pigs who seized control of "Animal Farm" (in George Orwell's classic modern fable) demonstrated so pithily, when philosophy becomes an instrument of control it ceases to be philosophy. "All animals are equal, but some are more equal than others," is a slogan that compounds conventional philosophic ambiguity with the cynicism of the modern propagandist. It announces the end of all philosophizing and the arrival of a mindless, purposeless imprisonment of will and intellect.[1]

It follows that if the tradition of political philosophy is to be revived in our time, it is also necessary to recognize the great changes registered in social history since philosophies became frozen into ideologies. In particular, it is essential to take account of the ways in which many of the goals espoused or predicted by philosophers of the past have in fact already come to pass. In some instances the very achievement of egalitarian goals has raised fresh possibilities of inequality. The coordination and control required in a Socialist society make large-scale bureaucratic hierarchy indispensable. Collective ownership, it is now obvious, does not preclude the rise of a new, managerial class. A similar paradox results from the acceptance of the belief that educational opportunities should be extended to all who can benefit from them. As a British sociologist has pointed out, in a work of social-science fiction, equality of opportunity may in the long run promote a new form of hierarchy, in his term, a "meritocracy," in which stratification will follow from ability and performance. Meritocracy, Michael Young contends, would arouse as much snobbery and envy as any class system, and the psychological insecurity of the lower classes would be worse than ever. In a conventional class system without equal opportunity, those who do not rise to the top can always blame their failure on circumstances. In a meritocracy they would have to face their own inadequacies squarely. "Educational injustice," Young's man of the future proclaims, "enabled people to preserve their illusions, inequality of opportunity fostered the myth of human equality."[1] Would most of them not find the truth too painful to bear?

In contemplating this prospect we can perhaps take comfort from the human capacity to find solace for comparative inadequacies, not only in illusions, but in the innumerable avenues of hope, escape, and security that crisscross every complex civilization. Plato's royal lie was a comparatively heavy-handed effort to take the sting out of inequality. Later generations have managed not to appear so deliberately deceptive. The belief in luck, as expressed in some forms of gambling, flourishes in the most advanced industrial societies. The quest for psychological security and acceptance and the encouragement of conformity to group norms seem to develop alongside the intensification of distinctions in rank and function. A complex society, moreover, offers so many opportunities for achievement that a man inadequate in one direction may easily excel in another. Where all these activities are valued almost interchangeably, few men need be made to feel the shame of a particular inferiority.

Plainly, the ideological debates over equality are becoming much less relevant in the advanced nations of the West than they were during the growing pains of industrialization, when scarcity was felt as a more acute problem, when the differences in education and opportunity were more dependent upon class, race, sex, and religion, and when some of the solutions proposed to meet these difficulties seemed to threaten the very fabric of society. But the irrelevance of the nineteenth century ideologies should not prevent us from recognizing that the values expressed in the philosophies of equality remain as relevant as ever, providing only that we address them to new-felt needs. Liberal egalitarians can take little comfort from the mounting intrusion of irrational appeals upon the deliberative process so essential to representative government, or from the increasing authority of technical specialists, or from the growing power of public and private governments to coerce recalcitrant individuals. Conservative critics of equality may properly remain concerned at the threat of mediocrity and banality and the dangers of a merely appetitive pursuit of happiness. Socialist egalitarians may well wish to direct the impulse to improvement beyond economic welfare to a corresponding development in popular moral and cultural standards and practices. More pluralistic personalities may well feel that all three traditions stand for values which, in one degree or another, a good society must take into account, and that all three stand against dangers which a good society must be careful to avoid. However these values are construed, the very fact of their continued existence—as values and not as outworn cliches or hypocritical rationalizations—may someday make more possible a lasting and creative mode of human coexistence, both domestic and international. The achievement of such a goal would more than repay any effort to restore the great tradition of political philosophy, even as this restoration would in turn justify the work of historical clarification as a necessary and even crucial preparing of the ground.

NOTES

Numerals following titles indicate the divisions of original texts, arranged in logical order; thus *Institutes of the Christian Religion,* 4.6, refers to book iv, chap. vi.

CHAPTER ONE

Three Concepts of Equality

1. J. G. Nicolay and J. Hay, eds., *Complete Works of Abraham Lincoln* (Harrogate, Tenn., 1894), address of June 26, 1857, pp. 330-331. Quoted by H. A. Myers, *Are Men Equal?* (Ithaca, New York, 1955), p. 89.

2. Address at Springfield, Ill., July 17, 1858, in Paul M. Angle, ed., *Created Equal? The Complete Lincoln-Douglas Debates of 1858* (Chicago, 1958), p. 82.

3. "Equality," in *Mixed Essays* (New York, 1880), p. 51.

4. *Ibid.,* p. 92.

5. *Liberty, Equality, Fraternity* (New York, 1873).

6. "Social Equality," *International Journal of Ethics,* 1: 261-288 (April 1891).

7. *What Social Classes Owe to Each Other* (New York, 1883), p. 41.

8. *Equality* (New York, 1897), p. 19.

9. *Les idées égalitaires* (Paris, 1899).

10. A. T. Hadley, *The Conflict Between Liberty and Equality* (New York, 1925).

11. *Equality* (London, 1931).

12. D. Thomson, *Equality* (Cambridge, England, 1949), p. 147.

13. Myers, *Are Men Equal?,* pp. 49-51.

14. "Equality," in *Proceedings of the Aristotelian Society,* New Series, vol. LVI, 1955-56 (London, 1956), p. 236.

15. *Ibid.,* pp. 313-314.

16. *Ibid.,* p. 317. Emphasis added.

17. "Conservative Thought," in K. Mannheim, *Essays on Sociology and Social Psychology,* trans. P. Kecskemeti (New York, 1953), pp. 105-106.

18. "Equality," *Proceedings,* p. 300.

19. See his introduction to *The Great Chain of Being* (Cambridge, Mass., 1948), pp. 14-17.

CHAPTER TWO

Ultimate and Operative: The Classical Dualism

1. *Medieval Political Theory in the West* (London, 1927), I, 8. Even Werner Jaeger's inspired commentary on the Platonic dialogues fails to distinguish between Plato's belief in natural hierarchy and his advocacy of equality on other grounds. See *Paideia: the Ideals of Greek Culture*, trans. G. Highet (New York, 1939-1944), II, 246, and *passim*. Leo Strauss makes a similarly indiscriminate generalization in claiming that egalitarian natural right was "rejected by the classics." *Natural Right and History* (Chicago, 1953), p. 118.

2. George H. Sabine and Stanley B. Smith note that "Stoic ethics and politics tend to fall into a radical dualism." In Stoic political theory "we have the perfect society of wise men, without institutions or organization, a pure ideal having no apparent relation to any society of actual human beings." Introduction to Marcus Tullius Cicero, *On the Commonwealth*, trans. Sabine and Smith (Columbus, Ohio, 1929), p. 25. See also J. Plamenatz, "Equality of Opportunity," *Aspects of Human Equality, Fifteenth Symposium of the Conference on Science and Religion* (New York, 1957). The Stoics and Epicureans, Plamenatz points out (p. 87), believed that "all men are by nature capable of virtue and happiness. But they never went on to say that they should therefore have equal rights and opportunities. They did not believe in political or legal or social equality."

3. For an exposition of Aquinas' theory of equality, demonstrating the coexistence in his system of "Spiritual equality" and "hierarchical society," see M. J. F. Ferguson, *The Philosophy of Equality*, in *The Catholic University of America Philosophical Studies*, LXVIII (Washington, 1943), 105-191.

4. *Laws*, 5.739, in *The Dialogues of Plato*, trans. B. Jowett (New York, 1937), II, 506.

5. *Republic*, 5.454-457, in *Dialogues* (Jowett), I, 715-718.

6. *Ibid.*, 4.432 (I, 695).

7. *Ibid.*, 8.557-558 (I, 816).

8. *Ibid.*, 8.561 (I, 820).

9. *Ibid.*, 8.562-563 (I, 821).

10. *Ibid.*, 8.546-557 (I, 804-815).

11. *Ibid.*, 8.564 (I, 822).

12. "Slavery in Plato's Thought," *The Philosophical Review*, 50:300 (May 1941).

13. See *ibid.*, p. 301.

14. See books 1 and 2.

15. See *The Politics of Aristotle*, 1.5.1254a.2, trans. E. Barker (Oxford, 1950), shortened version, pp. 14-15; 1.5.1254b.8 (p. 16).

16. *Ibid.*, 1.13.1260a.7-8 (pp. 43-44).

17. *Ibid.*, 4.8.1294a.9 (p. 208).

18. *Ibid.*, 2.7.1266b.5 (p. 77).

19. *Ibid.*, 3.11.1282a.14 (p. 147).

20. See, however, E. A. Havelock's attack upon Aristotle's doctrine of proportional equality as "an example of philosophic cannibalism. A serious theoretic position that men are historically equal and should be socially organized in such a way as to reflect this—is not rebutted in open fight, but turned inside out and then, in a more palatable form, swallowed into the system of its benevolent host,"—the theory of oligarchy. *The Liberal Temper in Greek Politics* (New Haven, 1957), p. 371. For an advocacy of propor-

tional equality which is clearly built out of a concern similar to that of Aristotle to chart a *via media* between equality and inequality, see the proposal of the Athenian spokesman in Plato's *Laws*, 6.756-757 *Dialogues* (Jowett), II, 518-519.

21. *The City of God*, 11.22, trans. M. Dods (New York, 1950, Modern Library), p. 365.

22. Dionysius Areopagita, *Oeuvres complètes du Pseudo-Denys l'Aréopagite*, trans. from the Latin by M. de Gandillac (Paris, 1943), pp. 84-85.

23. *Ibid.*, p. 88.

24. A. O. Lovejoy and George Boas, *A Documentary History of Primitivism and Related Ideas*, Vol. I: *Contributions to the History of Primitivism. Primitivism and Related Ideas in Antiquity* (Baltimore, 1935), p. 67.

25. Quoted *ibid.*, translated from Justin, *Historarium phillipicarum epitoma*, 43.1.3-4.

26. Quoted *ibid.*, p. 66, translated from *Cronosolon*, 13.

27. Lovejoy and Boas, *Primitivism*, p. 16.

28. *Ibid.*, p. 123.

29. *The Pursuit of the Millennium* (London, 1957), p. 200.

30. R. Bultmann, *The Theology of the New Testament*, trans. K. Grobel (New York, 1951), I, 309.

31. See Cohn, *Pursuit of the Millennium*, p. 203. Lovejoy, in "The Communism of St. Ambrose," *Essays in the History of Ideas* (Baltimore, 1948), points out that while Ambrose did not regard the communism of the ideal state of nature as having practical application, he was nevertheless sharply critical of economic inequalities and of avarice (p. 298, and *passim*).

32. *City of God*, 19.15 (p. 693).

33. *Ibid.*, p. 694.

34. *Ibid.*, 19.17 (p. 696).

35. Lovejoy and Boas, *Primitivism*, p. 81.

36. See George Boas, *Essays on Primitivism and Related Ideas in the Middle Ages* (Baltimore, 1948).

CHAPTER THREE

Equality in the Reformation

1. *An Open Letter to the Christian Nobility of the German Nation, Concerning the Reform of the Christian Estate* (1520), in Luther's *Three Treatises* (Philadelphia, 1943), p. 16.

2. *Ibid.*, p. 14.

3. *Ibid.*, p. 28.

4. *Medieval Papalism* (London, 1949), p. 81.

5. As the Hungarian canonist, Damasus, asserted: "the clerical order is more worthy than the flock of laity" (*ordo clericorum dignior est coetu laicorum*). Quoted *ibid.*, p. 97.

6. Zenzilianus de Cassanis offered a typical formulation: "Know, it is

the order of nature that not all are equal." (*Intellige, ordo enim naturae est, quod non omnes sint equales.*) Damasus, in his *Summa*, identified this order with the entire universe: "Neither can the universe subsist . . . unless it is guarded by an order of great differences." (*Nec universitas . . . poterat . . . subsistere nisi ordo magnae differentiae eam servaret.*) Quoted *ibid.*

7. *A Commentary on St. Paul's Epistle to the Galatians* (1535), ed. P. S. Watson (London, 1953), p. 501.

8. *Ibid.*

9. *Ibid.*, p. 213.

10. This conception is said to appear first in a letter from Luther to Spalatin in 1519. See A. T. W. Steinhaeuser's introductory comments, *Works of Martin Luther*, IV (Philadelphia, 1950), 73.

11. *Letter to the Christian Nobility*, p. 14.

12. *A Prelude on the Babylonian Captivity of the Church* (1520), in *Three Treatises*, p. 231.

13. *Ibid.*, p. 234.

14. *Letter to the Christian Nobility*, pp. 15-16.

15. *Ibid.*, pp. 21-22.

16. Cf. Ullmann, *Medieval Papalism*, p. 116.

17. *Babylonian Captivity*, pp. 230-231.

18. In *Three Treatises*, pp. 263-264.

19. *Letter to the Christian Nobility*, p. 24.

20. *Secular Authority: To What Extent it Should Be Obeyed*, trans. J. Schindel, in *Works of Martin Luther*, III (Philadelphia, 1930), 234.

21. *Ibid.*, p. 258.

22. *Ibid.*, p. 259.

23. *Ibid.*, p. 253.

24. *Ibid.*, p. 265.

25. *Ibid.*, pp. 237, 262.

26. See *The Twelve Articles*, in *Works*, IV, 213 (Article Three).

27. Quoted by P. Smith, *The Life and Letters of Martin Luther* (Boston, 1911), p. 153.

28. *A Reply to the Twelve Articles*, in *Works*, IV, 240.

29. *Ibid.*, p. 228.

30. The peasants' first Article reads as though it might have been copied out of Luther's own pamphlets: "We should have authority and power so that a whole community should choose and appoint a pastor, and also have the right to depose him, if he should conduct himself improperly." *Twelve Articles*, p. 211.

31. *Gesammelte Aufsätze zur Kirchengeschichte*, 3 vols. (Tübingen, 1927-1928), I, 366-375.

32. See *The Protestant Ethic and the Spirit of Capitalism*, trans. T. Parsons (New York, 1948), *passim*.

33. *Letter to the Christian Nobility*, p. 82. Luther was not so ahead of his time, however, that he left behind the medieval agrarian bias: "This I know well, that it would be more pleasing to God if we increased agriculture and diminished commerce." *Ibid.*, p. 108.

34. See Josef Pieper, *Leisure the Basis of Culture*, trans. A. Dru (New York, 1952), *passim*.

35. *Treatise on Christian Liberty*, p. 269.

36. *Letter to the Christian Nobility*, p. 73.

37. See *On Trading and Usury*, in *Works*, IV, 12-69.

38. *Ibid.*, pp. 59-60.

39. *Institutes of the Christian Religion* (1536), 4.6, trans. H. Beveridge (London, 1953), II, 357.

40. *Ibid.*, pp. 357-358.

41. *Ibid.*, 4.4 (II, 328).

42. *Ibid.*, 4.6 (II, 358).

43. *Ibid.*, 4.5 (II, 340).

44. *Ibid.*, 4.4 (II, 335).

45. *Reply by Calvin to Cardinal Sadolet's Letter* (1539), in *Tracts and Treatises on the Reformation of the Church*, vol. I, trans. H. Beveridge (Grand Rapids, Mich., 1958), p. 61.

46. *Institutes*, 4.9 (II, 407-408).

47. *Ibid.*, 4.20 (II, 651).

48. *Ibid.* (p. 652).

49. *Ibid.* (p. 653).

50. *Ibid.* (p. 654).

51. *Ibid.* (pp. 670-671).

52. *Ibid.* (p. 675).

53. *Ibid.* (p. 676). As ambiguous as Calvin's position undoubtedly is, he cannot be held responsible for the attitude George H. Sabine finds in the "initial form" of Calvinism, which, he asserts, "lacked all leaning toward liberalism, constitutionalism,

or representative principles." See *A History of Political Thought* (New York, 1955), p. 363.

54. *Institutes*, 3.23 (II, 227). Calvin uses the term here with explicit reference to Plato.

55. *Ibid.*, 3.21 (II, 206).

56. *Johannes Calvin; Rede zur Feier der 400, Widerkehr des Geburtstages Calvins* (Berlin, 1909), p. 10.

57. *Second Defense of the Pious and Orthodox Faith Concerning the Sacraments in Answer to the Calumnies of Joachim Westphal*, in *Tracts*, II, 343.

58. *Institutes*, 3.21 (II, 202).

59. *Articles Agreed Upon by the Faculty of Sacred Theology of Paris, in Reference to Matters of Faith at Present Controverted; with the Antidote* (1542), in *Tracts*, I, 76-77.

60. See T. F. Torrance, *Calvin's Doctrine of Man* (Grand Rapids, Mich., 1957), p. 16, for an elaboration of this point.

61. See especially *A Treatise on the Eternal Predestination of God* (1552), trans. H. Cole, in *Calvin's Calvinism*, vol. I (London, 1856), for Calvin's confutation of those who hold that faith is an acceptance of the Gospel open to anyone. Faith, Calvin declares, "flows from Divine election" (p. 3) and is therefore available only to the elect. See also *Institutes*, 3.2 (I, 475).

62. *Institutes*, 3.14 (II, 74).

63. *The Necessity of Reforming the Church* (1544), in *Tracts*, I, 159. Torrance, *Calvin's Doctrine of Man*, makes the noteworthy point that Calvin's doctrine of depravity ought not to be considered apart from his belief in God's merciful regeneration of fallen man. Calvin's intention is not only to "show us man's degradation before God" but to prevent us "from seeing man in his mere degradation," for this would be to dishonor God (p. 17). In this effort to exonerate Calvin from the charge that he considers man only in his depravity, Torrance is compelled almost to ignore Calvin's emphatic belief in predestination. Calvin's belief that God fulfills his original intention despite human depravity, Torrance writes, "is hardly consistent with the doctrine that some men are expressly predestined to damnation" (p. 93). See also p. 66.

64. *Institutes*, 3.7 (II, 9).

65. *Ibid.*, 3.9 (II, 26).

66. *Ibid.*, 3.7 (II, 13).

67. *Reply to Sadolet*, pp. 41-42.

68. *Necessity of Reforming the Church*, p. 160.

69. *Institutes*, 3.7 (II, 14).

70. *Ibid.*, 3.19 (II, 136).

71. *Ibid.*, 4.20 (II, 657).

72. Calvin himself makes possible this modification when he writes that, although the elect cannot be certain of their faith ("this belongs not to us, but to God only"), as members of his church they "feel firmly assured" in their minds that they "are set apart." *Institutes*, 4.1 (II, 283). As far as the organization of the church is concerned, Calvin did not take this feeling of assurance into account because of the difficulty of distinguishing the elect: "though none are enlightened into faith, and truly feel the efficacy of the Gospel, with the exception of those who are fore-ordained to salvation, yet experience shows that the reprobate are sometimes affected in a way so similar to the elect, that even in their own judgment there is no difference between them." *Institutes*, 3.2 (I, 478). See also H. Berger, *Calvins Geschichtsauffassung* (Zürich, 1955), pp. 116-118, for the view that Calvin did not intend the church of believers to be identical with the body of the elect.

73. H. A. Myers, *Are Men Equal?* (Ithaca, New York, 1955), p. 27. Myers asserts that for this reason

the doctrine of natural depravity has "never aided . . . equality in America." See also V. L. Parrington, *Main Currents in American Thought*, I (New York, 1927), 21, for a similar discussion of the rise of oligarchy out of Calvinism in America.

74. *Institutes*, 3.22 (II, 207).

75. See *A Defence of the Secret Providence of God* (1558), trans. H. Cole, in *Calvin's Calvinism*, II, 28.

76. *Thomas Müntzer, sein Leben und seine Schriften* (Jena, 1933), ed. O. H. Brandt, intro., p. 33.

77. Müntzer read Tauler and Seuse while under Lutheran influence, as well as the church histories of Eusebius and Hegesippus and various works on ecclesiastical law. A. Lohmann, *Zur Geistigen Entwicklung Thomas Müntzers* (Leipzig and Berlin, 1931), p. 9.

78. "For me the testimony of the Abbot Joachim is weighty." *Of the Fantastic Beliefs* (1524), in *Leben und Schriften*, p. 132.

79. *Explicit Unmasking of the False Beliefs of a Faithless World* (1524), *ibid.*, p. 177.

80. *Highly Provoked Defense and Answer to the Unspiritual, Soft-living Flesh in Wittenberg* (1524), *ibid.*, p. 192.

81. See Luther's letter to the princes of Saxony, *On the Rebellious Spirit* (1524), *ibid.*, pp. 202–210.

82. *The Confessions of Thomas Müntzer* (1525), *ibid.*, p. 82.

83. *Historie Thomä Müntzers*, *ibid.*, p. 42. On the authorship of this document, see Brandt's note, p. 223. As Brandt remarks, the work bears the distinct impress of the Lutheran camp.

84. *Ibid.*, p. 164.

85. *Ibid.*, p. 187.

86. *Ibid.*, p. 192.

87. *Der Deutsche Bauernkrieg* (1850), trans. M. J. Olgin as *The Peasant War in Germany* (London, 1947).

88. M. M. Smirin, *Die Volksreformation des Thomas Münzer und der grosse Bauernkrieg*, trans. from the Russian by H. Nichtweiss (Berlin, 1952), p. 659. Three other works on Müntzer, also from a Marxist point of view, have been published in East Germany since 1948.

89. Smirin, *Volksreformation*, p. 96.

90. *Spiritual and Anabaptist Writers*, ed. G. H. Williams and A. Mergall, vol. XXV, *The Library of Christian Classics* (Philadelphia, 1957), intro., p. 32.

91. *Gesammelte Aufsätze*, I, 420–467.

92. See especially C. Hinrichs, *Luther und Müntzer, ihre Auseinandersetzung über Obrigkeit und Widerstandsrecht* (Berlin, 1952).

93. Norman Cohn, *The Pursuit of the Millennium* (London, 1957), p. 271.

94. Troeltsch, *The Social Teaching of the Christian Churches* (1911), trans. O. Wyon (New York, 1931), II, 754.

95. *Ibid.*, p. 331.

96. *Ibid.*, p. 336.

97. See Williams, *Spiritual and Anabaptist Writers*, intro., p. 22.

98. Stadler, *Cherished Instructions on Sin, Excommunication, and the Community of Goods* (c. 1537), *Spiritual and Anabaptist Writers*, p. 278.

99. *Ibid.*, pp. 278-279.

100. *Ibid.*, p. 281.

101. *Ibid.*, p. 277.

102. *Ibid.*, p. 280.

103. *Ibid.*, pp. 281-282.

104. *Ibid.*, p. 283.

105. Cohn, *Pursuit of the Millennium*, p. xiv; for the Flagellants in Germany, see *ibid.*, pp. 127-129; for the Free Spirit doctrine of direct revelation, see *ibid.*, pp. 182-185, 186-189.

106. *Cherished Instructions*, p. 278.

107. See J. Chapman, "Mysticism (Christian, Roman Catholic)," *Encyclopedia of Religion and Ethics*, ed. J. Hastings (New York, 1917), IX, 99-101.

108. See Holl, *Gesammelte Aufsätze*, I, 425, 435. Quotation cited by Holl is from Luther's foreword to his translation of the *Magnificat* (1521), in *Werke*, ed. Paul Pietsch, VII (Weimar, 1897), 546.

109. *Explicit Unmasking, Leben und Schriften*, pp. 168-169.

110. Attributed to Müntzer by his contemporary, Johannes Agricola, in his *Exposition of the Nineteenth Psalm*. Brandt, note, *Leben und Schriften*, p. 248. In the *Explicit Unmasking* Müntzer accuses Luther and his followers of making faith depend upon knowledge of the Bible so that they can keep the common man (*der gemeine Mann*) from becoming equal to them. *Ibid.*, p. 165.

111. *Leben und Schriften*, intro. p. 24.

112. *Of the Fantastic Beliefs*, p. 129.

113. *Ibid.*

114. *Explicit Unmasking*, p. 170.

115. *Of the Fantastic Beliefs*, p. 130.

116. *Ibid.*, p. 129.

117. *Explicit Unmasking*, pp. 167-168.

118. *Protestation or Declaration of Thomas Müntzer . . . Concerning his Doctrine as to the Beginning of Right Christian Belief and Baptism* (1524), *Leben und Schriften*, p. 135.

119. *Highly Provoked Defense*, p. 200.

120. *Protestation*, p. 133.

121. *Thomas Müntzers Briefwechsel auf Grund der Handschriften und ältesten Vorlagen*, ed. H. Böhmer and P. Kirn (Leipzig and Berlin, 1930), p. 58.

122. See Cohn, *Pursuit of the Millennium*, chaps. vii, viii, pp. 149-194 ("An Élite of Amoral Supermen").

123. *Briefwechsel*, p. 148.

124. *Sermon Before the Princes* (1524), in Williams, *Spiritual and Anabaptist Writers*, p. 64.

125. *Ibid.*, p. 69.

126. *Letter to the Allstedt Bund* (1525), in *Leben und Schriften*, p. 75. The possible significance of the reference to Nimrod is noted by Cohn. In 1531, the contemplative Sebastian Franck, in a commentary on the spurious Fifth Epistle of Clement, had added to the traditional legendary association of Nimrod with evil the view that the distinction of mine and thine resulted from Nimrod's accession to power. See note in Cohn, *Pursuit of the Millennium*, p. 421, and quotation from Franck on p. 280.

CHAPTER FOUR

From Theology to Politics

1. The term "Puritan" is used here to describe a political and religious movement made up of groups with certain limited common objectives, but without ideological unity. If, as William Haller asserts, "the central dogma of Puritanism" is "an all-embracing determinism, theologically formulated as the doctrine of pre-destination," then the Levellers are not dogmatic Puritans. *The Rise of Puritanism* (New York, 1938), p. 83. Since Haller himself does not exclude the Levellers from this designation he apparently intends that the term be taken to have different meanings in different uses. It would seem preferable to use the term, as

Joseph Frank does, to refer not to any particular ideology but to a coalition of groups which shared at most "an originally common source of motivation." *The Levellers* (Cambridge, Mass., 1953), p. 253. For, as Frank has observed, "in fact, there seems to be no common denominator which can distinguish the members of the several Puritan coalitions from their various opponents." *Ibid.*, p. 254. A. S. P. Woodhouse, after pointing out many of the difficulties which attend the use of "Puritanism" as a designation, nevertheless argues that what is common to all Puritan groups is the ideal, derived from Calvin, of establishing the "holy community." *Puritanism and Liberty* (Chicago, 1951), intro., pp. 36-37. D. B. Robertson argues persuasively that the Levellers did not share the ideal of the "holy community." *The Religious Foundations of Leveller Democracy* (New York, 1951), p. 109. Even if Woodhouse is correct, the different understandings of "holy community" reduce the consensus of the various groups to a vague minimum.

2. Woodhouse, *Puritanism and Liberty*, pp. 68-69.

3. *Ibid.*, pp. 206-207.

4. *Ibid.*, pp. 68-69.

5. Woodhouse, however, contends that Luther did not intend his doctrine of spiritual equality to apply to church organization, which he regarded as something "indifferent and at the discretion of the civil magistrate." *Ibid.*, intro., p. 67.

6. This resemblance was noted by Harold Laski when he wrote to Justice Holmes of his surprise that "nothing has been made in the books of the really obvious fact" that Hobbes's "view of human nature is simply Calvinism set down in naturalistic instead of supernatural terms." *Holmes-Laski Letters, The Correspondence of Mr. Justice Holmes*

and Harold J. Laski (1916-1935), ed. M. D. Howe (Cambridge, Mass., 1953), p. 951.

7. John Lilburne, *Londons Liberty in chains discovered* (1646), quoted by P. Zagorin, *A History of Political Thought in the English Revolution* (London, 1954), p. 12.

8. *The Free-Man's freedom vindicated* (1646), excerpted, Woodhouse, *Puritanism and Liberty*, p. 317.

9. *The Power of Love* (1643), in W. Haller, *Tracts on Liberty in the Puritan Revolution, 1638-1647*, 3 vols. (New York, 1934), II, 280.

10. *Ibid.*, p. 282.

11. *Ibid.*, p. 302.

12. As Robertson points out (*Religious Foundations*, p. 53) the conception of natural law held by Lilburne shows the influence both of Sir Edward Coke and of St. Germain's *The Dialogue in English, betweene a Doctor of Divinitie and a Student in the Lawes of England* (1530-1531). The Levellers collapsed (or, as Robertson has it, "forgot,") the distinction between the moral law revealed in Scripture and the natural law written in every man's heart. Robertson, pp. 62, 71. Thus they referred to the "dictates of Divinity, Nature and Reason ingraven in our hearts" (*A Copy of a Letter* [addressed to Sir Thomas Fairfax], 1647, in D. M. Wolfe, ed., *Leveller Manifestoes of the Puritan Revolution*, New York, 1944, p. 220), and also to the moral law revealed in Scripture.

13. See Zagorin, *Political Thought*, p. 40. Although the Levellers rejected the communism of the Diggers, they agreed with them in advocating the return of the commons to the poor. See Richard Overton, *Certain Articles for the Good of the Commonwealth* (1647), in Wolfe, *Leveller Manifestoes*, p. 194.

14. *A Copy of a Letter* [attached to *The Case of the Army Truly*

Stated] (1647), in Wolfe, *Leveller Manifestoes*, p. 219. The idea also appears in Lilburne's letter to William Prinne (1644), in Haller, *Tracts on Liberty*, III, 182.

15. Report of the Putney debates, in Woodhouse, *Puritanism and Liberty*, pp. 55-56.

16. *The Power of Love*, p. 297.

17. Woodhouse, *Puritanism and Liberty*, intro., p. 69.

18. Robertson, *Religious Foundations*, p. 90.

19. What Charles A. Beard wrote of freedom applies also to the concept of equality: "Nearly all the fundamentals of government and liberty had been set forth or foreshadowed in the declarations of the English Levellers long before Locke ever published his celebrated treatises on government." Wolfe, *Leveller Manifestoes*, foreword, p. viii.

20. Christ reaffirmed this law, preaching "Righteousness & Justice" summed up in the Golden Rule. Lilburne, *Londons libertie*, p. 12.

21. Luther, *A Commentary on St. Paul's Epistle to the Galatians* (1535), ed. P. S. Watson (London, 1953), intro., pp. 24, 28.

22. Woodhouse, *Puritanism and Liberty*, p. 53.

23. *Ibid.*, pp. 55-56.

24. Wolfe, *Leveller Manifestoes*, p. 297.

25. *Ibid.*, p. 384.

26. *Ibid.*, p. 391.

27. *The Power of Love*, p. 280.

28. Woodhouse, *Puritanism and Liberty*, pp. 63-64.

29. *A Manifestation* (1649), in Wolfe, *Leveller Manifestoes*, p. 394.

30. *An Appeale* (1647), *ibid.*, p. 158.

31. *Ibid.*, p. 162.

32. *Ibid.*, p. 163.

33. *Ibid.*, p. 162.

34. *Ibid.*, p. 179.

35. *Ibid.*, p. 180.

36. Thomas Hobbes, *The Levia-*

than (1651), 1.15, ed. W. G. Pogson Smith (Oxford, 1947), pp. 117-118.

37. *Elements of Philosophy Concerning the Body* [selections from *De Corpore*] (1656), in M. W. Calkins, ed., *The Metaphysical System of Hobbes* (La Salle, Ill., 1948), p. 12. For the political importance of method see especially *Leviathan*, 2.20 (p. 160).

38. *Politique et philosophie chez Thomas Hobbes* (Paris, 1953), p. xvi. Describing a church, Hobbes wrote that it is "*a company of men professing Christian Religion, united in the person of one Soveraign; at whose command they ought to assemble, and without whose authority they ought not to assemble.*" *Leviathan*, 3.39 (p. 362).

39. *Leviathan*, intro., p. 9.

40. *Ibid.*, 2.17 (p. 132).

41. *Ibid.*, intro., p. 8.

42. *Leviathan*, 2.28 (p. 246).

43. *De Cive* (1642), English version, ed. S. P. Lamprecht (New York, 1949), p. 9.

44. See *Leviathan*, 1.4 (pp. 29-31).

45. *Ibid.*, 2.18 (p. 134).

46. *Ibid.*, 2.19 (p. 149).

47. *Ibid.*, 3.38 (p. 348).

48. *Ibid.*, 3.38 (p. 350).

49. *Ibid.*, 3.38 (pp. 356-357).

50. *Ibid.*, 1.13 (p. 94).

51. *Ibid.*, 1.8 (p. 57).

52. *Ibid.*, 1.5 (p. 33).

53. *Ibid.*, 1.13 (pp. 94-95).

54. *The Elements of Law Natural and Politic* (1650), 1.8.5, ed. F. Tönnies (Cambridge, 1928), pp. 26-27.

55. *De Cive*, 2.10.11 (p. 123).

56. *Elements of Law*, 1.9 (pp. 27-34).

57. *Ibid.*, 1.9.21 (pp. 36-37).

58. *Leviathan*, 1.13 (p. 95).

59. *Ibid.*, 1.14 (p. 108).

60. See *ibid.*, 3.42 (p. 381), and 2.21 (p. 163).

61. *Ibid.*, 2.21 (p. 168).

62. *The English Works of Thomas Hobbes of Malmesbury*, ed.

W. Molesworth, 11 vols. (London, 1839-1845), VII, 158.

63. *Leviathan*, 2.18, (p. 137).

64. Gerrard Winstanley, *A Watch-word to the City of London and the Army* (1649), in *The Works of Gerrard Winstanley*, ed. G. H. Sabine (Ithaca, New York, 1941), p. 323.

65. *Truth Lifting Up its Head Above Scandals* (1649), *Works*, p. 124.

66. *The Saints Paradice* [Abstract] (1648), *Works*, p. 93.

67. *The New Law of Righteousness* (1648), *ibid.*, p. 159.

68. *A New-Yeers Gift for the Parliament and Armie* (1650), *ibid.*, p. 377.

69. *Fire in the Bush* (1650), *ibid.*, p. 458.

70. *Ibid.*, p. 453.

71. *New Law of Righteousness*, p. 153.

72. *Ibid.*, p. 226.

73. *The True Levellers Standard Advanced* (1649), *Works*, p. 262.

74. *Saints Paradice*, p. 96.

75. *Truth Lifting Up its Head*, p. 105.

76. *New Law of Righteousness*, p. 200.

77. *Fire in the Bush*, p. 453.

78. *Truth Lifting Up its Head*, p. 105. This revealing remark, as well as the overwhelming evidence in Winstanley's writings for the view that he identifies reason with mystical understanding, has failed to impress modern students of Winstanley who approach him from a Marxist point of view. David W. Petegorsky, in his *Left-wing Democracy in the English Civil War* (London, 1940), p. 124, asserts that after Winstanley's early pamphlets, "though he is still concerned exclusively with spiritual problems, his argument is that of a progressive rationalist." In a few months, Petegorsky contends, Winstanley went through a re-markable development from a mystical to a rational theology (p. 124), from which he emerged a practical communist (p. 138). Christopher Hill, in *Gerrard Winstanley, Selections from his Works*, ed. L. Hamilton (London, 1944), intro., p. 6, pursues the same line of analysis even further: "To priestly obscurantism and deception Winstanley opposes education, rational science with its feet on the earth." The fact is that, as Sabine has observed, mysticism is "involved in everything Winstanley either said or did." *Works*, intro., p. 27. His advocacy of practical (vocational) education and of "empirical" science is based upon a mystical understanding of knowledge as experienced belief and a condemnation of "imagined," i.e., rational, understanding. It is mysticism and not ordinary rationalism, however paradoxical this may seem, which stands behind Winstanley's insistence that "every one who speaks of any Herb, Plant, Art or Nature of Mankind, is required to speak nothing by imagination, but what he hath found out by his own industry and observation in tryall." *The Law of Freedom in a Platform, or True Magistracy Restored* (1652), *Works*, p. 564.

79. *Saints Paradice*, pp. 93-94.

80. *Fire in the Bush*, p. 476.

81. *Ibid.*, p. 474.

82. *Law of Freedom*, p. 579.

83. *The True Levellers Standard*, p. 261.

84. *Ibid.*, p. 262.

85. *Ibid.*, p. 263.

86. *Saints Paradice*, p. 95.

87. *New Law of Righteousness*, p. 227.

88. *Truth Lifting Up its Head*, p. 107.

89. *New Law of Righteousness*, p. 181.

90. *Ibid.*, pp. 201-203.

91. *Ibid.*, pp. 182-183.

92. *New-Yeers Gift*, pp. 378-379.
93. *Law of Freedom*, p. 515.
94. *Ibid.*, pp. 504-508.
95. *Ibid.*, p. 510.
96. *Ibid.*, p. 513.
97. *Ibid.*, p. 524.
98. *Ibid.*, p. 527.

99. *Ibid.*, p. 535.
100. *New Law of Righteousness*, p. 158.
101. *Law of Freedom*, pp. 540-541.
102. *Ibid.*, p. 542.
103. *Ibid.*, p. 553.

CHAPTER FIVE

Equality and Enlightenment

1. Cf. Henri Michel, *L'idée de l'état* (Paris, 1896), pp. 10-17, and H. J. Laski, *The Rise of European Liberalism* (London, 1936), pp. 210-224.

2. *Encyclopédie, ou Dictionnaire Raisonné des Sciences, des Arts, et des Métiers*, 17 vols. (Paris, 1751-1765), V, 415, "Égalité Naturelle," by M. le Chevalier de Jaucourt.

3. *The Spirit of the Laws* (1748), 8.3, trans. T. Nugent (New York, 1949, Hafner paperback), p. 111.

4. *Ibid.*, 5.5 (pp. 44-45).

5. *Philosophic Dictionary* (1769), trans. P. Gray (New York, 1962), I, 245-247, "Égalité."

6. *De l'Homme* (1772), in *Oeuvres complètes* (Paris, 1818), II, 71. Quoted by F. E. Manuel, "From Equality to Organicism," *Journal of the History of Ideas*, 17: 54 (January 1956).

7. Locke, *The Second Treatise on Government* (1690), 5.31-33, in *Two Treatises on Government* (New York, 1947, Hafner paperback), pp. 136-137.

8. See the provocative and stimulating but not quite persuasive argument of Leo Strauss (*Natural Right and History*, Chicago, 1953, pp. 165-166) that it was Locke, not Hooker, who was really "judicious." F. J. Shirley justly observes that while Hooker "helped to formulate the political philosophy of Liberalism," he did so "all unwittingly." *Richard*

Hooker and Contemporary Political Ideas (London, 1949), p. 201.

9. *Laws of Ecclesiastical Polity* (1593), 2.8.4 (London, 1954, Everyman's Library), I, 310.

10. *Ibid.*, 2.8.5 (I, 311).
11. *Ibid.*, Preface 3.10 (I, 102).
12. *Ibid.*, 3.8.15 (I, 322).
13. *Ibid.*, 3.8.18 (I, 324).
14. *Ibid.*, Preface 2.1 (I, 80).
15. *Ibid.*, Preface 2.4 (I, 83).
16. *Ibid.*, Preface 2.4 (I, 86).
17. *Ibid.*, Preface 2.4 (I, 84).
18. *Ibid.*, Preface 3.3 (I, 96).
19. *Ibid.*, Preface 3.10 (I, 101).
20. *Ibid.*, Preface 3.13 (I, 103).
21. *Ibid.*, 1.2.4 (I, 152-153).
22. *Ibid.*, 1.10.1 (I, 188).
23. *Ibid.*, 1.10.14 (I, 199).
24. *Ibid.*, 1.8.11 (I, 184-185).
25. Hooker even suggests that men are perfectible. "In their spring" men are utterly ignorant, but "they grow by degrees, till they come at length to be even as the angels themselves are." *Ibid.*, 1.6.1 (I, 166).
26. *Ibid.*, 1.10.4 (I, 190-191).
27. *Laws of Ecclesiastical Polity*, 8.2.8, in *The Works of That Learned and Most Judicious Divine, Mr. Richard Hooker*, ed. Isaac Walton (Oxford, 1845), II, 499.
28. *Ecclesiastical Polity*, 1.10.8 (London, 1954), I, 194-195.
29. *Ibid.*, 3.11.20 (I, 357).
30. *Ibid.*, 3.11.20 (I, 356).
31. *Ibid.*, 1.9.7 (I, 193).
32. *Ibid.*, 1.16.6 (I, 228).

33. See D. B. Robertson, *The Religious Foundations of Leveller Democracy* (New York, 1951), p. 52.

34. In a critical comment upon Parker's *A Discourse of Ecclesiastical Politie* (1669), Locke wrote that either sovereignty descends only to the rightful heir of Adam or "all government, whether monarchical or other, is only from the consent of the people." Quoted by M. Cranston, *John Locke: a Biography* (London, 1957), pp. 132-133.

35. "With sense-perception showing the way, reason can lead us to the knowledge of a law-maker or of some superior power to which we are necessarily subject." *Essays on the Law of Nature* (1660), trans. W. von Leyden (Oxford, 1954), IV, 155.

36. *Ibid.*, p. 183.
37. *Ibid.*, p. 185.
38. *Ibid.*, p. 115.
39. *Ibid.*, p. 135.
40. *Ibid.*, p. 161.

41. *On the Conduct of the Understanding* (1697), in *The Works of John Locke* (London, 1812, Bohn Library), sect. 2, p. 26. Locke adds: "Though this be so, yet I imagine most men come very short of what they might attain unto, in their several degrees, by a neglect of their understandings."

42. Locke, *Second Treatise*, 2.4 (p. 122).

43. *Ibid.*, 6.63 (p. 151).
44. *Ibid.*, 6.54 (p. 147).
45. *Ibid.*, 6.57 (p. 148).
46. *Ibid.*, 5.34 (p. 137). See also 5.27 (p. 134).
47. *Ibid.*, 5.36-50 (pp. 138-145).

48. A.-N. de Condorcet, *Sketch for a Historical Picture of the Progress of the Human Mind* (1795), trans. J. Barraclough (London, 1955), ninth stage, p. 128.

49. *Ibid.*, p. 130.
50. *Ibid.*, p. 129.
51. *Ibid.*, fourth stage, p. 71.

52. *Ibid.*, sixth stage, p. 83, seventh stage, p. 96.
53. *Ibid.*, eighth stage, pp. 100-102.
54. *Ibid.*, ninth stage, p. 126.
55. *Ibid.*, eighth stage, p. 105.
56. *Ibid.*, ninth stage, p. 142.
57. *Ibid.*, tenth stage, pp. 173-174.
58. *Ibid.*, p. 179.
59. *Ibid.*, p. 174.
60. *Ibid.*, ninth stage, p. 131.
61. *Ibid.*, pp. 130-131.
62. *Ibid.*, tenth stage, p. 179.
63. *Ibid.*, p. 181.
64. *Ibid.*, p. 182.
65. *Ibid.*, p. 183.
66. *Ibid.*, pp. 183-184.
67. *Ibid.*, p. 194.
68. *Ibid.*, pp. 187-188.
69. *Ibid.*, p. 189.
70. *Ibid.*, p. 179.

71. A. O. Lovejoy has persuasively demonstrated that despite Rousseau's stated disagreements with Hobbes the psychological theory of the *Discourse on Inequality* bears a strong resemblance to the Hobbesian view of human nature. The state of nature, which Rousseau is supposed to have pictured as a state of peace, is actually, as Lovejoy points out, a term which comprehends four distinct phases, only the first of which is a state of peace—the peace of brute animals, however, not of man in his distinctively human aspects— and the last of which, the one immediately preceding the compact to form political society, is "little more than a replica of the state of nature pictured in the *Leviathan*." Lovejoy, "The Supposed Primitivism of Rousseau's *Discourse on Inequality*," in *Essays in the History of Ideas* (Baltimore, 1948), p. 33. Hobbism, as Robert Derathé notes, had a "seductive" attraction for Rousseau. *Jean-Jacques Rousseau et la science politique de son temps* (Paris, 1850), p. 108.

72. *A Discourse on the Origin of Inequality* [Among Men] (1755),

trans. G. D. H. Cole, in *The Social Contract and the Discourses* (New York, 1950, Everyman's Library), p. 199.

73. *Ibid.*, p. 281.

74. The partisans of revolution were able to read the *Discourse* without succumbing to its apolitical conclusions, apparently because they read it in the light of their own preconceptions. Sébastien Mercier, in his *De Jean Jacques Rousseau considéré comme l'un des premiers auteurs de la révolution* (Paris, 1791), argues that although Rousseau "satirized" civilized society (*la société policée*), he did so only to point the way toward the improvement of actual conditions. Rousseau recognized that civilization will be an improvement over the state of nature "only when social man will have received all of his perfections." The advantages of the state of nature cannot compare with those of the "truly civilized" man, who would enjoy the virtues of a highly developed reason, of "sensibility, probity, justice, filial piety, paternal and conjugal love, patriotism, devotion to moral good." It is therefore a mistake, Mercier argues (pp. 18-20, n. 1), to think that Rousseau considered man happier in nature than he would be in a truly civilized society.

75. *Discourse on Inequality*, p. 193.

76. *Ibid.*, pp. 191-193. It seems certain that by moderns Rousseau meant Hobbes, Cumberland, and Pufendorf (see *ibid.*, p. 202), and possibly all or most of the other modern natural law theorists.

77. *Ibid.*, p. 198.

78. *Ibid.*, p. 208.

79. *Ibid.*, p. 176.

80. From *The Confessions of Jean-Jacques Rousseau* (1782-89), trans. J. M. Cohen (London, 1953), p. 362.

81. *Discourse on Inequality*, p. 200.

82. *Ibid.*, p. 233.

83. *Ibid.*, p. 236.

84. "In the end, then, it is this Hobbesian (and partly Mandevillian) social psychology that—even more than the primitivistic tradition represented by Montaigne and Pope —prevented the evolutionistic tendency in the thought of the *Discourse* from issuing in a doctrine of universal progress, in a faith in *perfectibilité*. Man being the kind of creature that he is, the inevitable culmination of the process of social development is a state of intolerable evil." Lovejoy, "The Supposed Primitivism of Rousseau's *Discourse*," p. 33.

85. *Discourse on Inequality*, p. 237.

86. *Ibid.*, p. 247.

87. *Ibid.*, p. 271.

88. *Ibid.*, pp. 247-248.

89. *Ibid.*, pp. 221, 230-232.

90. *Ibid.*, p. 232.

91. *Ibid.*, p. 233.

92. *Ibid.*, p. 241.

93. *Ibid.*, p. 251.

94. *Ibid.*, p. 263.

95. *Ibid.*, p. 268.

96. *Ibid.*, p. 270.

97. *Ibid.*, p. 249.

98. *Ibid.*, p. 265.

99. *Ibid.*, p. 176.

100. *Ibid.*, p. 185.

101. *Rousseau Juge de Jean-Jacques* (1776; Frankfurt on Main, 185-), p. 313.

102. *The Heavenly City of the Eighteenth-Century Philosophers* (New Haven, 1932), p. 29.

103. Alfred Espinas, *La philosophie sociale du XVIII° siècle et la révolution*, pp. 86-87, points out that in eighteenth century France every church service taught that, before the fall, men lived in equality and happiness; that sin had caused the introduction of private property; that the poor were dignified in the order of grace, the rich suspect. Espinas concludes that this "Christian dogma of the state of nature and of the inequality derived from sin was there-

fore for almost everyone a sort of axiom at the time when Rousseau, Morelly and Mably began to write." Three of the more or less Socialist philosophers, Jean Meslier, Gabriel de Bonnot de Mably, and Thomas Raynal, were clergymen of low rank.

104. André Lichtenberger, *Le socialisme au XVIIIe siècle* (Paris, 1895), uses the designation so broadly that it becomes almost a synonym for "critical philosophers." A number of figures emerge from his study as more or less Socialist: Meslier, Mably, Brissot de Warville, Simon N.-H. Linguet, Raynal, Mercier, and Retif de la Bretonne.

105. *Doutes proposées aux philosophes économistes sur l'ordre naturel et essentiel des societés politiques,* in *Collection complète des oeuvres de Mably,* ed. Arnoux, 15 vols. (Paris, 1794-1795), XI, 12.

106. *Ibid.,* pp. 8-11.
107. *Ibid.,* p. 12.
108. *Ibid.,* p. 15.
109. *Ibid.,* p. 12.
110. *Ibid.,* pp. 27-28. "The philosopher who, upon entering the palace of a rich voluptuary, cries to himself, 'What things I do not need!' Is he not closer to happiness than the possessor of these insipid and gluttonous superfluities?" *De la législation ou principes des lois,* in *Oeuvres,* IX, 13. Linguet, in vol. II, p. 223, of his *Réponses aux docteurs modernes* (London, 1771), also directed against the Physiocrats, describes the idyllic communist state of nature as a "community of privation." Quoted by A. Lichtenberger, *Le socialisme utopique* (Paris, 1898), p. 93.
111. *Doutes,* p. 14.
112. *De la législation,* pp. 93-95.
113. *Ibid.,* p. 107.
114. *Ibid.,* p. 151.
115. *Doutes,* p. 3.
116. *Ibid.,* p. 9.
117. *Ibid.,* pp. 10-11.

118. *De la législation,* p. 52.
119. *Doutes,* p. 18.
120. *De la législation,* p. 59.
121. *Doutes,* p. 11.
122. *Ibid.,* pp. 44-45.
123. *Ibid.,* pp. 58-59.
124. *Ibid.,* p. 37.
125. *Ibid.,* p. 50.
126. *De la législation,* p. 98.
127. *Ibid.,* p. 101.
128. *Ibid.,* p. 109.
129. *Ibid.,* p. 120.
130. *Ibid.,* pp. 140-143.
131. *Ibid.,* p. 229.
132. *Ibid.,* p. 224.
133. *Code de la nature, ou le véritable esprit des lois* (1755), ed. G. Chinard (Paris, 1950), p. 159.
134. *Ibid.,* p. 160.
135. *Ibid.,* p. 166.
136. *Ibid.,* p. 169.
137. *Ibid.,* p. 168.
138. *Ibid.*
139. *Ibid.,* p. 171.
140. *Ibid.,* p. 186.
141. *Ibid.,* p. 187.
142. *Ibid.,* p. 190.
143. *Ibid.,* pp. 197-199.
144. *Ibid.,* pp. 283-284.
145. *Ibid.,* p. 212.
146. *Ibid.,* p. 284.
147. *Ibid.,* p. 218.
148. *Ibid.,* p. 290. He does not anticipate that such shortages will be constant. "The world is a table sufficiently garnished for all the guests." *Ibid.,* p. 167.
149. *Ibid.,* pp. 297-301.
150. *Ibid.,* p. 321.
151. *Défense générale de Babeuf devant la haute-cour de Vendôme* (1793), in V. Advielle, *Histoire de Gracchus Babeuf et du Babouvisme* (Paris, 1884), II, 316. Babeuf thought Diderot, not Morelly, the author of the *Code de la nature.*
152. *Défense générale,* p. 43, and *passim.*
153. *Correspondance de Babeuf avec Dubois de Fosseux* (1785-1788), in Advielle, *Histoire,* II, 193-194.

154. *Défense générale*, p. 38.
155. *Correspondance*, pp. 194-195.
156. *Défense générale*, p. 41.
157. *Correspondance*, p. 195.
158. *Ibid.*, p. 194.
159. *Manifesto of the Equals*, in *Histoire*, I, 197-199.
160. *Ibid.*, p. 198.
161. From a brochure written in

1796, in *La doctrine des égaux, extraits des oeuvres complètes*, ed. A. Thomas (Paris, 1906), p. 75.
162. *Ibid.*, p. 79.
163. From *Tribun du Peuple* (1796), in *La doctrine des égaux*, pp. 61-62. See also *Défense générale*, p. 40.

C H A P T E R   S I X

The Liberal Crisis

1. *Representative Government* (1861), in *Utilitarianism, Liberty, and Representative Government* (New York, 1951, Everyman's Library), p. 383.
2. See E. Halévy, *The Growth of Philosophic Radicalism*, trans. M. Morris (London, 1928), pp. 45-46.
3. *Ibid.*, pp. 50-51.
4. Quoted from Bentham, *Works*, ed. J. Bowring (Edinburgh, 1838-1843), III, 230, in Halévy, *ibid.*, p. 366.
5. "Enfranchisement of Women" (1851), in *Dissertations and Discussions, Political, Philosophical, and Historical* (London, 1859), II, 429.
6. *Ibid.*, p. 423.
7. *Autobiography* (London, 1873), pp. 231-232.
8. "The Claims of Labour" (1845), in *Dissertations*, II, 196.
9. *Ibid.*, p. 197.
10. "Vindication of the French Revolution of February, 1848, in reply to Lord Brougham and others" (1849), in *Dissertations*, II, 385.
11. *Ibid.*, pp. 385-386.
12. *Ibid.*, p. 386.
13. "The Claims of Labour," *Dissertations*, II, 198.
14. *Ibid.*, p. 202.
15. *Ibid.*, p. 206.
16. "Vindication," *Dissertations*, II, 388.

17. *Ibid.*, pp. 388-389.
18. *Ibid.*, p. 389.
19. *Ibid.*, p. 390.
20. *Ibid.*, p. 394.
21. *Ibid.*, p. 395.
22. "Social Equality," *International Journal of Ethics*, 1: 261-288 (April 1891).
23. *Utilitarianism*, in *Utilitarianism, Liberty, and Representative Government* (New York, 1951, Everyman's Library), p. 42.
24. "Vindication," *Dissertations*, II, 395-397.
25. *Autobiography*, p. 167.
26. *Representative Government*, p. 267.
27. "The Claims of Labour," *Dissertations*, II, 210-211.
28. "M. de Tocqueville on Democracy in America" (1840), in *Dissertations*, II, 3.
29. *Ibid.*, p. 3.
30. *Ibid.*, p. 62.
31. *Ibid.*, p. 64.
32. *Ibid.*, p. 67.
33. *Ibid.*, pp. 69-70.
34. *Ibid.*, p. 13.
35. *Ibid.*, p. 15.
36. *Ibid.*, pp. 14-15.
37. *Ibid.*, p. 15.
38. *Ibid.*, p. 20.
39. *Ibid.*, p. 21.
40. *Ibid.*, p. 37.
41. *Ibid.*, pp. 20-21.

42. "Bentham" (August 1838), in *Dissertations*, I, 381.

43. "M. de Tocqueville," *Dissertations*, II, 73, 80.

44. *Ibid.*, pp. 67-68.

45. Appendix, *Dissertations*, I, 470.

46. *Utilitarianism*, p. 12.

47. *Ibid.*, p. 17. Emphasis added.

48. *Ibid.*, p. 73.

49. *Ibid.*, pp. 78-79.

50. *Principles of Sociology*, III (London, 1897), 516.

51. *Social Statics* (1850), in *Social Statics Together with The Man Versus the State* (New York, 1892), p. 62. Significantly this passage appears at the outset of a discussion of private property.

52. David G. Ritchie, *The Principle of State Interference* (London, 1891), p. 83.

53. *Principles of Sociology*, I (London, 1880), 618 (*a* and *b*).

54. *Social Statics*, p. 36.

55. *Ibid.*, p. 54.

56. *Ibid.*, pp. 65-66.

57. *Ibid.*, p. 66. Emphasis added.

58. *Ibid.*, pp. 66-67. See also pp. 58-59.

59. *Ibid.*, pp. 7-8.

60. *Principles of Sociology*, III, 505-506.

61. "From Freedom to Bondage," in *Essays Scientific, Political and Speculative* (London, 1892), III, 448.

62. *The Man Versus the State*, p. 369.

63. *Social Statics*, p. 150.

64. *The Man Versus the State*, p. 369.

65. *Principles of Sociology*, III, 528.

66. "From Freedom to Bondage," *Essays*, III, 454.

67. *Ibid.*, p. 463.

68. *Ibid.*, pp. 455-456.

69. *Social Statics*, p. 76.

70. *The Data of Ethics* (London, 1881), p. 18.

71. *Ibid.*, p. 19.

72. *Ibid.*, p. 20.

73. *Ibid.*, p. 147.

74. "From Freedom to Bondage," *Essays*, III, 563.

CHAPTER SEVEN

The Conservative Paradox

1. *The Old Regime and the French Revolution* (1856), trans. Stuart Gilbert (New York, 1955, Vintage paperback), p. 20.

2. *Recollections*, trans. A. T. de Mattos, ed. J. P. Mayer (London, 1948), p. 79.

3. *Democracy in America* (1835), trans. H. Reeve, rev. F. Bowen, P. Bradley (New York, 1944, Vintage paperback), I, 3. The "observations" are made of the United States, but Tocqueville adds that the same tendency is just as visible in Europe.

4. *Ibid.*, p. 341.

5. *Oeuvres complètes d'Alexis de Tocqueville*, 2nd. ed. (Paris, 1866), VIII, 338ff, cited by J. P. Mayer, *Alexis de Tocqueville* (New York, 1960), p. 15.

6. See *Old Regime*, p. 21. Despite certain resemblances to Burke, Tocqueville's observations frequently differ from those of the author of *Reflections on the French Revolution*. Thus, whereas Burke had excoriated the important role played by lawyers in the revolutionary legislature—they were, he said, petty, litigious, and untrustworthy—Tocqueville counted them as, on the whole, among the most reliable supports of stability and order. (See *Democracy in America*, I, 283-285).

7. *Democracy in America*, II, 37.

8. *Ibid.*, I, 15. Emphasis added.

9. "When equality of conditions succeeds a protracted conflict between the different classes of which the elder society was composed, envy, hatred, and uncharitableness, pride and exaggerated self-confidence seize upon the human heart, and plant their sway in it for a time. This, *independently of equality itself*, tends powerfully to divide men . . . That sort of intellectual freedom which equality may give, ought, therefore, to be very carefully distinguished from the anarchy which revolution brings." *Democracy in America*, II, 7-8 (emphasis added). For other reflections on the distinction between the temporary effects of revolution and the more lasting effects of equality, see also *ibid.*, pp. 221 and 332. Tocqueville's observation that Americans were fortunate in being "born equal" without having to become so by revolution (*ibid.*, p. 108), should be weighed against this distinction. The absence of an old regime meant simply that America would be spared the temporary dislocations attendant upon violent upheaval. These insights of Tocqueville have served Louis Hartz, in *The Liberal Tradition in America* (New York, 1955), as the basis for a comparative analysis of the development of democracy in America, France, and England. Tocqueville himself did not contend that the absence of feudalism would make for a radical uniqueness in American development. Because of the overriding importance he gave to the organizing principle of the historical period—which was common to both continents—he confined himself to suggesting that the American development was likely to be more "natural" than the European, and to pointing out isolated instances in which tradition and circumstance produced different incidental effects.

10. *Democracy in America*, I, 7.
11. *Ibid.*, p. 6.
12. *Ibid.*, II, 34-35.
13. Quoted by A. Rédier, *Comme disait M. de Tocqueville* (Paris, 1925), p. 46.
14. *Democracy in America*, I, 7. Emphasis added.
15. *Oeuvres complètes*, V, 425ff, quoted by Mayer, *Alexis de Tocqueville*, p. 30. Translation altered and emphasis added.
16. *Old Regime*, p. 13; for a similar discussion of historical causality see *Democracy in America*, II, 91-93.
17. *Ibid.*, pp. 31-32.
18. *Ibid.*, p. 176.
19. Tocqueville's list of the events responsible for the rise of equality includes a number which he does not explicitly link to the failure of the aristocracy, such as the invention of firearms, which made the noble and vassal equal on the field of battle; the invention of printing and the introduction of a postal system, which made knowledge and inflammatory ideas accessible to all; the proclamation by Protestantism that "all men are equally able to find the road to heaven"; and the discovery of America. *Democracy in America*, I, 5-6. Otherwise, the most consequential of the events which he discusses are all traced, with varying directness, to the door of the aristocracy.
20. *Ibid.*, p. 4. Emphasis added.
21. *Ibid.*, p. 5.
22. *Old Regime*, p. vii.
23. *Democracy in America*, I, 5.
24. *Old Regime*, p. 30.
25. *Democracy in America*, II, 220-221.
26. Cf. Melvin Richter, "A Debate on Race, The Tocqueville-Gobineau Correspondence," *Commentary*, 25: 151-160 (February, 1958), for a similar view. Tocqueville, Richter observes (p. 153), "would have preferred to live in a stable society

ordered on aristocratic principles, for he believed that men—all men—were most comfortable when living under a hierarchical system with clearly drawn class lines. But he could see no possibility whatever of reversing the process of social levelling set off by the French Revolution. Hence he sought to do what he could toward the application of his moral principles to the egalitarian society in which he found himself."

27. *Old Regime*, chap. xii, pp. 120-137.

28. *Ibid.*, p. 121.

29. *Recollections*, pp. 11-12.

30. *Democracy in America*, II, 43

31. *Ibid.*, p. 35.

32. *Ibid.*, pp. 104-105.

33. *Old Regime*, p. xii.

34. See *Democracy in America*, vol. II, chap. vi, pp. 30-31, on democrats' "secret admiration" of the discipline and unity of the Roman Catholic Church.

35. See *ibid.*, chap. xxi, pp. 94-98.

36. *Ibid.*, p. 86.

37. *Ibid.*, p. 77.

38. *Ibid.*, chap. xi, pp. 50-55.

39. *Ibid.*, p. 252.

40. *Old Regime*, p. x.

41. *Ibid.*, part II, chap. xi, pp. 108-120.

42. *Democracy in America*, II, 141.

43. *Ibid.*, p. 25.

44. *Old Regime*, p. xi.

45. *Democracy in America*, I, 7.

46. *Ibid.*, p. 11.

47. *Ibid.*, p. 10.

48. *Ibid.*, p. 204.

49. *Ibid.*, II, 111.

50. *Ibid.*, I, 6.

51. From *Oeuvres complètes*, vol. IX; cited in *Recollections*, pp. 10-11.

52. *Democracy in America*, II, 265-269.

53. *Ibid.*, p. 160.

54. See *Old Regime*, p. 79; *Democracy in America*, I, 49-53.

55. *Democracy in America*, I, 391.

56. "The Present Age" (1846), in

R. Bretall, *A Kierkegaard Anthology* (Princeton, N. J., 1946), p. 260.

57. *Ibid.*, p. 265.

58. Kierkegaard, *On Authority and Revelation, The Book on Adler, or a Cycle of Ethico-Religious Essays* (1848), trans. W. Lowrie (Princeton, N. J., 1955), postscript, p. 195.

59. *Ibid.*, preface no. 3, p. xxii.

60. "The Present Age," p. 269.

61. *On Authority and Revelation*, p. xxv.

62. *Ibid.*, pp. xxv-xxvi.

63. *Ibid.*, p. xxvi.

64. Stirner, *The Ego and His Own* (*Der Einzige und sein Eigentum*, 1844), trans. S. T. Byington (New York, 1907), p. 152.

65. *Ibid.*, p. 154.

66. *Ibid.*, pp. 229-230.

67. *Ibid.*, p. 340.

68. *Ibid.*, pp. 249-250.

69. *Ibid.*, p. 323.

70. Friedrich Nietzsche, *Beyond Good and Evil* (1886), trans. H. Zimmern, in *The Philosophy of Nietzsche* (New York, 1927), p. 497.

71. Nietzsche, *Thus Spoke Zarathustra* (1883-1885), part II, in *The Portable Neitzsche*, trans. W. Kaufmann (New York, 1954), pp. 212-213.

72. *Ibid.*, part IV, p. 357.

73. Quoted from *Werke, Musarionausgabe* (Munich, 1920-1929), xvi, 374, in W. Kaufmann, *Nietzsche, Philosopher, Psychologist, Antichrist* (New York, 1956, Meridian paperback), p. 262.

74. *Zarathustra*, part IV, p. 383.

75. See *The Genealogy of Morals* (1887), trans. H. B. Samuel, *The Philosophy of Nietzsche*, p. 664n.

76. *Ibid.*, p. 643.

77. *Ibid.*, pp. 663-664.

78. *Zarathustra*, part II, pp. 211-214.

79. *Ibid.*, part I, pp. 160-163.

80. *Genealogy*, p. 665. In the Samuel translation "Übermensch" is rendered "Superman."

81. *Zarathustra*, part I, p. 130.

82. *Ibid.*, part I, p. 155.

83. *Totem and Taboo*, in *The Basic Writings of Sigmund Freud*, trans. A. A. Brill (New York, 1938), p. 867. See also p. 875. Philip Rieff, *Freud: the Mind of the Moralist* (New York, 1959), pp. 190-191, suggests that Freud probably derived this notion of mental evolution from anthropologists, such as E. B. Tylor, who had been influenced by English Comtians.

84. "One of the Difficulties of Psycho-Analysis" (1917), in *Collected Papers*, trans. J. Riviere (London, 1953), IV, 351-352. See also "Resistance to Psycho-Analysis" (1925), *ibid.*, V, 173.

85. "We must admit that this ideal prevention of all neurotic illness would not be advantageous to every individual. A good number of those who now take flight into illness would not support the conflict [between instinctual drives and the need for their restriction] . . . but would rapidly succumb or would commit some outrage which would be worse than if they themselves fell ill of a neurosis." "Future Prospects of Psycho-Analytic Therapy" (1910), *ibid.*, II, 294.

86. *Group Psychology and the Analysis of the Ego*, trans. J. Strachey (New York, 1949), p. 2. It should be noted that the term "group psychology" is a translation of "Massenpsychologie."

87. "Why War?" (1932), letter to Albert Einstein, in *Collected Papers*, V, 284.

88. *The Future of an Illusion*, trans. W.-D. Robson-Scott (London, 1949), p. 12.

89. *Totem and Taboo*, p. 916.

90. *Ibid.*, pp. 921-925. Cf. the exegesis of this section in Rieff, *Freud: the Mind of the Moralist*, pp. 192-199. The reinstatement of the primal father was, Rieff notes, "at least in symbolic form . . . as natural as his disposition." *Ibid.*, p. 194. Herbert Marcuse has offered what amounts to an elaboration of Freud's theory with an historical dimension added. "From the slave revolts in the ancient world to the socialist revolution, the struggle of the oppressed has ended in establishing a new, 'better' system of domination." *Eros and Civilization, a Philosophical Inquiry into Freud* (Boston, 1955), p. 90. Marcuse explains that as social authority replaces individual authority, "the father, restrained in the family and in his individual biological authority, is resurrected, far more powerful, in the administration which preserves the life of society, and in the laws which preserve the administration." *Ibid.*, p. 91.

91. *Totem and Taboo*, p. 917.

92. "Why War?" *Collected Papers*, V, 286.

93. "Some Psychological Consequences of the Anatomical Distinction between Sexes" (1925), *ibid.*, V, 197.

94. "Libidinal Types" (1931), *ibid.*, V, 250.

95. The role of suggestion in all relations of dominance is indicated by an analogy which Freud draws between being in love and hypnosis. There is only "a short step," he writes, from one to the other. "There is the same humble subjection, the same compliance, the same absence of criticism, towards the hypnotist just as towards the love object." The hypnotist, Freud explains, has "stepped into the place of the ego ideal." *Group Psychology*, p. 77.

96. *Ibid.*, p. 42.

97. *Ibid.*, p. 43.

98. "Why War?" *Collected Papers*, V, 275.

99. *Ibid.*, p. 278.

100. *Totem and Taboo*, p. 917.

101. *Ibid.*, p. 920.

102. *Ibid.*, pp. 920-921.
103. *Ibid.*, p. 922.
104. *Group Psychology*, p. 95.
105. *Ibid.*, p. 92.
106. *Ibid.*, p. 89. Emphasis added.
107. *Ibid.*, pp. 44-45.
108. *Ibid.*, p. 43.
109. *Ibid.*, p. 56.
110. *Ibid.*, pp. 102-103.
111. *Ibid.*, pp. 86-87.
112. *Ibid.*, p. 88.
113. "Why War?" *Collected Papers*, V, 283. In arguing that the overcoming of scarcity offers an opportunity for diminishing repression (*Eros and Civilization*, pp. 92-134), Marcuse ignores this specific denial by Freud of the view that aggressiveness is a function of material scarcity.

114. *New Introductory Lectures on Psychoanalysis*, trans. W. J. H. Sprott (New York, 1933), p. 231.
115. Marcuse reduces the Freudian theory of domination to the control and restraint of gratification and argues that as mankind matures intellectually and increases its material wealth the need for domination diminishes. *Eros and Civilization*, p. 153. This argument ignores the theory of domination propounded in *Group Psychology*, according to which domination remains necessary regardless of advances in rationality and social welfare.
116. *Beyond the Pleasure Principle* (1920), trans. J. Strachey (New York, 1950), pp. 79-80.
117. *Ibid.*, p. 57.

CHAPTER EIGHT

The Socialist Dilemma

1. Included in G. W. F. Hegel, *Early Theological Writings*, trans. T. M. Knox and R. Kroner (Chicago, 1951).
2. One of the *Economic-Philosophic Manuscripts* (1844), translated by R. Dunayevskaya and published as Appendix A of her *Marxism and Freedom* (New York, 1958), pp. 290-303.
3. "The Positivity of the Christian Religion," in *Early Theological Writings*, pp. 88-89.
4. Marx and Engels, *The German Ideology* (1846), parts I and II, ed. R. Pascal (New York, 1947), p. 25.
5. *Love, Power and Justice; Ontological Analysis and Ethical Applications* (New York, 1954), p. 22. See also his *Systematic Theology*, I (Chicago, 1951), 234.
6. In *Early Theological Writings*, p. 308.
7. *Ibid.*, p. 271.
8. *Ibid.*, p. 270.
9. *Ibid.*, p. 265.

10. "Love," *ibid.*, p. 308.
11. The theme of love and justice (domination) which is so central for the young Hegel has been revived in the recent work of Paul Tillich and Herbert Marcuse, both of whom have intellectual roots in Marxism and in Hegel. Tillich, having originally concluded that Marx was a better "executor" (*Vollstrecker*) of the young Hegel than Hegel himself because Marx recognized the economic character of alienation, has now returned to a more Hegelian view, using the terms which the young Hegel employed. For Tillich's development, see "Der Junge Hegel und das Schicksal Deutschlands," in *Hegel und Goethe, Zwei Gedenkreden, Sammlung Gemeinverständlicher Vorträge und Schriften aus dem Gebiet der Theologie und Religionsgeschichte*, No. 158 (Tübingen, 1932), and his more recent *Love, Power and Justice*. Marcuse, having concluded in his

study of Hegel that with Hegel philosophy as such comes to an end, has gone to Freud to explore the theme of love and domination. See his *Reason and Revolution, Hegel and the Rise of Social Theory* (New York, 1954), and *Eros and Civilization, a Philosophic Inquiry into Freud* (Boston, 1955).

12. Hegel also uses the same formula in *The Philosophy of History*. See *The Philosophy of Hegel*, ed. C. J. Friedrich (New York, 1953), p. 93. H. C. Lea's account of Joachim's doctrines in *A History of the Inquisition of the Middle Ages* (New York, 1906), vol. III, indicates the striking resemblances between his and early Hegelian thought. Among other distinctions, Joachim believed that "in the first state there was knowledge, in the second piety, in the third will be plenitude of knowledge; the first state was servitude, the second was filial obedience, the third will be liberty; the first state was passed in scourging, the second in action, the third will be in contemplation; the first was in fear, the second in faith, the third will be in love; the first was of slaves, the second of freemen, the third will be of friends." (*ibid.*, p. 15).

13. The chief difference, for Hegel, between Judaism and Kantian ethics is that Judaism prescribes subjection "under the law of an alien Lord," while the Kantian subjection to law is a "self-coercion" under "a law of one's own." "Spirit of Christianity," p. 244.

14. *Ibid.*, p. 218.

15. *Ibid.*, p. 230.

16. *Ibid.*, p. 222.

17. *Ibid.*, pp. 224-225.

18. *Ibid.*, p. 225.

19. *Ibid.*, p. 232.

20. *Ibid.*, pp. 234-235.

21. *Ibid.*, pp. 235-236.

22. Hegel does not emphasize the point to the extent that he does in the *Phenomenology*, but even here it is clearly suggested that social existence is incompatible with the passive love of the beautiful soul. See *The Phenomenology of Mind* (1807), trans. J. B. Baillie (London, 1949), chap. iii, part C, pp. 642-679.

23. "Spirit of Christianity," pp. 236-237.

24. *Ibid.*, p. 235.

25. *Ibid.*, pp. 238-239.

26. *Ibid.*, p. 239.

27. *Ibid.*, p. 240. Translator's footnote.

28. *Ibid.*, p. 250.

29. *Ibid.*, p. 251.

30. *Ibid.*, p. 252.

31. *Ibid.*, pp. 252-253. Similar imagery recurs in the *Phenomenology* in the discussion of the unhappy consciousness: "The statues ... are now corpses in stone whence the animating soul has flown ... The tables of the gods are bereft of spiritual food and drink, and from his games and festivals man no more receives the joyful sense of his unity with the divine being." *Phenomenology*, chap. vii, part C, p. 753.

32. "Spirit of Christianity," p. 262.

33. *Ibid.*, p. 264.

34. *Ibid.*, p. 245. Cf. Marcuse, *Eros and Civilization*, pp. 226-237, on the self-limiting nature of Freudian *Eros*. In Marcuse's exegesis of Freud this serves to support the argument that external repressive authority is unnecessary for social order. Tillich, *Love, Power and Justice*, p. 15, brings out the difference between love and justice in a way which captures precisely what Hegel meant: "Justice is expressed in principles and laws none of which can ever reach the uniqueness of the concrete situation ... But it is love which creates participation in the concrete situation."

35. "Spirit of Christianity," p. 247.

36. *Ibid.*, p. 266. Emphasis added.
37. *Ibid.*, p. 268.
38. *Ibid.*, p. 273.
39. *Ibid.*, p. 278.
40. *Ibid.*, p. 280.
41. *Ibid.*, p. 281.
42. *Ibid.*, p. 284. Bracketed word supplied by Knox. Cf. Tillich, *Love, Power and Justice*, p. 12: The distinction of love from power leads to "separation of the political from the religious and the ethical and to the politics of mere compulsion."
43. "Spirit of Christianity," p. 287. Bracketed phrase supplied by Knox.
44. *Ibid.*, p. 291. Bracketed word supplied by Knox.
45. *Ibid.*, p. 293.
46. *Ibid.*, p. 295. Nietzsche had a similar conception of the inadequacy of the believer: "The man of faith, the 'believer' of every kind, is necessarily a dependent man—one who cannot posit himself as an end, one who cannot posit any end at all by himself. The 'believer' does not belong to *himself*, he can only be a means, he must be *used up*, he requires somebody to use him up . . . Every kind of faith is itself an expression of self-abnegation, of self-alienation." *The Antichrist* (1888), in *The Portable Nietzsche*, pp. 638-639. But it is evident that, unlike Hegel, Nietzsche did not regard faith as a step toward the ultimate overcoming of alienation.
47. "Spirit of Christianity," p. 301.
48. *Phenomenology*, chap. vii, part C, p. 750.
49. "Spirit of Christianity," pp. 260-284.
50. *Ibid.*, p. 249.
51. *Ibid.*, pp. 256-258.
52. *Ibid.*, pp. 289-291.
53. *Phenomenology*, chap. vii, part C, p. 763.
54. Frank E. Manuel, *The New World of Henri Saint-Simon* (Cambridge, 1956), pp. 299-302.
55. *Ibid.*, pp. 237-242.

56. *Ibid.*, p. 308.
57. From a letter of Enfantin and Bazard, Saint-Simon's disciples, to the President of the Chamber of Deputies, Oct. 1, 1830, quoted in A. Gray, *The Socialist Tradition, Moses to Lenin* (London, 1947), p. 168.
58. *Le nouveau monde industrielle et sociétaire*, vol. VI of *Oeuvres complètes de Charles Fourier* (Paris, 1841-1848), p. 10.
59. Quoted, from *Théorie de l'unité universelle*, by E. Fournière, in *Les théories socialistes au XIXᵉ siècle; de Babeuf à Proudhon* (Paris, 1904), p. 132.
60. Cited by Fournière, *Théories socialistes*, p. 131.
61. *Nouveau monde*, p. 62.
62. "Toast à la révolution," *Idées révolutionnaires* (Paris, 1850), pp. 255-259.
63. *Idée générale de la révolution au XIXᵉ siècle*, vol. III of *Oeuvres complètes*, ed. C. Bouglé and H. Moysset, 16 vols. (Paris, 1923-1939), p. 73.
64. *Idée générale*, intro. A. Berthod, p. 30. See also *De la célébration du Dimanche considérée sous les rapports de l'hygiène publique, de la morale, des relations de famille et de cité*, vol. V of *Oeuvres complètes*, p. 61.
65. *Idée générale*, pp. 173-174.
66. *Ibid.*, p. 166.
67. *Philosophie du progrès*, vol. XIII of *Oeuvres complètes*, p. 81.
68. *Idée générale*, p. 187.
69. *Philosophie du progrès*, p. 80.
70. *Ibid.*, p. 118.
71. Letter to T. A. Sorge (Oct. 19, 1877), *The Correspondence of Marx and Engels, 1846-1895*, ed. D. Torr (New York, 1937), p. 350.
72. *Correspondence*, p. 337.
73. *Herr Eugen Dühring's Revolution in Science* [*Anti-Dühring*] (1878), trans. E. Burns (New York, 1939), pp. 104-105.
74. *Ibid.*, p. 107.

75. *Ibid.*, pp. 108-109.
76. *Ibid.*, p. 110.
77. *Ibid.*, p. 111.
78. *Ibid.*, p. 113.
79. *Ibid.*, pp. 113-114.
80. *Ibid.*, p. 117.
81. *Ibid.*, p. 118.
82. *The Poverty of Philosophy* (1847), trans. H. Quelch (Chicago, 1920), p. 54.
83. Cited, *Poverty of Philosophy*, pp. 75-77, from Bray's *Labour's Wrong and Labour's Remedy; or, The Age of Might and the Age of Right* (1839), reprinted by London School of Economics and Social Science (London, 1931).
84. *Poverty of Philosophy*, p. 85.
85. *Ibid.*, p. 48.
86. *Ibid.*, p. 57.
87. Letter to P. Annankov (Dec. 28, 1846), *Correspondence*, p. 157.
88. *Poverty of Philosophy*, p. 56.
89. *Critique of the Gotha Programme*, ed. C. P. Dutt (New York, 1938), p. 8.
90. *Ibid.*, p. 9.
91. Marx and Engels, *The German Ideology*, p. 7.
92. *Ibid.*, pp. 27-28.
93. *Ibid.*, p. 112.

94. *Gotha Programme*, pp. 9-10.
95. *Ibid.*, p. 10. Emphasis added.
96. Engels, *The Origin of the Family, Private Property, and the State* (1884), (New York, 1942), p. 87.
97. *Ibid.*, p. 88.
98. *Ibid.*, p. 163.
99. *Anti-Dühring*, p. 114.
100. *Ibid.*, p. 115.
101. *Ibid.*, p. 118.
102. *German Ideology*, pp. 21-22.
103. *Ibid.*, p. 21.
104. *Ibid.*, p. 22.
105. Letter to Conrad Schmidt (Aug. 5, 1890), *Correspondence*, pp. 472-473.
106. *Origin of the Family*, p. 57.
107. *Ibid.*, pp. 65-66.
108. *Ibid.*, p. 58.
109. *Ibid.*, p. 64.
110. *Ibid.*, pp. 66, 73.
111. "Private Property and Communism," p. 299.
112. *Ibid.*, p. 300.
113. *Ibid.*, p. 290.
114. *Ibid.*, p. 291.
115. *Ibid.*, pp. 291-292.
116. *Ibid.*, p. 297.
117. *Ibid.*, p. 293.

CHAPTER NINE

Equality and the Decline of Political Philosophy

1. See as a commentary on his *Animal Farm* (New York, 1946) Orwell's discussion of modern propaganda in "Politics and the English Language," *Collected Essays* (New York, 1957, paperback), pp. 162-176.
2. Michael Young, *The Rise of the Meritocracy 1870-2033* (London, 1958), p. 85.

Index of Names

Harvard Political Studies